Desserts and Wines
by Lenôtre & Olivier Poussier

First published in 2002 under the title *Desserts et Vins*
by Editions Solar, Paris
This edition published in 2004 by Mitchell Beazley, an imprint
of Octopus Publishing Group Limited,
2–4 Heron Quays, London E14 4JP.

A CIP catalogue record for this book is available from the
British Library.

ISBN: 1 84000 954 3

The author and publishers will be grateful for any information
which will assist them in keeping future editions up-to-date.
Although all reasonable care has been taken in the preparation
of this book, neither the publishers nor the author can accept
any liability for any consequences arising from the use thereof,
or the information contained therein.

Commissioning Editor: Hilary Lumsden
Executive Art Editor: Yasia Leedham-Williams
Production Director: Julie Young
English Translation by JMS Books LLP

Typeset in Gill Sans

Printed and bound by Mame imprimeur à Tours in France

Lenôtre
In association with Philippe Gobet

Olivier Poussier
Voted Best Sommelier in The World 2000

Desserts and Wines

Exquisite combinations to delight the palate

Photographs by Yutaka Yamamoto

Styling by Valérie Lhomme

MITCHELL BEAZLEY

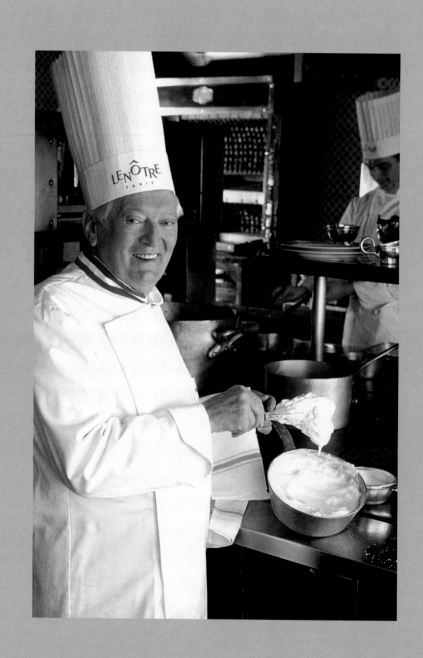

Preface

I was delighted when Olivier Poussier asked me to write the preface for his book and accepted all the more readily as he is also a friend of longstanding. His career has been exemplary and a resounding success. An impressive fund of knowledge built up during his travels throughout the world, his qualities (like those of a flawless vintage wine), and his skill as a speaker make him much sought after when it comes to expert advice on matching wines to main courses and desserts. For me, he is the epitome of courage, determination, and honesty.

A true pioneer in his field, his book represents a new stage in the art of living as he invites his readers to create subtle harmonies between wines and desserts. This is where I discovered how well a Coteaux de l'Aubance Les Fontenelles complements a delicious farmhouse apple tart (*tarte paysanne aux pommes*) that my brother Marcel and I were taught to make by our mother when we were children. This is just one of the recipes to have been magnificently presented by master chef Philippe Gobet (Meilleur Ouvrier de France in 1993) and the lecturers of the École Lenôtre in Paris, of which he is also the director. Together, they wanted to bring these recipes – from the traditional to the modern – within everyone's reach.

The following pages will help you choose wines that complement a particular dessert, which is just as important as choosing a wine to accompany a main course. Your guests will be surprised and delighted by the sweet complicity between a Bonnezeaux and an almond cream brioche with candied pears (*moelleux aux amandes et poires confites*), or a Corsican lemon liqueur (*cédratine*), and a lemon meringue tart made with sweetened shortcrust pastry (*tarte sablée au citron meringuée*). This is a book that makes a major contribution to the art of entertaining.

Gaston Lenôtre

Contents

Yellow and
White Fruit

Peach Flan

(Flan aux pêches)

This very sweet dessert calls for wines with carefully controlled sweetness. Late-harvest wines are ideal for achieving this balance as their acidity provides a subtle contrast to the sugar. Although produced using different grape varieties in two different European regions, the maturity of the Gewurztraminer (Alsace) and the Scheurebe Auslese (Austria) is virtually identical. The first, which has a more exotic flavour when the grapes are allowed to botrytize and overripen, develops exuberant hints of lychee and roses giving way to livelier touches of spice and yellow fruit (late-ripening peach and candied apricot). Because it is not as sweet as a wine produced using a selection of nobly rotted grapes, which would be too sugary for this dessert, its acidity offsets the sweetness of the flan and greatly heightens its flavour. The Scheurebe Auslese has a similar aromatic palette and provides an equally delicious accompaniment for the peaches.

SERVES 8
Preparation time: 25 minutes
Cooking time: 25 minutes

FOR THE PASTRY CASE AND
FLAN FILLING
200g (7oz) Sweetened
   Shortcrust Pastry (see
   page 26)
2 eggs + 2 egg yolks
80g (3oz) caster sugar
200ml (7fl oz) single cream

FOR THE PEACHES
300g (10oz) caster sugar
1 vanilla pod, split lengthways
juice of 1 lemon
1 litre (1¾ pints) water
800g (1¾lbs) yellow peaches
50g (1¾oz) honey

Preparing the pastry case and peaches

Roll out the pastry to a thickness of 2mm (1⁄16 inch) and use it to line a greased flan dish with fluted edges. Chill in the refrigerator.

Add the caster sugar, vanilla pod, and lemon juice to the measured water and bring to the boil. Remove from the heat and plunge the peaches into the syrup. Cover with greaseproof paper and leave until completely cold.

Remove the peaches, reserving 100ml (3½fl oz) of the syrup. Peel the peaches, cut in half and then pan-fry the halves in the honey until they turn a lovely golden colour.

Making and cooking the flan

Beat the eggs together with the sugar, single cream and measured syrup. Arrange the peach halves, cut side down, on the pastry case and cover with the beaten egg mixture.

Bake for about 25 minutes in a preheated oven – 170°C (325°F), Gas Mark 3 – until the flan has set.

Serve hot or cold.

Serving temperature

Gewurztraminer Burg Vendange Tardive 1997, Domaine Marcel Deiss: 10°C (50°F).

Neusiedlersee Scheurebe Auslese 1998, Alois Kracher: 10°C (50°F).

Late-harvest wines from Alsace

The Vendange Tardive or VT (late-harvest) and Sélection de Grains Nobles or SGN (selection of nobly rotted grapes) – labels have been officially recognized since March 1, 1984. Since then, new wine laws have further complicated the already difficult conditions under which these labels are obtained. Moreover, this type of wine is only produced in certain vintage years since it requires a particular set of climatic conditions – a combination of mist and sunshine – that favour the development of Botrytis cinerea (noble rot). This uncertain method of production accentuates the variable concentration and balance of these wines. When harvested, the grapes must contain a minimum level of alcohol, depending on the varieties used: fourteen degrees for Riesling and Muscat and 15.3 degrees for Gewurztraminer and Pinot Gris. The grapes also have to be harvested by hand and chaptalization (the addition of sugar) is forbidden. A prior declaration of harvest must be submitted to the INAO (French National Institute for AOC and AOVDQS wines) and is not usually approved until at least eighteen months after harvest.

GEWURZTRAMINER BURG VEN-DANGE TARDIVE 1997, DOMAINE MARCEL DEISS

Jean-Michel Deiss is a perfectionist who is very demanding when it comes to producing wines that represent his local terroir. He has carried out groundbreaking work in the field of moderate yields and soil management and his vines are cultivated entirely according to biodynamic methods. His wines achieve high levels of purity and perfection. This late-harvest Gewurztraminer is produced on the fertile clay soil of the Burg vineyard. The nearby forests of the Vosges mountains, the heaviness and depth of the soil, and the south-facing exposure make this wine-growing area ideally suited to the production of great wines for laying down. The aromatic expression of this particular vintage is remarkably delicate, with overtones of exotic spices and even a hint of mineral. The mouth is harmonious, sweet, and delicate. In short, it is a beautifully fresh and classy wine.

Neusiedlersee Scheurebe Auslese (Austria)

Neusiedlersee, the leading wine-growing sub-region of Burgenland, lies on the eastern shore of Lake Neusiedl, in Eastern Austria. It is a fairly flat region with a soil composed of loess, gravel, and sand. The climatic conditions make it ideally suited to the production of sweet and nobly rotted wines since warm late summers and the ambient humidity, due to the proximity of the lake, favour the development of botrytis. The wines are classified according to their level of sweetness, with Auslese containing a minimum sugar concentration of 14.5 degrees. Their sweetness and balance is therefore extremely delicate. In Austria, Kabinett and Prädikatswein wines (the class to which this wine belongs) cannot be chaptalized. The Scheurebe variety (also known as Samling), used in Germany and Austria, is a hybrid of the Riesling and Sylvaner varieties.

NEUSIEDLERSEE SCHEUREBE AUSLESE 1998, ALOIS KRACHER

This late-harvest wine is of the highest quality. Like the Gewurztraminer described above, the remarkable balance of acidity, sugar, and alcohol makes this wine ideal as an accompaniment to this dessert as it has sufficient acidity to counter the sweetness of the flan. Scheurebe grapes develop some interesting aromas when they become overripe and botrytized.

Apricot Clafoutis

(Clafoutis aux abricots)

The baked apricot of the clafoutis develops a delicious sweetness and juiciness that can only be fully complemented by a concentrated, golden-yellow wine with strong hints of stewed fruit. In the mouth, both the wines chosen have a sensation of opulence, luxuriance, and a sugary exuberance that goes wonderfully well with this traditional dessert from the Limousin region. While the fortified Muscat de Rivesaltes brings out the flavour of the fruit, the Moscato di Pantelleria, made from raisined grapes, pays homage to the complete dessert. The first is pervaded by the slightly mentholated notes of Muscat, hints of peonies, roses, and fresh grapes, and its sweetness blends harmoniously with that of the apricots, creating a perfect combination based on a delicious fruity freshness. The Moscato di Pantelleria, on the other hand, with its overtones of stewed fruit, apricot, and candied mandarins, tends to echo the flavour of the baked fruit.

SERVES 8

Preparation time: 30 minutes

Cooking time: 25 minutes

FOR THE FRUIT

50g (1¾oz) flower honey

50g (1¾oz) butter

500g (1lb 2oz) fresh apricots, washed, halved, and stoned

FOR THE BATTER

4 eggs + 2 egg yolks

15g (½oz) flour

140g (5oz) caster sugar

375ml (13fl oz) single cream

1 tablespoon apricot liqueur

FINISHING

40g (1½oz) butter

40g (1½oz) granulated sugar

30g (1oz) flaked almonds

40g (½oz) icing sugar

Preparing the fruit and batter

Melt the honey and butter in a non-stick pan. Add the apricot halves and cook rapidly, taking care that the fruit doesn't brown and that it remains slightly firm. Remove from the heat and put to one side.

Beat the eggs, together with the flour and caster sugar, in a round-bottomed mixing bowl. Then gently incorporate the single cream and apricot liqueur.

Cooking the clafoutis

Grease eight individual oven-proof ramekins, sprinkle with sugar and pour a little of the batter into each one. Bake in a preheated oven – 170°C (325°F), Gas Mark 3 – for 6 minutes, then remove and divide the apricots between the ramekins.

Cover with the rest of the batter and sprinkle with flaked almonds. Return to the oven and bake for about 14 minutes.

Dust with a little icing sugar and bake for a further 4 minutes.

Finishing

Remove the clafoutis from the oven and check they are cooked by inserting the point of a knife – the blade should come out clean.

Leave to cool on a wire cake rack before dusting with more icing sugar.

Serving temperature

Muscat de Rivesaltes 1999, Domaine Cazes: 10°C (50°F).

Moscato Passito di Pantelleria, Pietro Colosi: 10°C (50°F).

Muscat de Rivesaltes

Unlike other French VDN (*vin doux naturel*) wines, this appellation, which covers the *département* of Pyrénées-Orientales, is based on Muscat grapes grown in France. It is also the only one to combine two varieties of Muscat – Muscat of Alexandria and Muscat à Petits Grains – each adding its own particular aromatic palette. The wine's natural sugar content is the same as for all other VDN wines, *i.e.* a minimum of 252g per litre when harvested, with an obligatory minimum level of residual sugar of 100g per litre. The method for making these white wines is the same as for all AOC Vin Doux Naturel wines based on Muscat. The grapes are harvested when ripe. During fermentation, pure wine alcohol (ninety-six degrees) is added to the must at between five and ten per cent of must volume. This stops the natural fermentation process and preserves some of the freshness of grapes that have not been allowed to overripen. The differences between the Muscats lie mainly in the type of soil, the maturity of the grapes, and the skill and expertise of the producer. Most Muscats de Rivesaltes are drunk young, but they are also interesting after a few years. Wines from the best-quality appellations are complex and pleasant (Domaine Cazes is a noteworthy producer).

MUSCAT DE RIVESALTES 1999, DOMAINE CAZES

The Cazes family owns the best vineyard and produces the finest naturally sweet wines in the *département*, to the point that you forget you are drinking a fortified wine. Producing a good *vin doux naturel* is a real art – the fortification process or *mutage*, which involves adding neutral alcohol to fresh or fermenting grape must, has to be carefully controlled. If it is carried out too soon it can destroy the flavour of the fruit; too late and it risks highlighting the alcohol. On this estate, it is an extremely delicate operation. The Cazes family reigns supreme in its field and the Muscat de Rivesaltes 1999, with its notes of late-ripening peaches, lemons, and oranges, is truly superb. The palate is harmonious and well-balanced, with plenty of fruity freshness.

Moscato Passito di Pantelleria (Italy)

The tiny Italian island of Pantelleria lies to the south of Sicily, near the coast of Tunisia. It is an arid volcanic island, with no natural source of water. The only crops grown are olive trees and vines, or, to be exact, the Zibibbo grape variety. Some growers maintain that this is in fact the Muscat of Alexandria, while others, like Salvatore Murana, one of the appellation's leading producers, regard it as a related variety that has undergone several changes over the centuries. Whatever its origins, it is used to produce sweet wines with differing sugar contents. The winemaking process for this appellation is simple. The *passito* designation indicates that the grapes have been overripened and dried, either on the vine or on straw to concentrate the sugars, and implies a minimum natural sugar content of 21.5 degrees. The pressed juice is then added to Muscat juice that has been fermented normally, a process reminiscent of the Hungarian Tokaji-method. *Passito* winemakers blend wines with different sugar contents in order to obtain a finer balance.

MOSCATO PASSITO DI PANTELLERIA, PIETRO COLOSI

The Colosi family, better known for their Malvasia delle Lipari, a sweet wine from the island of Salina, also produce Moscato Passito di Pantelleria. The vines are grown in small individual hollows to protect them from the salt-laden sea winds and maintain humidity. The grapes are left to overripen and dry on the vine and then sun-dried for ten days on the rocks. Fermentation takes place at low temperatures in stainless-steel vats. The wine contains 120g of residual sugar per litre and is aged for twelve months in vats. This Pantelleria has strong overtones of apricot with hints of candied mandarins and other candied fruits.

Pear and Almond Tart

(Tarte aux poires et aux amandes)

This tart is a subtle blend of almond cream and pears, whose delicate flavour should be complemented by wines with a controlled sweetness and restrained exuberance. The Quarts de Chaume 1989, with its aromas of tart apples, quinces, and greengages – that become more pronounced with age – goes extremely well with the pears. In the mouth, a touch of minerality with hints of gentian, plant roots, and linden blossom offset the sugars and create a perfect balance between the sweetness of the almond cream and the cleanness and final acidity of the wine. The Cotnari Grasa offers a match based on a subtle balance, with more strongly oxidized notes of yellow fruit, furniture polish, honey, and herbal liqueurs. It is a complex wine with a wide range of aromatic elements and a sweetness that respects the flavour and texture of the tart.

SERVES 8

Preparation time: 40 minutes

Cooking time: 35 minutes

Chilling: 2 hours

FOR THE SHORTCRUST PASTRY

220g (8oz) flour

100g (3¾oz) softened butter

pinch table salt

20g (¾oz) icing sugar

1 beaten egg

1 tablespoon cold water

FOR THE ALMOND CREAM

50g (1¾oz) softened butter

50g (1¾oz) caster sugar

50g (1¾oz) ground almonds

1 egg

1 teaspoon cornflour

1 teaspoon vintage rum

FOR THE TOPPING

8 Williams' pear halves in syrup

50g (1¾oz) apricot jam

Making the shortcrust pastry

Place the flour, butter, salt, and icing sugar in a large mixing bowl and rub in the butter with your fingertips until you have a light, crumbly texture and the fat has been evenly dispersed. Add the beaten egg and measured water and mix to a firm dough. Use your hands to bring the dough together in a ball and chill for 2 hours in the refrigerator.

Making the almond cream

Cream the butter and sugar until you have a smooth, creamy mixture. Add the ground almonds, egg, cornflour, and rum, and use a balloon, rotary, or electric hand whisk to obtain a smooth, even texture.

Cooking and finishing

Roll out the pastry thinly and use it to line a greased 22-cm (8½-inch) flan ring.

Thinly slice the pear halves in syrup. Put the almond cream into a piping bag and cover the base of the pastry case with the cream before arranging the sliced pears in overlapping rows. Bake in a preheated oven – 170°C (325°F), Gas Mark 3 – for about 35 minutes and then leave the tart to cool on a wire pastry rack.

Warm the apricot jam and use it to glaze the surface of the tart.

Chill in the refrigerator until ready to serve.

Serving temperature

Quarts de Chaume, Château Bellerive 1989: 10°C (50°F).

Cotnari Château Cotnari Grasa VSOC CIB 1993: 10°C (50°F).

Quarts de Chaume AOC

Quarts de Chaume is a nobly rotted *grand cru* (top-ranked wine) from Coteaux du Layon. This superb appellation covers an area of forty hectares in the *commune* of Rochefort-sur-Loire, around the tiny village of Chaume. Its name derives from the fact that, in the past, the local overlord demanded one quarter (*quart*) of his tenant farmers' harvest in exchange for the right to farm and cultivate his land. The soil is schistose, with slight variations in the Quarts, Rouères and Vau vineyards. The yield is low – a maximum of twenty-five hectolitres per hectare. Like Bonnezeaux in 1951, Quarts de Chaume obtained AOC status in 1954. The wine is characterized by its great subtlety and delicacy, with a wonderful balance of residual sugars and great harmony on the palate. On this soil, Chenin excels itself, achieving great class and a high level of purity.

QUARTS DE CHAUME, CHATEAU BELLERIVE 1989

For the last few years, this twelve-hectare vineyard has been run by Michel Malinge. The Quarts de Chaume 1989, produced by former owner Jacques Lalanne, expresses itself in a palette that is both mature and mineral, with hints of plum and rhubarb, and a touch of herbal tea. It is a vintage of raisined rather than nobly rotted grapes. The mouth is superbly sweet and mellow, with the sweetness offset by a delicious acidity and expansive mineral flavours. This is an attractive wine with a wonderful future.

Cotnari

Cotnari is a very old appellation from the north of Moldavia (Romania), where it is known as "the pearl of Moldavia". Its vineyards lie on chalky hillsides in the form of an amphitheatre, at an altitude of between 100 and 400 metres (328–1,312 feet). The region has a continental climate, with cold winters and hot summers. The main vine stock, Grasa, is related to Muscat and favours the development of botrytis. The secondary grape varieties –

Feteasca Alba, Francusa and Tamaioasa Romaneasca – are used to produce separate wines that are then blended. There is every reason to believe that the earliest written records (fifteenth century) of vintages made from the selective picking of noble-rotted grapes include references to the Cotnari vineyards. Unfortunately, they are now under threat due to lack of funding and two very severe bouts of frost in the year 2000.

COTNARI CHATEAU COTNARI GRASA VSOC CIB 1993

Château Cotnari is made entirely from Grasa, a beautifully defined grape variety that produces very well-balanced wines. This 1993 blend has a well-controlled sugar content. The grapes are harvested at seventeen degrees potential alcohol and the straw-coloured wine rests on a balance of 12.2 degrees alcohol and 78g of residual sugar per litre. The nose has hints of white and yellow – almost candied – fruit, with undertones of acacia honey, rhubarb, quinces, and plums. The wine has a well-balanced palate, with well-integrated sweetness and good acidity.

Peach and Vanilla Parcels

(Croustillant de pêches à la vanille)

The crispness of these pastry parcels, filled with white peaches and flavoured with cinnamon and star anise, calls for a wine in which texture is as important as taste. Two wines meet this requirement, each in their own way. The sweetness of the Muscat de Beaumes-de-Venise, absorbed by the crunchiness of the pastry, and the subdued frothiness of the Moscato d'Asti, ideally suited with its crispness and sweetness, provide textural sensations that go wonderfully well with those of the dessert. Strongly marked by raisining, the Clos des Bernardins has little of the mentholated flavour of fresh Muscat. Its high level of maturity gives it a rich topaz colour and aromas that are strongly reminiscent of candied oranges, apricots, and yellow peaches. The Moscato d'Asti, a sparkling wine made from the Moscato Bianco variety (Muscat Blanc à Petits Grains), is also pervaded by aromas of yellow fruit and makes an ideal partner that is best enjoyed at lunchtime.

SERVES 8

Preparation time: 25 minutes

Cooking time: 10 minutes

FOR THE PARCELS

8 white peaches

2 vanilla pods, split lengthways

50g (1¾oz) butter

8 sheets of filo pastry

8 macaroons

80g (2¾oz) raspberry jam

FOR THE CINNAMON SYRUP

100g (3¾oz) caster sugar

1 cinnamon stick

1 star anise

80ml (2¾fl oz) water

SERVING

1 tablespoon icing sugar

200ml (7fl oz) raspberry coulis

1 litre (1¾pints) vanilla
   ice-cream

Preparing the peaches

Immerse the peaches in boiling water for one minute, remove carefully with a slotted spoon and plunge into iced water. Peel and leave to one side on absorbent kitchen paper.

Preparing the parcels and syrup

Scrape the pulp from the inside of the vanilla pods with the tip of a knife. Add the pulp to the butter and melt over a low heat. Then spread the mixture evenly over the sheets of filo pastry.

Add the sugar, cinnamon stick, star anise, and vanilla pods to the measured water, bring to the boil and leave to infuse.

Making the parcels

Place a macaroon in the centre of each sheet of pastry and top with a teaspoon of raspberry jam and a peach. Fold the pastry to form a parcel and tie the top of each parcel with a piece of string.

Bake the parcels for about 10 minutes in a preheated oven – 160°C (320°F), Gas Mark 2–3.

Finishing

Take the parcels out of the oven and arrange on small individual plates. Remove the strings, drizzle with the warm, sieved syrup and dust with icing sugar.

Serve with raspberry coulis and vanilla ice-cream.

Serving temperature

Muscat de Beaumes-de-Venise Clos des Bernardins 2000: 10°C (50°F).

Moscato d'Asti Bricco Quaglia 2001, Giorgio Rivetti: 8°C (47°F).

...w and white fruit...

Muscat de Beaumes-de-Venise AOC

In France, Muscat de Beaumes-de-Venise is one of the AOC Vin Doux Naturel appellations produced in the *département* of Vaucluse, near the mountains known as the Dentelles de Montmirail and the villages of Cairanne, Rasteau, and Gigondas. The name of the appellation is a reference to the tiny caves (*balmes* in the Provençal dialect) nestling in these mountains, while *Venise* derives from the name of the former papal state of the Comtat Venaissin (reintegrated into France in 1791). The predominately clay-and-chalk soil in this area enables the Muscat à Petits Grains to attain an exceptional degree of maturity. The appellation includes several different types of wine that vary in richness and concentration, depending on the producers. The winemaking method is the same as for all VDN wines, which are legally required to contain a minimum of 110g of residual sugar per litre.

MUSCAT DE BEAUMES-DE-VENISE CLOS DES BERNARDINS 2000

The twenty-two-hectare estate owned by the Castand family is one of the flagships of the appellation, with seventeen hectares of vines devoted to the production of this delicious nectar. Louis Castand was responsible for the AOC quality label obtained in 1945. The property is situated in the foothills of Mont Ventoux where the extremely thin soil lies above sandy molasse. The style of the Clos des Bernardins Muscats is very different from that of the wines produced on other estates in this area – they are characterized by a stronger flavour of candied and overripe fruit with hints of late-ripening peaches and stewed apricots. Although the 2000 vintage has a residual sugar level of 117g per litre, this does not detract from its harmony and freshness. In fact, it is one of the finest expressions of the appellation.

Moscato d'Asti DOCG

The Moscato d'Asti appellation is produced in the Italian provinces of Asti, Cuneo, and Alessandria. Made from white Muscat grapes, Moscato d'Asti differs, in its very conception, from Asti Spumante. It must have a minimum eleven degrees of potential alcohol when harvested and the must is fermented according to the Charmat method, *i.e.* the fermentation is carried out in hermetically sealed vats. It is bottled when it has five to six degrees of alcohol. This method produces a sparkling wine with fine bubbles, a creamy texture, an intensely fruity palette and a luscious mouth-feel. Moscato d'Asti and Asti Spumante share the dubious honour of being Italy's second largest appellation, in terms of volume, after Chianti, produced in Tuscany. It is therefore important to take great care when choosing one of these wines, and the reputation of the producer should be a determining factor.

MOSCATO D'ASTI BRICCO QUAGLIA 2001, GIORGIO RIVETTI

Giorgio Rivetti produces a superb Moscato d'Asti from grapes grown on chalky soil. This very attractive wine is clean and full-flavoured, achieving a good balance of sugars with 100g of residual sugar per litre. The bubbles are fine and creamy, and the palate sweet and smooth. Its aromatic notes of yellow fruit make it a particularly suitable partner for the peach parcels.

Yellow Peach Tart with Flaky Pastry

(Tarte feuilletée aux pêches jaunes)

The flavours of this peach dessert are more reminiscent of nectarines and apricots and call for wines pervaded by aromas of well-ripened, juicy yellow fruit and yellow-fruit preserves, regardless of their high levels of residual sugar. The flaky pastry of the tart in fact balances the sugars in the mouth and goes well with rich wines, for example a Barsac or a *vin santo* from Tuscany. The Barsac has an aromatic palette of candied apricots, late-ripening peaches, candied oranges, and yellow fruit, with wonderful undertones of vanilla and cream caramel added by oak-ageing. The sugar-rich, low-alcohol Vin Santo, with its aromas of dried apricots, peach preserve, and even hazelnuts, pine kernels, and sesame seeds (there's a touch of controlled oxidation), also makes an ideal match.

SERVES 8

Preparation time: 30 minutes

Cooking time: 40 minutes

Chilling: at least 1½ hours

300g (10oz) Flaky Pastry
   (see page 52)
200g (7oz) Almond Cream
   (see page 17)
8 yellow peach halves in syrup
50g (1¾oz) icing sugar
50ml (2fl oz) strawberry or
   raspberry syrup
50g (1¾oz) crushed green
   pistachios

Preparing the pastry case

Roll out the pastry to a thickness of 2mm (⅟₁₆ inch) and chill in the refrigerator for at least 1 hour.

Use a plate to cut out a circle, 22cm (8½ inches) in diameter, and then cut the edges with a knife to give the circle the shape of a daisy.

Line a greased 20-cm (8-inch), straight-edged flan dish with the flaky pastry and chill in the refrigerator for 30 minutes.

Prick the base all over with a fork, cover with greaseproof paper and fill the pastry case with dried baking beans. Bake blind for 20 minutes in a preheated oven – 170°C (325°F), Gas Mark 3.

Finishing

Soften the almond cream slightly in the microwave or remove from the refrigerator 20 minutes beforehand. Cut the peaches into quarters.

Take the pastry case out of the oven, remove the beans and greaseproof paper, and leave to cool. Cover the base with almond cream and arrange the peach quarters on top.

Increase the oven temperature to 180°C (350°C), Gas Mark 4 and bake the tart for 15 minutes. Dust with icing sugar and bake for a further 5 minutes. Remove from the oven and leave to cool.

Brush the fruit with the strawberry or raspberry syrup. Reduce a little of the syrup from the peaches until it thickens and use it to lightly glaze the fruit.

Sprinkle with pistachios and chill in the refrigerator until ready to serve.

Serving temperature

Barsac Château Doisy-Védrines 1989, Casteja: 10°C (50°F).

Vin Santo Chianti Classico Fattoria di Felsina 1996: 12°C (53°F).

Barsac

Whereas Barsac wines are legally allowed to use the "Sauternes" appellation, the reverse does not apply and the "Barsac" appellation can only be used by châteaux situated in the Barsac region. The chalky soil of the Barsac vineyards is in fact very distinctive and the wines produced here have a wonderfully aromatic expression and well-balanced flavour. Their sweetness and mellowness is better integrated than in Sauternes, and a good-quality Barsac has freshness and harmony. A number of châteaux producing Barsac are worthy of mention – Château Climens for its exceptional harmony and delicacy, Châteaux Doisy-Védrines and Doisy-Daîne for their subtlety, and Château Coutet for its superb "Cuvées Madame". Sauternes and Barsacs are produced from very low yields – a legal maximum of twenty-five hectolitres per hectare. However, for the top vintages, the yield is in the region of twelve to twenty hectolitres per hectare.

BARSAC CHATEAU DOISY-VEDRINES 1989, CASTEJA

This second *grand cru classé* (classed great growth) is produced on an exceptional estate, run by successive generations of the Casteja family, in the heart of the Barsac appellation. The vine stock comprises eighty per cent Sémillon and twenty per cent Sauvignon Blanc. Doisy-Védrines has consistent class and sophistication. Year after year, this label maintains its high standard, with a noticeable emphasis on delicacy and balance. The years 1988, 1989, and 1990 were three truly exceptional years, while 1997 (a very successful vintage) and 2001 are also well worth tasting. This golden, straw-coloured wine has a candied, almost roasted, nose with aromas of apricot purée and candied oranges. The palate is dense, rich, and beautifully sweet, while the alcohol is controlled by a fine acidity that provides a beautifully fresh backbone.

Vin Santo Chianti Classico DOCG (Italy)

This appellation has just acquired DOCG (*Denominazione di Origine Controllata e Garantita*) status, the Italian label of excellence. It produces wines by raisining (*passito*), a process that involves laying the grapes out to dry on racks in lofts, where they are exposed to natural temperatures. Today, producers can also use a controlled supply of warm air to desiccate the grapes and concentrate the sugars. After this period of obligatory drying, the grapes must be pressed between December 1 of the year of harvest and March 31 of the following year. The wine is aged in small barrels known as *caratelli*, sealed with clay mortar and stored under the rafters for a minimum of three years, four for the *riserva* (reserve). The wine is therefore exposed to climatic variations – winter cold and summer heat – and the results are extremely variable. The grape varieties used are fifty per cent Sangiovese and fifty per cent Trebbiano, Malvasia del Chianti, and Grechetto. Vin Santo ("holy wine") comes in varying degrees of sweetness and has a minimum alcohol content of sixteen degrees. The difficulties of the winemaking process and limited production make it an expensive wine.

VIN SANTO CHIANTI CLASSICO FATTORIA DI FELSINA 1996

Fattoria di Felsina lies to the south of the village of Castelnuovo Berardenga, within the Chianti Classico appellation, on the edge of the Chianti dei Colli Senesi vineyards. The estate produces a range of top-quality wines, including a superb *vin santo* produced according to traditional methods from white Malvasia and Trebbiano grapes. It is an extremely complex wine, with hints of dried fruit, candied orange peel, gingerbread, candied yellow fruit, and fruit jellies. It has a strong, luscious, sugary mouth and a long, lingering persistence.

Candied Pear Tart

(Tarte aux poires confites)

In this dessert, the delicate hints of white fruit are complemented by two wines that provide a fine balance of flavours. The Vouvray 1989 is an extremely subtle vintage with a wide aromatic palette – rich with the fragrance of loft-stored apples, cider apples, quinces, rhubarb, and linden blossom – that pays homage to the delicate flavour of the pears. There is nothing exotic or exuberant about this wine, but it is made from a grape variety (Chenin Blanc) that evokes the flavour of overripe white fruit and expresses itself more beautifully in the Loire region than anywhere else in the world. The Beerenauslese is a top-quality botrytized wine that combines maturity, and acidity. As with the Chenin Blanc the balance of sweetness, acidity, and alcohol is well-controlled. In this combination, the fullness of the wine echoes the honeyed sweetness of the dessert, while its acidity offsets and enhances the sugariness of the tart and the pastry absorbs the wine's residual sugar.

SERVES 8

Preparation time: 30 minutes
Cooking time: 25 minutes
Chilling: 3 hours

FOR THE SWEETENED
SHORTCRUST PASTRY

110g (4oz) softened butter
pinch table salt
110g (4oz) icing sugar
4 large egg yolks
250g (9oz) flour

FOR THE FILLING

4 large pears
60g (2oz) acacia honey
1 vanilla pod, split lengthways
8 prunes, stoned and halved
30g (1oz) flaked almonds
20g (¾oz) icing sugar

FOR THE CREAM

2 eggs + 2 egg yolks
1 teaspoon vanilla sugar
40g (1½oz) granulated sugar
200ml (7fl oz) single cream

Making the pastry case

Mix the butter, salt, and icing sugar until you obtain a smooth, creamy texture. Fold in the egg yolks and then add the flour and mix briskly. Shape the pastry into a ball, wrap in clingfilm, and chill in the refrigerator for at least 2 hours.

Roll out the pastry to a thickness of 2mm (1/16 inch) and use it to line a greased flan dish with fluted edges. Chill in the refrigerator for 1 hour.

Preparing the filling

Wash and peel the pears and cut into pieces. Pour the honey into a non-stick pan. Add the pears and vanilla pod and leave to cook over a low heat for 20 minutes, until the juice has completely evaporated and the fruit is slightly caramelized. Add the prunes and remove from the heat.

Making the cream

Using a balloon, rotary or electric hand whisk, beat the eggs together with the vanilla sugar, granulated sugar, and single cream.

Finishing

Bake the pastry case blind for 6 minutes in a preheated oven – 180°C (350°F), Gas Mark 4. Remove from the oven and arrange the fruit in the pastry case. Cover with the cream, sprinkle with flaked almonds, and bake for about 20 minutes at 170°C (325°F), Gas Mark 3.

Remove the tart from the oven, place on a wire cake rack and leave to cool for 20 minutes before dusting lightly with icing sugar.

Serving temperature

Vouvray Premier Tri Haut-Lieu 1989, Domaine Huet: 10°C (50°F).

Wachau Beerenauslese 2000 Freie Weingartner: 10°C (50°F).

Vouvray AOC

Vouvray has been an AOC wine since 1936. The Vouvray wine-growing area incorporates eight villages on the north bank of the river Loire. It produces some truly superb wines using the Chenin Blanc grape variety grown on predominantly clay-and-chalk (known locally as *tuffeau*) and clay-and-silica (*perruche*) soils. In good years, the situation of the vineyard – near the Loire and Brenne rivers – favours the development of botrytis. In the Vouvray area, the Chenin Blanc grape expresses itself in every possible type of wine – slightly sparkling, sparkling, dry, medium-dry, and sweet – with purity, delicacy, and elegance. The botrytized wines, produced only in great vintage years, achieve high levels of concentration and an excellent balance. Their ageing capacity is truly sensational and the 1947, 1921, and even 1871 vintages have been a source of exquisite pleasure.

VOUVRAY PREMIER TRI HAUT-LIEU 1989, DOMAINE HUET

The Domaine Huet is run by Noël Pinguet, a great winemaker who is painstaking, meticulous, and modest, and one of the charismatic figures of the Vouvray appellation. He has gradually converted the estate to the use of biodynamic methods and has some truly exceptional vineyards – Le Mont, Clos du Bourg, and Haut-Lieu. His wines are renowned for their high quality and great purity – 1989 was a particularly good year whose very hot summer produced wines that owed more to raisining than noble rot. This extremely delicate Vouvray has an aromatic nose of stewed apples, quinces and linden blossom. The palate is full, mellow, and well-balanced, rich with the flavours of plum and rhubarb. The freshness is truly remarkable.

Wachau

Wachau's vineyards, some of the prettiest in the world, are situated in Niederösterreich (Lower Austria), the country's leading wine region. With 1,448 hectares of vines, it also has the country's sixth largest vine stock. The vineyards lie on the north and south banks of the Danube, near the towns of Spitz and Dürnstein, to the west of Vienna. The vines are cultivated on predominantly volcanic soil, on terraces stretching for a distance of sixteen kilometres (ten miles). It is impossible not to be affected by the sheer beauty of these vineyards. The wines produced in the region are ripe and fresh – this is the home of Riesling and Grüner Veltliner – and tend to be dry rather than sweet. Sweet wines are few and far between and the year has to be really favourable for the production of raisined or botrytized wines.

WACHAU BEERENAUSLESE 2000 FREIE WEINGARTNER

In its own way, the Freie Weingartner cooperative, situated in the town of Dürnstein, is an example to the entire wine world. Its members are all fully trained and the wines are made to perfection, with quality taking precedence over quantity. This particular blend has a Beerenauslese level of maturity with a minimum of eighteen degrees potential alcohol. It was produced using grapes grown on silica, mica and basalt soils, and harvested on November 15, 2000. It is a blend of grapes grown on different plots, comprising thirty per cent Riesling, thirty per cent Grüner Veltliner, thirty per cent Müller-Thurgau, five per cent Chardonnay, and five per cent Pinot Blanc. The wine is fermented in barrels and matured in wood for six months. With ninety-nine grams of residual sugar per litre and an acidity of 6.8g this is a superbly well-balanced wine.

Farmhouse Apple Tart

(Tarte paysanne aux pommes)

This delicious combination of crisp pancakes and melting, slightly tart Reinette apples calls for wines that highlight the simplicity of the apples. The controlled sweetness of the Coteaux de l'Aubance makes it an ideal candidate, especially the 1999 vintage – a good year for overripening – in which the aroma is strongly pervaded by notes of cooked apples. Made from Chenin Blanc, its subtlety provides a perfect complement for the delicate flavour of white-fruit desserts. With this Coteaux de l'Aubance, you breathe in the aroma of sweet, juicy loft-stored apples, with just a hint of minerality, spices, and honey. A slight bitterness of valerian and gentian creates an interesting balance. With its high sugar content and no trace of the aroma of old wooden barrels, Eric Bordelet's sweet cider is truly exceptional. Its wonderful flavour of really ripe, fresh, and richly scented apples makes it an ideal accompaniment for this dessert.

SERVES 6

Preparation time: 30 minutes

Cooking time: 35 minutes

4 large Reinette apples
50g (1¾oz) dried white grapes
2 eggs
60g (2oz) granulated sugar
1 teaspoon vanilla sugar
100ml (3½fl oz) milk
100ml (3½fl oz) single cream
2 teaspoons Calvados
4 thin pancakes
butter for greasing
1 tablespoon icing sugar

Preparing the fruit

Wash and peel the apples and cut into medium-sized cubes. Plunge the dried grapes into boiling water and then cool immediately in cold, running water. Put to one side.

Making the tart

Beat the eggs, together with the granulated and vanilla sugar, in a large mixing bowl. Then beat in the milk, single cream and, finally, the Calvados.

Line the bottom of a greased 18-cm (7-inch) flan dish with one of the pancakes and then arrange the other pancakes in an overlapping layer to form the sides of the tart. Arrange the cubes of apple and the dried grapes in the bottom of the dish, cover with the egg mixture and bake for about 35 minutes in a preheated oven – 160°C (320°F), Gas Mark 2–3.

Leave to cool on a wire cake rack. Dust with icing sugar before serving.

Serving temperature

Coteaux de l'Aubance Les Fontenelles, Domaine de Haute-Perche, Christian Papin: 10°C (50°F).

Cidre Doux, Château de Hauteville, Éric Bordelet: 8°C (47°F).

Coteaux de l'Aubance AOC

Like the river Layon, the Aubance, which flows to the south of the French town of Angers, gives rise to the early morning mists that favour the development of botrytis. The wine-growing area of Coteaux de l'Aubance, which obtained AOC status in 1936, incorporates ten villages. Chenin is the only grape variety used and the wines, produced on schistose soil, are mellow and well-rounded. In certain years, growers can produce some exceptional botrytized wines, but under unexceptional conditions it is enough for a Coteaux de l'Aubance to be well-balanced, pleasant, and not overly sweet. In spite of its limited production, this appellation is gaining in quality and recognition with a style of wine in which freshness and harmony are the main criteria.

COTEAUX DE L'AUBANCE LES FONTENELLES, DOMAINE DE HAUTE-PERCHE, CHRISTIAN PAPIN

Christian Papin and his wife run a vineyard in Saint-Melaine-sur-Aubance – fourteen hectares of vines planted on schistose soil. Together they ensure the quality of the selection process and take great care to produce wines that are well-rounded, fresh, full-flavoured, and well-balanced. With their pure, delicate, and not overly sweet wines, they hold the key to this appellation and the secret of the best sweet Loire wines. The 1999 vintage of this Les Fontenelles *cuvée*, produced from fairly young vines, has a great deal of elegance. The nose has a rich aroma of plums and pears with a hint of mineral, while the mouth – full- and well-rounded – is relieved by a pleasant acidity. The whole is extremely fresh, with a superb persistence in the mouth.

Cider

Cider is produced by fermenting fresh apples in the form of fresh must and/or a concentrate. Concentrated must can be added to the fresh must provided the concentrate does not exceed fifty per cent of the total volume. Today, France has two ciders with AOC status, obtained on March 19, 1998 – Cidre de Cornouailles, from Finistère, and Cidre du Pays d'Auge, from the *départements* of Calvados, Eure, and Orne. The designation can only be used for a restricted number of villages. Cider is usually produced using different types of apples – tart, bitter-sweet, sweet, acidulous – grown as half-standard or tall standard trees, depending on the density of trees per hectare. The yield from pressing is limited to 750 litres (165 gallons) per tonne of fruit and the juice is not topped up during the slow fermentation process – a minimum period of six weeks must be observed between the date of pressing and bottling. Cider must have an acquired alcohol content greater than 3.5 degrees and a carbon dioxide (CO_2) content greater than three grams per litre.

CIDRE DOUX (SWEET CIDER) CHATEAU DE HAUTEVILLE, ERIC BORDELET

Eric Bordelet – a professional sommelier who has worked in the restaurant of top Parisian chef Alain Passard – has been growing apples and producing cider since 1992. His orchards lie in southern Normandy, in the continuation of the Domfront region and on the borders of the *départements* of Mayenne and Orne. The estate – 10.5 hectares of schistose and silt-and-clay soils planted with twenty varieties of apples and fourteen varieties of pears – is cultivated according to biodynamic methods, with complete respect for nature. The cider is clear and clean, with a fresh aroma of well-ripened, juicy apples and a well-rounded mouth relieved by a superb acidity. Its freshness is deliciously thirst quenching.

Almond Cream Brioche with Candied Pears

(Moelleux aux amandes et poires confites)

With their aromas of candied pears, loft-stored apples, rhubarb, and juicy Williams' pears, overmature, botrytized Chenin Blanc wines make an ideal accompaniment to this delicious combination of candied pears and almond cream. The Bonnezeaux Château de Fesles – mature yet still fresh – is a perfect choice, especially the 1997 vintage, a year of wonderfully well-balanced wines. Its sugar content is beautifully controlled and its delicacy ideally suited to the creamy almond filling and sweet white fruit. The Ermitage Flétri, a dessert wine from the Valais region of Switzerland, is also made from botrytized grapes. It is finely balanced, with hints of white fruit – cooked apples and pears – that provide a subtle and delicate match for this dessert.

SERVES 8

Preparation time: 30 minutes

Cooking time: 30 minutes

FOR THE ALMOND CREAM BRIOCHE

8 slices brioche

200g (7oz) Almond Cream (see page 17)

30g (1oz) flaked almonds

50g (1¾oz) icing sugar

200ml (7fl oz) Vanilla Sauce (see page 174)

FOR THE PEARS IN VANILLA SYRUP

8 Williams' pears

1 litre (1¾ pints) water

300g (10oz) granulated sugar

2 vanilla pods, split lengthways

zest of 1 lemon, removed in a single strip

FOR THE CREAM CARAMEL

100ml (3½fl oz) water

200g (7oz) caster sugar

100ml (3½fl oz) single cream

Preparing the pears

Peel the pears but don't remove the stalks. Place the measured water, sugar, vanilla pods, and lemon zest in a saucepan and bring to the boil. Plunge the whole pears into the pan and leave to simmer for 20 minutes over a low heat.

Remove from the heat and leave to cool on a bed of ice.

Making the almond cream brioche

Place the brioche slices on a baking sheet and drizzle with 2 tablespoons of the pear syrup. Cover each slice with a thin layer of almond cream, sprinkle with flaked almonds and dust with icing sugar. Bake in a preheated oven – 190°C (375°F), Gas Mark 5 – for about 10 minutes.

Making the cream caramel

Pour the measured water into a saucepan, add the sugar, mix, and cook for about 8 minutes over a moderate heat until you obtain a dark-brown caramel. Then add the warm single cream to reduce the temperature and give the caramel the correct consistency. Remove from the heat and put to one side.

Finishing

Dip each slice of almond brioche into the vanilla sauce and arrange on small individual plates. Put a warm pear on each slice and cover with cream caramel.

Pour a little vanilla sauce onto each plate and decorate with a piece of the vanilla pod used to cook the pears.

Serving temperature

Bonnezeaux Château de Fesles 1997, Bernard Germain: 10°C (50°F).

Ermitage Flétri 2000, Nicolas Zufferey: 10°C (50°F).

Bonnezeaux AOC

Along with Quarts de Chaume, Bonnezeaux is the other *grand cru* of Coteaux du Layon. The appellation is only produced in the *commune* of Thouarcé and covers an area of some 100 hectares of schistose soil interspersed with igneous rhyolite and siliceous phthanite deposits. Yields are low, set at a maximum of twenty-five hectolitres per hectare. Compared with other sweet and botrytized wines, Bonnezeaux has a remarkable capacity for controlling the natural sugars and, in spite of its strength and maturity, is exceptionally delicate. Its balance, even when young, is incredible.

BONNEZEAUX CHATEAU DE FESLES 1997, BERNARD GERMAIN

This magnificent property is the symbol of the appellation and its Château de Fesles 1947 a truly unforgettable vintage. The estate was run by the Boivin family until 1990, when it was bought by Gaston Lenôtre. He built a winery worthy of the great wine-growing estates but the years between 1991 and 1995 were difficult. The weather did nothing to help produce good-quality nobly rotted wines and the efforts of the new owner went unrewarded. In 1995, he

sold the estate to Bernard Germain, a native of Bordeaux who owns the Château Yvon-Figeac vineyard in the St-Emilion wine area and who produced two excellent vintages of nobly rotted wines in 1996 and 1997. The quality of the selection process, fermentation in wood and a long period of ageing in new wooden barrels have given this Château de Fesles its great class and style.

Wines from the Valais

The vineyards of the Valais, which cover an area of 5,000 hectares, represent the largest wine-producing region in French-speaking Switzerland and indeed the entire country. Although the production of shrivelled, nobly rotted grapes remains low, the results are excellent, with a number of top growers producing some truly superb wines — Marie-Thérèse Chappaz, Benoît Dorsaz, Christophe Abbey, Fabienne Cottagnoud, Dominique Rouvinez and Jean-René Germanier. However, because the climate of the Valais is continental, with cold winters and usually very hot summers, wines produced by raisining represent a higher proportion than botrytized wines. The technique of raisining can be carried out on the vine or under controlled atmospheric

conditions. Ermitage Blanche is the Swiss name for the Marsanne grape variety, which "raisins" relatively easily in this climate. With the Rhône rising in the St Gotthard mountains and the Valais vineyards lying on the north and south banks of the river, it is not uncommon to find Marsanne and Syrah enjoying a privileged situation in this region.

ERMITAGE FLETRI 2000, NICOLAS ZUFFEREY

Nicolas Zufferey runs a wine estate at Sierre and produces some superb wines that are wonderfully clean and straightforward — the whites are pure and mineral, the reds ripe and full-flavoured. This particular *cuvée* was produced from overripe Marsanne (Ermitage Blanche) grapes grown on gravelly soil with a high proportion of chalky sand, at an altitude of around 600 metres (1,968 feet). The average age of the vine stock is twenty years, and the planting density 10,000 vines per hectare. The grapes are overripened on the vine and harvested in December. This Ermitage was matured entirely in oak barrels — with about one-third new wood — for a year.

Meringue with Peaches and Armagnac

(Dacquoise aux pêches à l'Armagnac)

With its smooth, creamy topping on a crisp, sugary base, this dessert is both sweet and complex. The fruity and candied aromas of the peaches, with discreet undertones of Armagnac, are beautifully set off by the light, almond meringue of the Dacquoise. The white Floc de Gascogne makes an ideal partner for the yellow fruit since, although it is fortified and probably less digestible than a naturally fermented wine, this traditional dessert from southwestern France calls for a wine that is also typical of the region. The Armagnac, through its affinity with the fortified *floc*, also meets this criterion. The Navarra, which comes from a wine-growing region that is not so far away from the home of the Dacquoise, also provides the perfect complement in terms of taste and aroma. The light suppleness, slightly exotic smoothness, and voluptuous fragrance of the wine go wonderfully well with the sweetness of the dessert and candied aromas of the peaches.

SERVES 8

Preparation time: 40 minutes

Cooking time: 43 minutes

FOR THE MERINGUE

75g (2½oz) ground almonds

125g (4½oz) icing sugar

3 egg whites

30g (1oz) granulated sugar

40g (1½oz) whole almonds, finely chopped

FOR THE PEACH COMPOTE

3 yellow peaches

50g (1¾oz) granulated sugar

1 vanilla pod, split lengthways

FOR THE CHIBOUST CREAM

3 egg whites

50g (1¾oz) granulated sugar

200g (7oz) Confectioners' Custard (see page 157)

2 tablespoons Armagnac

SERVING

icing sugar

200ml (7fl oz) peach coulis

Making the meringue

Mix the ground almonds with 75g (2½oz) of the icing sugar.

Use a balloon, rotary, or electric hand whisk to beat the egg whites and granulated sugar until they form stiff peaks. Carefully fold in the almond and icing sugar mixture and then add the finely chopped almonds. Spoon the meringue mixture into a piping bag with a smooth nozzle.

Pipe eight rounds, each 7cm (2¾inches) in diameter and 2-cm (¾-inch) thick, onto a greased baking sheet and dust with the rest of the icing sugar.

Bake in a preheated oven – 180°C (350°F), Gas Mark 4 – for about 15 minutes. Remove the meringues from the oven and put to one side.

Making the peach compote

Peel and stone the peaches and cut into slices. Place in a saucepan with the sugar and vanilla pod and cook for 30 minutes over a low heat. Remove from the heat and put to one side.

Making the Chiboust cream

Use a balloon, rotary, or electric hand whisk to beat the egg whites and granulated sugar until they form stiff peaks.

Whisk the confectioners' custard and Armagnac in a large mixing bowl and then use a spatula carefully to incorporate the beaten egg whites.

Finishing

Decorate the centre of the meringues with peach compote, cover with the Armagnac-flavoured Chiboust cream and dust with icing sugar.

Caramelize under a preheated grill for about 30 seconds and serve immediately with a little peach coulis.

Serving temperature

Floc de Gascogne Blanc, Château de Tariquet: 10°C (50°F).

Navarra Vendimia Tardia Colección 125: 10°C (50°F).

Floc de Gascogne

Floc de Gascogne is a dessert wine that obtained AOC status in 1990. Its area of production corresponds to the geographical region of the Armagnac, Ténarèze, and Haut-Armagnac appellations. The grape varieties used in white Floc are Baroque, Colombard, Folle Blanche, Gros Manseng, Petit Manseng, Sémillon, Sauvignon, and Ugni Blanc. Before it is fortified (muté) with unclassified Armagnac (eighteen months old), the grape must has to have a sugar content equal to 170g per litre. The brandy must have a minimum alcohol content of fifty-two degrees and come from the same property that produces the floc. It must be added to the unfermented grape must before fermentation takes place and the mixture be allowed to rest for a minimum of nine months. The final alcohol content is between sixteen degrees and eighteen degrees. Dessert wines cannot leave the cellar before the September 1 of the year following the year of harvest.

FLOC DE GASCOGNE BLANC CHATEAU DE TARIQUET

White Château de Tariquet is made according to the traditional method and consists of thirty per cent Ugni Blanc, thirty per cent Colombard and forty per cent Gros Manseng. The dominance of this last grape variety gives the wine its aromatic potential. The flocs produced by the Château de Tariquet are fortified with pure Folle Blanche brandy, produced and distilled on the property. The brandy is well-integrated in this extremely delicate wine, with a harmonious palate, and a well-controlled sweetness.

Navarra DO

This Spanish DO (Denominación de Origen) wine is produced south of Pamplona, in a region bounded by the Pyrénées to the north and the river Ebro to the south. Although the mountains rise to a height of 1,400 metres (4,593 feet), the vines are planted at an altitude of between 200 and 500 metres (656–1,640 feet). The region's three northernmost areas – Baja Montana, Valdizarde, and Tierra Estella – are the hilliest and coolest, the nearby Pyrénées accounting for their wide variations in temperature and the fact that they are not affected by drought. The areas of Ribera Alta, in the centre, and Ribera Baja, in the south, near the town of Tudela, are much hotter and more arid. Production is also higher in these areas, with rosés representing the greater proportion of the wines produced, followed by red and then white wines. The grape varieties used – Macabeo, Malvasia, Garnacha (Grenache), Moscatel (Muscat), and Chardonnay – are grown on the clay-and-gravel soil of this predominantly limestone region.

NAVARRA VENDIMIA TARDIA COLECCION 125

The Chivite estate is one of the oldest wine producers in Navarra. Its vines cover an area of 400 hectares in the region of Tierra Estella and its rosés have won international acclaim. This particular blend is made from overripe or botrytized Muscat grapes. The vines, which are thirty years old, are harvested between late October and early November, and the wine is fermented in French oak barrels and aged for a period of nine months. This 1999 vintage is a beautiful golden-yellow colour and has a delicious and slightly exotic nose of candied oranges and lemons. With a soft, harmonious palate, this wine is extremely delicate without being excessively sweet.

Baked Peaches with Rosemary

(Pêches rôties au romain)

This dessert calls for aromatic wines that complement the flavour of the peaches. With their notes of well-ripened yellow fruit, sweet or nobly rotted white wines made from Muscat are an obvious choice. In the mouth, the wine must echo the sweetness of the dessert while at the same time providing a contrast with its acidity. When the Muscat Blanc à Petits Grains is well-ripened or raisined, the wine has hints of candied oranges and stewed citrus fruit, as well as fresher, slightly mentholated, resinous, and spicy notes that blend with the camphorated aroma of the rosemary and the slight pungency of the pine honey. This blend of aromas is at its best with the Muscat du Cap Corse and the Muscat from the Peloponnese in Greece, rich with the flavour of candied citrus fruit and yellow fruits.

SERVES 8

Preparation time: 40 minutes
Cooking time: 30 minutes

FOR THE BAKED PEACHES

8 large, ripe peaches
2 litres (3½ pints) water
50g (1¾oz) fresh butter
50g (1¾oz) pine honey
100ml (3½fl oz) dry white wine
2 vanilla pods, split lengthways
8 fresh rosemary sprigs

FOR THE NUT CRUMBLE

20g (¾oz) flour
15g (½oz) butter
20g (¾oz) granulated sugar
20g (¾oz) ground hazelnuts

SERVING

750ml (1¼ pints) vanilla
  ice-cream
1 tablespoon crushed green
  pistachio nuts

Preparing the peaches

Plunge the peaches into the boiling, measured water for 10 seconds. Remove and plunge into iced water and then peel with a small knife. Put to one side.

Melt the butter in a pan, add the peaches and brown lightly. Add the pine honey and leave to cook until the fruit has caramelized. Gradually deglaze with the dry white wine until you obtain a smooth syrup. Then add the vanilla pods and rosemary sprigs. Reduce the syrup over a low heat, spooning it over the peaches at regular intervals.

Making the crumble

Mix the flour, butter, sugar, and ground hazelnuts together with your fingertips and crumble the mixture onto a greased baking sheet.

Bake for 12 minutes in a preheated oven – 170°C (325°F), Gas Mark 3.

Remove from the oven and put to one side.

Finishing

Place a baked peach in each individual dessert dish, sprinkle with the nut crumble and drizzle the cooking syrup from the peaches over the crumble.

Add a scoop of vanilla ice-cream, decorate with one of the rosemary sprigs and sprinkle with crushed, green pistachios.

Serving temperature

Muscat du Cap Corse 2000, Domaine Antoine Arena: 9–10°C (48–50F).

Rion of Pátras 1998, Thanasis Parparousis: 10–11°C (50–52°F).

Muscat du Cap Corse AOC

This appellation, which obtained AOC status in 1993, is the crowning glory of a long local tradition of *vins doux naturels* made from Muscat Blanc à Petits Grains, centred around a region in northern Corsica. This region incorporates two wine areas that have given their name to the Patrimonio and Cap Corse appellations. The wines acquire different expressions, depending on the exposure and type of soil on which the vines are grown. Muscat grapes in the Cap Corse area are mostly planted on granite soil, while the soil in the Patrimonio area is mainly clay and chalk with some granite. The skill and techniques of each individual wine-grower are also contributory factors. In France, there are currently seven AOC Vin Doux Naturel wines based on the Muscat grape variety. The Muscat du Cap Corse was the last to be granted AOC status, at a time when the composition and gustatory balance of *vins doux naturels* were being re-evaluated. The minimum level of residual sugar, set at ninety-five grams per litre, has greatly improved the quality of this type of wine, giving rise to the remarkable delicacy and elegance that characterize this Muscat du Cap Corse. Contrary to popular belief, it is also a wine that ages well.

MUSCAT DU CAP CORSE 2000, DOMAINE ANTOINE ARENA

Antoine Arena, a perfectionist when it comes to wine-growing, runs an eleven-hectare vineyard in the heart of the Patrimonio appellation. His Muscat 2000 has a rich aromatic palette pervaded by the aroma of late-ripening peaches, with hints of citrus fruit and citron, highlighted by a green freshness that complements the flavour of the rosemary. The mouth is sweet, mellow, and full, reminiscent of apricots, while the gustatory balance between sugar, acidity and alcohol is truly remarkable. The wine also has a wonderful lingering persistence.

Rion of Pátras OPE

Produced in the northwest of the Peloponnese, on the shores of the Gulf of Corinth, this OPE wine (the Greek equivalent of the French AOC system) is one of three appellations in the region made from Muscat Blanc à Petits Grains and classified as dessert wines. Unfortunately, it is now under threat due to progressive urbanization.

RION OF PATRAS 1998, THANASIS PARPAROUSIS

Thanasis Parparousis produces naturally sweet (*i.e.* unfortified) wines. The method is permitted by Greek wine legislation provided the grapes are ripe enough when harvested – 252g of sugar per litre and 300g per litre after raisining. The grapes are planted at an altitude of 600 metres (1,968 feet), that not only enables them to ripen for longer but also, and above all, to conserve some of their acidity. When harvested, they are raisined in well-ventilated sheds or lofts where they are exposed to day- and night-time temperatures. After four or five days' drying, the grapes are pressed and fermented. The 1998 vintage is a golden-yellow colour, with a remarkably delicate nose pervaded by aromas of apricots, candied oranges, and clementines. The palate is round, full, and beautifully harmonious. The wine is full-flavoured, concentrated, and yet subtle, with an acidity that makes you forget the 110g of residual sugar per litre. In short, this Muscat is a sheer delight.

Mirabelle Plums and Blackcurrants in Citronella Syrup

(Nages de mirabelles et cassis à la citronelle)

The golden-yellow mirabelle plum is a delicate fruit whose subtle flavour should not be overshadowed by the accompanying wine. Two neutral wines – one based on Chenin Blanc, the other on Riesling – allow the fruit to give free rein to its flavours. The Savennières 1997 is a high-quality vintage of sweet, botrytized wine. When botrytized, Chenin Blanc is not particularly aromatic but has discreet hints of plums, rhubarb, quinces, and pears, a touch of candied fruit and an acidity that goes well with small stone fruit. The balance of sugar and acidity is superb. The German Riesling meets the same criteria since the grapes are harvested when extremely ripe. Both wines are characterized by their freshness and neutrality and create a fine mineral accompaniment based on purity.

SERVES 8

Preparation time: 15 minutes

Cooking time: 6 minutes

Chilling: 1 hour

FOR THE FRUIT

500g (1lb 2oz) plums, washed and de-stoned

100g (3¾oz) blackcurrants, with stalks removed

juice of half a lemon

FOR THE SYRUP

100g (3¾oz) granulated sugar

1 vanilla pod, split lengthways

1 citronella sprig, cut into several pieces (or verbena, lemon balm, melissa)

400ml (14fl oz) water

Preparing the plums

Place the plums in a large mixing bowl, sprinkle with the lemon juice and put to one side.

Making the syrup

Place the sugar, vanilla pod, pieces of citronella and measured water in a saucepan and bring to the boil. Leave to infuse for 5 minutes before adding the plums.

Bring to the boil, cover, remove from the heat and leave to cool. Then add the blackcurrants and chill in the refrigerator for 1 hour.

Serve in small individual bowls.

Serving temperature:

Savennières Clos du Papillon 1997, Cuvée d'Avant, Pierre Soulez: 10°C (50°F).

Riesling Eiswein Zeltingen Himmelreich 1998, Selbach-Oster: 10°C (50°F).

Savennières AOC

The Savennières appellation obtained AOC status in 1952. The vines that produce this top-ranked white wine from the Loire Valley occupy a privileged site on the north bank of the river, about seven-kilometres (four-miles) west of Angers. Their south-facing exposure ensures maximum daily sunshine, making it possible to produce wonderfully mature wines, while the schistose soil adds freshness and a touch of minerality. The appellation, which is extremely consistent and of an excellent overall standard, has a number of quality vineyards. Savennières wines are fresh and delicate, with a strength controlled by their minerality. Here, the Chenin Blanc grape reigns supreme and produces ultra-pure wines which, at their best, age extremely well. Unfortunately, they are often drunk too young – the term "mellow" doesn't feature in the official designation. However, history has proved that, in good years, the appellation is capable of producing superb nobly rotted wines. This was the case in 1997, a great vintage year when several producers made some truly exquisite wines. These include the Clos de Coulaine 1997, with its wonderful concentration and delicacy, and the equally delicate Clos du Papillon 1997 from Pierre Soulez.

SAVENNIERES CLOS DU PAPILLON 1997, CUVEE D'AVANT, PIERRE SOULEZ

Château de Chamboureau is run with a master's hand by Pierre Soulez who owns a large part of the Roche-aux-Moines estate. He makes several excellent blends within the appellation. The Clos du Papillon is so-called because the vineyard is shaped like the wings of a butterfly (*papillon*). Pierre Soulez has two hectares on the "left wing", near the River Loire. In 1997, this particular *cuvée* was affected by botrytis. The grape harvest began in the second week of October; when the sugar content was 17.5 degrees, the wine was fermented in barrels and matured until February 1999. It has great delicacy and is not dominated by noble rot. The syrupiness in the mouth is offset by the minerality added by the soil. It has a balance of 13.5 degrees alcohol and forty grams of residual sugar per litre.

Mosel-Saar-Ruwer

The Riesling grape variety expresses itself more beautifully in the Mosel-Saar-Ruwer region than anywhere else in the world. The vines are planted on the steep hillsides overlooking the Mosel, Saar and Ruwer rivers in northern Germany. This is a great wine-growing region, both in terms of surface area and the number of talented winemakers – Egon Müller Scharzhof, J.J. Prüm, Dr. Loosen, Markus Molitor, Fritz Haag, Selbach-Oster. It stretches from the right bank of the Mosel in Luxembourg, along the course of the river to the German city of Koblenz, forming one of the most beautiful vineyard landscapes in the world. On these schistose soils, Riesling has a truly exquisite expression and the wines are pure, clean, and flawless. The sweet wines produced here can have a disconcerting balance – often low in alcohol, they have an acidity that provides contrast and above all makes them agreeable and harmonious in the mouth. Mosel-Saar-Ruwer is living proof that, in a northern climate, grapes can still be ripe and full-bodied on a relatively low potential alcohol.

RIESLING EISWEIN ZELTINGEN HIMMELREICH 1998, SELBACH-OSTER

The Selbach-Oster vineyards lie in the beautiful wine area of Bernkastel, on the lower Mosel, near the villages of Zeltingen and Graach. The grapes for this Eiswein 1998 were harvested around November 6, 1999, from eighty-year-old, non-grafted Riesling vines planted on steep, stony slopes of Devonian schist, and fermented slowly in stainless-steel vats. The wine has a superb balance – eight degrees alcohol for a residual sugar content of 250g per litre and an underlying acidity of 13.1 degrees – and the whole is expressed with complete delicacy and harmony.

Red Fruit

Raspberry Sorbet Macaroons

(Macarons glacés aux framboises)

The contrasting elements of this delicate dessert call for wines that complement its texture as well as its flavour. It is fascinating to try and match the crunchiness of the macaroons with the effervescence of a sparkling wine, and you've found the perfect accompaniment if the wine is also pervaded by strong aromas of red fruit. This perfection is achieved with the Rubis Demi-Sec, a red wine with a slightly purple hue, a subdued, creamy frothiness, and flavours reminiscent of fallen red fruit – cherries, blackcurrants, and raspberries. A truly delicious combination for summer afternoons. The second choice is a little more disconcerting and places much greater emphasis on the aromatic elements of the combination. The Tacoronte-Acentejo from Tenerife is a superb ruby-red wine that releases a wonderful fragrance of slightly peppery, spicy red fruit with a touch of balsamic vinegar. These aromas go perfectly with the sugar of the macaroons, while the tannic structure of the wine offsets the sweetness of the dessert.

SERVES 6

Preparation time: 30 minutes
Cooking time: 20 minutes
Freezing: 30 minutes

FOR THE MACAROONS

180g (6¼oz) icing sugar
100g (3¾oz) ground almonds
2 egg whites
20g (¾oz) granulated sugar
10 drops red food colouring

FOR THE RASPBERRY SORBET

500g (1lb 2oz) well-ripened
  raspberries
100g (3¾oz) icing sugar
juice of half a lemon

SERVING

seasonal fresh fruit
Red Fruit Coulis (see page 119)

Making the macaroons

Mix the icing sugar and ground almonds. Use a balloon, rotary, or electric hand whisk to beat the egg whites, gradually adding the granulated sugar, until they form stiff peaks. Then incorporate the red food colouring and the mixed almonds and icing sugar, stirring gently with a wooden spoon.

Spoon the mixture into a piping bag with a smooth nozzle and pipe small rounds of mixture onto a greased baking sheet.

Bake for about 20 minutes in a preheated oven – 170°C (325°F), Gas Mark 3 – until the macaroons are well-risen and have a crunchy texture.

Take the baking sheet out of the oven and remove the macaroons from the sheet.

Making the raspberry sorbet

Blend the raspberries, icing sugar, and lemon juice in a food processor or using a balloon, rotary, or electric hand whisk.

Strain the mixture through a sieve, pour into an ice-cream maker, and leave to churn for 15 minutes.

Pour into a container with an airtight lid and put in the freezer for 30 minutes.

Finishing

Spread a little raspberry sorbet on the flat surface of the macaroons and stick them together in pairs.

Serve with fresh fruit and red fruit coulis.

Serving temperature

Rubis Demi-Sec Bouvet-Ladubay: 9°C (48°F).

Bodegas Insulares de Tenerife, Viña Norte Tinto 1999, Dulce Humboldt: 13–14°C (55–57°F).

RUBIS DEMI-SEC BOUVET-LADUBAY

Unlike Italy, which produces a number of sparkling red wines – Lambrusco from Emilia-Romagna and Lombardy, Vernaccia di Serrapetrona from Marche, and Brachetto d'Acqui from Piedmont – France is not renowned for this type of wine. However, there is a Touraine Mousseux appellation that makes sparkling reds from Cabernet Franc grapes harvested in the wine areas of Bourgueil, Chinon, and Saint-Nicolas-de-Bourgueil. The Rubis *cuvée*, a blended wine from Touraine and Anjou, is produced using a must of forty per cent Gamay and sixty per cent Cabernet Franc. The Bouvet-Ladubay wine house in Saint-Hilaire-Saint-Florent is owned by the Taittinger Champagne house. It produces some very fine still and sparkling wines, including the Cuvée Saphir, which is well-made in spite of the number of bottles produced, and the extremely complex and delicate Cuvée Trésor, one of the best sparkling reds produced by the appellation. The Cuvée Rubis is initially made like a traditional red wine. After bottling, a *liqueur de tirage* (a blend of sugar and yeasts) is added to start a second fermentation. It then undergoes a process known as *remuage*, which involves turning the bottles daily and gradually tipping them upside down so that any sediment collects in the neck of the bottle. This is followed by *dégorgement*, the "disgorging" or removal of the sediment, and *dosage* with a *liqueur d'expédition* containing forty grams of sugar per litre that turns the wine into a *demi-sec*. The wine remains in the cellar for eighteen to twenty-four months.

Tacoronte-Acentejo DO

Valle de la Orotava, Abona, Valle de Güímar, Ycoden-Daute-Isora, and Tacoronte-Acentejo are the five appellations of Tenerife, the largest of the Canary Islands, which has some 8,115 hectares of vines planted on volcanic soil. Tacoronte-Acentejo, on the northernmost tip of the island, has an arid climate tempered by the winds and trade winds of the Atlantic Ocean. In this area, the vines – unaffected by phylloxera and therefore non-grafted – are planted at an altitude of 1,000 metres (3,280 feet). The red wines, which represent eighty-five per cent of production, are made from the Negramoll and Listán Negro grape varieties, while the whites are made from Listán Blanco, Gual, Verdello, Malvasía, Moscatel, and Vijariego.

BODEGAS INSULARES DE TENERIFE, VINA NORTE TINTO 1999, DULCE HUMBOLDT

The Viña Norte wine cooperative has more than 500 members and boasts an ultra-modern winery. The Dulce Humboldt blend is made from the Listán Negro grape variety with a small amount (one per cent) of Negramoll. The wine is fortified, aged in oak for nine months, and has a residual sugar content of 101g per litre.

Red Fruit Crumble

(Crumble aux fruits rouges)

This dish very evidently calls for a red wine to echo the flavour of the fruit.
It must have a residual sugar content to complement the crunchiness of the
crumble, and even a touch of spiciness to reflect the notes of cinnamon in the
dessert. The wines chosen are both fortified and go equally well with the acidity
of the fruit and the sweetness of the crumble topping. The Banyuls is well-rounded
and pleasant, with a controlled sweetness pervaded by aromas of cherries and
strawberries. The Anton Bredell "Port" Wine 1998 is a superbly sweet wine that
makes a similar accompaniment to the Banyuls – it has the same fruity flavour –
while retaining the unmistakable character of a port wine. It may have a little
less delicacy and freshness, but still goes wonderfully well with this dessert in
which even the acidity of the bilberries is beautifully offset by the controlled
sweetness of the wine.

SERVES 8

Preparation time: 30 minutes

Cooking time: 25 minutes

Standing: 1 hour

FOR THE CRUMBLE

100g (3¾oz) flour

80g (3oz) ground almonds

100g (3¾oz) soft brown sugar

80g (3oz) butter, melted

half teaspoon ground cinnamon

FOR THE RED FRUIT

200g (7oz) strawberries,
  washed and hulled

150g (5¼oz) raspberries

100g (3¾oz) bilberries

20g (¾oz) vanilla sugar

Making the crumble

Mix the flour with the ground
almonds, brown sugar, and ground
cinnamon. Add the melted butter
and incorporate with a wooden
spoon until the mixture has a
crumbly texture.

Leave to stand for one hour in a
cool place.

Sprinkle the crumble mixture onto
a greased baking sheet and bake
in a preheated oven – 170°C (325°F),
Gas Mark 3 – for about 20 minutes,
until it turns a lovely golden colour.

Remove from the oven and put to
one side.

Preparing the red fruit

Cut the strawberries in half, carefully
mix with the rest of the fruit, and add
the vanilla sugar.

Transfer the fruit to a fairly large
saucepan and cook for 2 minutes over
a high heat. Remove from the heat,
leave until lukewarm, and then spoon
into individual glass bowls.

Finishing

Sprinkle the cooked crumble mixture
over the fruit and serve immediately.

Serve with vanilla ice-cream (optional).

Serving temperature

Banyuls Vintage 2000, Cuvée Léon
Parcé, Domaine de la Rectorie,
Marc et Thierry Parcé: 14°C (57°F).

Anton Bredell "Port" Wine, Bredell
Wine Estate 1998, Stellenbosch:
14°C (57°F).

Banyuls AOC

This old AOC appellation, on the Roussillon shores of the Mediterranean, incorporates the villages of Collioure, Port-Vendres, Cerbère, and Banyuls. Banyuls produces various types of *vins doux naturels*. The whites may not be of the same standard as the reds, but they still have a certain charm. The reds include the *rancios* – whose prolonged maturation in oxidative conditions gives them a chocolatey taste, with notes of roasted coffee beans and dried fruit – and the early bottled *rimages* with their intense, deep-purple colour and dominant aromas of spicy red fruit – candied cherries and figs. Wine legislation requires that fifty per cent of Banyuls AOC be Grenache Noir (seventy-five per cent for Banyuls Grand Cru) but the proportion is generally much higher than this, often almost one hundred per cent, with up to ten per cent of additional grape varieties (Carignan, Syrah, Cinsault). The yield must not exceed thirty hectolitres per hectare.

BANYULS VINTAGE 2000, CUVEE LEON PARCE, DOMAINE DE LA RECTORIE, MARC ET THIERRY PARCÉ

Marc and Thierry Parcé run this magnificent twenty-hectare estate according to a simple philosophy – respect for the terroir. The quality of their Collioure and Banyuls wines makes them the finest examples of these appellations. For the Banyuls, the emphasis is on harmony, fruit, and fullness of flavour. Banyuls wines are fortified while the must is still on the skins – a process known as *mutage sur grains*, which produces their complexity and also makes them an ideal accompaniment for this dessert as it brings out the tannins to offset any excess sweetness. In this particular vintage, however, ninety to 100 grams of well-balanced residual sugar per litre highlight the purity of the red fruit. The Banyuls Cuvée Léon Parcé 2000 is characterized by its beautiful ruby-red colour and deep-purple reflections. The nose has aromas of well-ripened cherries, sugared strawberries, and mild spices. The palate is round, pleasant, and rich, with perfect balance of flavours. The sweetness is well-controlled, with the tannic relief balancing the residual sugars. The whole is fine and delicate.

Stellenbosch

The Stellenbosch region, which accounts for 15.6 per cent of South Africa's wine production, is regarded as the country's leading producer of quality wines. The vines are planted in the valleys and on hillsides, a location much better suited to the production of well-balanced wines. The soil is less fertile and the yields are therefore less prolific, while the altitude – up to 600 metres (1,968 feet) – creates the cooler conditions that favour the production of fine wines. The sandy soil and sandstone of western Stellenbosch make this an ideal red wine area. However, without the cooling influence of False Bay, the region's climate would be far too hot to produce fine, subtle wines. South Africa has a great tradition of fortified wines. This is not only due to the ideal climatic conditions but also the existence of such inland regions as Robertson and Worcester, each with their own particular characteristics. The overexposure of the vineyards, combined with the hot climate, tends to produce wines rich in alcohol, to the point of being unbalanced. This prompted the decision to make the fortified port-type wines to which the local climate is so well-suited. The schistose soils of the Stellenbosch region, the Cape Town and Durbanville areas, and even the Breede River Valley Region, favoured the introduction of Chenin Blanc and Portuguese varieties, which has resulted in the production of quality fortified wines.

ANTON BREDELL "PORT" WINE, BREDELL WINE ESTATE 1998, STELLENBOSCH

Anton Bredell is particularly well-known for his fortified and red wines. His "Port" Wine 1998 has an intense deep-purple colour and an exceptional palate of black and red fruit (blackberries, blackcurrants, cherries in eau-de-vie), liquorice, and mild spices. The concentration is remarkable, and completely fresh. Rich, generous, and harmonious, the wine is exquisitely concentrated and delicate. Its refreshing and thirst-quenching fruitiness make this an extremely drinkable wine.

Strawberry Mille-feuille

(Mille-feuille aux fraises)

Fruit is the keynote of this summer dessert with its contrasting flavours and textures. Strawberry mille-feuille certainly calls for rich, robust red wines with strong notes of red fruit – the flaky pastry absorbs any excess sugar in the mouth. The Rasteau Vintage and Spanish Jumilla are a perfect aromatic match for the fruit. The first, based on Grenache Noir grapes, was aged in non-oxidative conditions and has an array of aromas: of Morello cherries, ripe cherries, strawberries, and bilberries. The Jumilla is made from Monastrell (Mourvèdre) and this Bodegas Olivares blend is slightly fortified, with hints of red fruit and spices. Although less rich than the Rasteau, it develops a wonderful sweetness that provides a perfect complement for the dessert and creates a delicious combination of sweet, sun-ripened fruit.

SERVES 10

Preparation time: 1 hour
Cooking time: 35 minutes
Chilling: 8 hours

FOR THE FLAKY PASTRY

15g (½oz) table salt
220ml (8fl oz) water
500g (1lb 2oz) butter
500g (1lb 2oz) flour

FOR THE FILLING

300g (10oz) Confectioners'
   Custard (see page 157)
200ml (7fl oz) whipped cream
500g (1lb 2oz) strawberries,
   washed and hulled

TO DUST

icing sugar

Making the flaky pastry

Dissolve the salt in the measured water and add 75g (3oz) of melted butter. Pour onto the flour, mix to a dough and knead for 1 minute. Chill the pastry in the refrigerator for 3 hours. Shape the remaining butter into a slab, 12 × 12cm (4¾ × 4¾ inches).

Remove pastry from the refrigerator and roll out into a square, 20 × 20cm (8 × 8 inches). Place the butter on the pastry and fold in the edges. Roll the pastry into a rectangle, 40cm (16 inches) long, and fold in three. Turn the pastry and repeat the process. Leave to stand for 1 hour in the refrigerator.

Repeat the whole rolling-and-folding process twice more and leave to stand for another hour in the refrigerator.

Roll out and fold the pastry once more and chill for 3 hours in the refrigerator.

Baking the flaky pastry

Roll out the pastry to a thickness of 2mm (1/16 inch), forming a rectangle.

Place on a greased baking sheet, prick the surface all over with a fork and bake in a preheated oven – 180°C (350°F), Gas Mark 4 – for 20 minutes.

Cover with a baking sheet to prevent the pastry rising too much and leave to cook for a further 15 minutes. Dust with icing sugar and caramelize for 2 minutes at 230°C (450°F), Gas Mark 8.

Preparing the filling

Whisk the confectioners' custard to a smooth, creamy consistency and then fold in the whipped cream. Cut the strawberries in half.

Finishing

Cut the flaky pastry into three strips. Spread the cream filling on two of the strips and top with strawberries. Place the "filled" strips one on top of the other and cover with the third strip of pastry.

Dust with icing sugar and cut into ten pieces.

Serving temperature
Rasteau Vintage 1999, Domaine de la Soumade, André Roméro: 12–14°C (53–57°F).

Jumilla Olivares Dulce Monastrell 1998, Bodegas Olivares: 12–14°C (53–57°F).

Rasteau AOC Vin Doux Naturel

Rasteau, Sablet, and Cairanne are three villages in the Vaucluse region that have a well-established reputation for the quality of their Côtes du Rhône-Villages. Together they form the Rasteau (AOC Vin Doux Naturel) appellation which produces two types of *vins doux naturels*. One is an intensely red wine characterized by fragrances of well-ripened red and black fruit with hints of spices, the other – produced in oxidative conditions and aged in large oak barrels (*foudres*) – is an amber-coloured wine with hints of cocoa, dried fruit, and coffee. According to its official designation, Rasteau must be made from ninety per cent Grenache Noir, Gris or Blanc. Yields cannot exceed thirty hectolitres per hectare and the wine must be aged for at least a year.

RASTEAU VINTAGE 1999, DOMAINE DE LA SOUMADE, ANDRE ROMERO

In his Rasteau vineyard, André Roméro produces wines of character – fleshy and concentrated with a beautifully preserved fruitiness. While his various *cuvées* of Côtes du Rhône-Villages are of a remarkable standard, his Rasteaux are quite simply the best. Made from 100 per cent Grenache Noir grapes, fortified before pressing and aged in vats, this Vintage 1999 is fleshy, well-balanced, and concentrated with the aroma of red fruit. Its tannic structure adds harmony by enhancing the sweetness of the wine.

Jumilla (Spain)

Jumilla is a DO (Denominación de Origen) appellation that lies in the north of the province of Murcia and the southeast of Albacete, in southeastern Spain. It produces mainly robust reds and a few white wines, although the climate is too hot for the production of really refreshing white wine. This is a hilly region, rising to 600 metres (1,968 feet) in places, with an arid climate and a low rainfall of around 300 millimetres (twelve inches) per year. Yields are low, between twelve and fifteen hectolitres per hectare. The principal grape varieties are Monastrell (Mourvèdre), Garnacha Tinta (Grenache Noir), and a local variety, Cencibel. It is not unusual, in this region, for mature grapes to have a sugar content of sixteen degrees or more.

JUMILLA OLIVARES DULCE MONASTRELL 1998, BODEGAS OLIVARES

This 1998 blend was produced entirely from extremely ripe Monastrell grapes. After being fermented in stainless-steel vats, the wine was fortified with Monastrell *marc* brandy and aged for several months in oak barrels. It has an intense, deep-ruby colour and a nose dominated by red fruit. The palate offers a harmonious blend of sugar and alcohol, while the tannic structure offsets the sweetness of the wine. This is a high-quality vintage with an amazingly fruity concentration and a long, lingering persistence.

Almond Cream and Cherry Tartlets

(Mirliton aux cerises)

The red fruit calls for a mild, slightly sweet rosé or red wine. These qualities are extremely important when choosing a wine to accompany a cherry dessert since the sweetness and mildness are a product of the balance between sugar, acidity, and alcohol. Although very different, the two wines chosen complement the acidity preserved by the cooked fruit and the slight flavour of cherry stones highlighted by the almonds. The controlled sweetness of the Cabernet de Saumur, a rosé made from the two Cabernets, Franc and Sauvignon, creates a fine lunch-time partner for these tartlets filled with cherries and almond cream. The Recioto, an unusual and particularly concentrated wine, also makes an ideal accompaniment for the dessert since the acidity of the — Morello or Montmorency — cherries offsets the sweetness of the wine, while the pastry absorbs any excess sugar. This is a traditional and truly delicious dinner-time combination.

SERVES 10

Preparation time: 20 minutes

Cooking time: 25 minutes

Chilling: 30 minutes

FOR THE ALMOND CREAM FILLING

220 g (8oz) double cream

220 g (8oz) Almond Cream (see page 17)

140g (5oz) granulated sugar

20g (¾oz) vanilla sugar

6 eggs

1 dessertspoon orange-flower water

FOR THE TARTLETS AND CHERRY FILLING

400g (14oz) fresh, stoned cherries

500g (1lb 2oz) Flaky Pastry (see page 52)

50g (1¾oz) flaked almonds

50g (1¾oz) icing sugar

Making the almond cream filling

Use a balloon, rotary, or electric hand whisk to mix the fresh cream, almond cream, granulated sugar, and vanilla sugar in a large mixing bowl.

Add the eggs one at a time and then incorporate the orange-flower water.

Preparing and baking the tartlets

Roll out the flaky pastry to a thickness of 2mm (¹⁄₁₆ inch) and cut out ten circles 10cm (4 inches) in diameter. Place the pastry circles in ten greased 8-cm (3¼-inch) tartlet tins and chill in the refrigerator for 30 minutes.

Half-fill the pastry cases with the almond cream, top with the cherries and sprinkle with flaked almonds. Bake in a preheated oven — 180°C (350°F), Gas Mark 4 — for 20–25 minutes. Remove the tartlets from the oven and dust with icing sugar. Serve cold.

Serving temperature

Cabernet de Saumur, Domaine de la Tour-Grise 2000, Philippe Gourdon: 12°C (53°F).

Recioto della Valpolicella 1995, Romano Dal Forno: 12°C (53°F).

Cabernet de Saumur

This unassuming appellation obtained its certification in 1957. It produces rosé wines made from grapes harvested in the Saumur wine area, where the vine stock is Cabernet Franc and Cabernet Sauvignon. This type of light, delicate rosé is extremely pleasant if the wine is of good quality and fully mature. The fragrance produced by the aromatic concentration of the two grape varieties is complex and intense, gradually expressing a sensation of juicy, full-flavoured fruit. The maximum level of residual sugar is ten grams per litre.

CABERNET DE SAUMUR, DOMAINE DE LA TOUR-GRISE 2000, PHILIPPE GOURDON

Philippe Gourdon runs a vineyard near Puy-Nôtre-Dame, twenty-three hectares of vines cultivated according to biodynamic methods on predominately clay and chalk soil. This 2000 vintage, made entirely from the Cabernet Franc grape variety and produced by bleeding, has an intense, deep-pink colour with a vivid luminosity. The nose expresses ripeness, acidity and aromatic freshness. The palate is fresh, full, and thirst quenching, with an immediate well-ripened fruitiness – the acidity of Morello cherries, with notes of Kirsch, sugared strawberries, and grenadine syrup. In the mouth, the wine echoes the aromatic elements of the dessert, with an aftertaste of mineral acidity that highlights and heightens the flavour. This is a well-balanced wine that is dry, light, and delicate.

Recioto della Valpolicella DOC (Italy)

The Valpolicella appellation, in the Italian wine region of Veneto, is divided into two main areas – Valpolicella Classico, the traditional heart of the appellation, and Valpentena. The vine stock – Corvina Veronese, Rondinella, Molinara, and Rossignola – are all indigenous to the region, which produces a wide range of different wines, from the simple Valpolicella, through Amarone, to the rare and highly acclaimed Recioto. The Amarone and Recioto wines produced by the top growers are not only, and incontestably, the best in the Veneto, but also some of the best in Italy. Recioto is a sweet, tannic, unfortified wine made from raisined grapes. Since the grapes from which it is made have a very low yield and raisining is a long and unpredictable process, Recioto is not produced every year and can therefore be very expensive. The grapes are harvested when fully ripe and left to dry in well-ventilated rooms or lofts, a process that dehydrates (desiccates) them and concentrates their sugars.

They are then pressed and fermented before being aged for at least two years in oak. The minimum alcohol content required for the appellation is fourteen degrees, although it is often higher, while the level of residual sugar varies according to the vintage year. This wine can be drunk young, but is equally delicious when allowed to age a little.

RECIOTO DELLA VALPOLICELLA 1995, ROMANO DAL FORNO

Romano Dal Forno, whose wines have won him international acclaim, is certainly one of Italy's most passionate and brilliant producers. He owns an extremely beautiful vineyard near Illasi, in the Classico area, and built his magnificent winery with his own hands. Fermentation begins in March and is a lengthy process, with the wines remaining in the vats for about thirty-six months and sometimes even longer. Recioto is not marketed for at least five or six years. This Recioto della Valpolicella 1995 was made from sixty per cent Corvina Veronese, fifteen per cent Rondinella, and twenty-five per cent Croatina. The grapes were raisined for 150 days producing a residual sugar content of seventy-five grams per litre. This is, therefore, a sweet and very pleasant wine that immediately complements the cherries. This harmony begins in the soil since, in the Veneto, cherry and other fruit trees are planted among the vines and Recioto is traditionally regarded as the ultimate classic accompaniment for cherry desserts.

Almond Shortcrust Raspberry Tartlets

(Sablés amandines aux framboises)

In this dessert, the contrast between the sugar, acidity, and flavour of the raspberries and the sweetness of the almond filling calls for delicate wines with subtly balanced sugars. The Cabernet d'Anjou is an extremely aromatic rosé, pervaded by fragrances of strawberries and raspberries, with a sweetness that allows it to partner this dessert without detracting from its purity. It makes an ideal lunch-time complement, unlike the Ruster Ausbruch, which is better suited to an evening meal. This second choice, from the Austrian region of Burgenland, is a wine made from botrytized Pinot Noir. It has strong overtones of cherries – in eau-de-vie, fruit preserved in Kirsch, Morello cherries – and a residual sugar level of 100–120g per litre. However the aroma of Morello cherries and tannic quality of the wine offset its excess sweetness, making it an excellent accompaniment for this raspberry dessert.

SERVES 8

Preparation time: 20 minutes

Cooking time: 25 minutes

Chilling: at least 3 hours

FOR THE TARTS

250g (9oz) Sweetened Shortcrust Pastry (see page 26)

150g (5¼oz) Almond Cream (see page 17)

20g (¾oz) double cream

50g (1¾oz) Confectioners' Custard (see page 157)

FOR THE FILLING

500g (1lb 2oz) fresh raspberries

100g (3¾oz) raspberry jam

Making the pastry cases

Roll out the shortcrust pastry to a thickness of 3mm (⅛ inch) and then cut out circles 10–12cm (4–4½ inches) in diameter.

Place the pastry circles in greased tartlet tins, 8–10 cm (3¼–4 inches) in diameter, and chill in the refrigerator for at least 1 hour.

Use a balloon, rotary, or electric hand whisk to mix the almond cream, double cream, and confectioners' custard together in a large mixing bowl.

Fill the pastry cases with the mixture and bake in a preheated oven – 160°C (320°F), Gas Mark 2–3 – for 25 minutes.

Finishing

Take the tartlets out of the oven, remove from the tins, and leave to cool on a wire cake rack. Use a pastry brush to spread a little raspberry jam on each tartlet and top with tightly packed fresh raspberries.

Warm the rest of the jam and pour over the fruit topping.

Chill in the refrigerator for at least 2 hours.

Serving temperature

Cabernet d'Anjou 2001, Domaine Vincent Ogereau: 10°C (50°F).

Ruster Ausbruch Pinot Noir 1999, Feiler-Artinger: 10°C (50°F).

Cabernet d'Anjou AOC

This appellation only produces rosé wines from grapes harvested in the Anjou AOC wine area. The grape varieties used are Cabernet Franc and Cabernet Sauvignon, and the wines are *demi-sec* and even semi-sweet in some years. The level of residual sugar must be at least ten grams per litre, but the general average is as much as seventeen grams or more. At their best, these wines pay homage to the fruit from which they are made, through their sweetness in the mouth and their fullness of flavour on the palate. Of all the rosés produced in France, these are the only ones that become more interesting with age, undoubtedly due to their high level of residual sugar.

CABERNET D'ANJOU 2001, DOMAINE VINCENT OGEREAU

Vincent Ogereau owns a vineyard in the heart of the Coteaux du Layon. His passion and dedication make him one of the top three producers in the Loire region. This Cabernet d'Anjou 2001 is made entirely from Cabernet Sauvignon grapes grown on the schistose soil of Saint-Lambert-du-Lattay and harvested on carefully selected plots devoted exclusively to the production of rosé wine. This fact is well-worth mentioning since rosés are more often produced by bleeding a vat of red wine, and the aroma and flavour of this vintage is largely due to the traditional and highly selective process used by the vineyard. This mature and wonderfully well-balanced wine – twenty-eight grams of residual sugar per litre and an alcohol content of 11.5 degrees – is produced without chaptalization, and fermentation is stopped naturally by the cold. The end product is a wine that is full-flavoured, pleasant, and refreshing.

Neusiedlersee Ruster Ausbruch

Rust is a charming village on the western shore of Lake Neusiedl in the wine region of Burgenland, in Eastern Austria. Since the early seventeenth century, it has produced exceptional nobly rotted wines made from various white and a few red grape varieties. "Ausbruch" is etymologically related to the Hungarian term *aszú*, the sticky paste made from selected grape varieties and used in the production of Tokaji wines. Both the Hungarian and Austrian wines were developed at about the same time in the seventeenth century. Ausbruch wines fall within the official designation for the Austrian Prädikatswein class, somewhere between Beerenauslese and Trockenbeerenauslese (TBA), and have a minimum of 19.7 degrees' potential alcohol. These surprisingly concentrated and well-balanced wines are among the best nobly rotted wines in the world.

RUSTER AUSBRUCH PINOT NOIR 1999, FEILER-ARTINGER

Warm, late summers, and the humidity due to the proximity of Lake Neusiedl, favour the development of botrytis. This wine area is remarkable for its increasing production of sweet and even nobly rotted blends from red grape varieties. This involves something of a risk because red grapes are usually fairly fragile during the development of noble rot. It tends to reduce the colour and flavour of the fruit, making it difficult to produce wines with pure fruity notes. However, the Feiler-Artinger vineyard has proved itself perfectly well-able to make a quality red wine from botrytized grapes. The twenty-five-hectare estate grows thirteen different grape varieties, and Hans Feiler and his son Kurt are two of the best producers in Rust. With an alcohol content of thirteen degrees and 110g of residual sugar per litre, this Pinot Noir 1999 is more than just interesting. The fruit expresses itself in a beautifully intense aroma of Kirsch and Morello cherries, while the palate is rich, mellow, and extremely well-balanced.

Chilled Strawberry and Orange-flower Soup

(Soupe de fraises à la fleur d'oranger)

Although Champagne doesn't usually make a very good accompaniment for a dessert, in this instance it is extremely successful. The acidity of the strawberry soup, whose sugar is offset by the lime juice, works wonderfully well with the dry Champagne, which has a tangible note of sweetness on the nose and in the mouth – aromas of cultivated and wild strawberries – and a smooth, creamy frothiness. The much sweeter Schilfwein The Red One, is an Austrian wine made from desiccated grapes. Its light ruby colour is due to overripening, which causes the grapes to lose their colour. Its aromas of Kirsch, sugared strawberries, raspberries, and mild spices combine harmoniously with the sweetness, aromatic intensity, and acidity of the strawberries. Served in small quantities, it adds a note of freshness to the fruit-compote element of the dessert.

SERVES 8

Preparation time: 15 minutes

Chilling: 2 hours

600g (1lb 5oz) large
    strawberries, washed, hulled,
    and halved
150g (5¼oz) wild strawberries,
    washed and hulled
60g (2oz) granulated sugar
juice of 2 limes
200ml (7fl oz) orange juice
50ml (2fl oz) orange-flower
    water
1 tablespoon strawberry syrup
2 fresh mint sprigs

Preparing the fruit

Mix the strawberries together in a large mixing bowl, add the granulated sugar and lime juice and chill in the refrigerator for at least 1 hour.

Finishing

Pour the orange juice, orange-flower water, and strawberry syrup over the strawberries and mix carefully with a wooden spoon.

Sprinkle with mint leaves and chill in the refrigerator for another hour. Serve well chilled.

Serve with yoghurt ice-cream or red-fruit sorbet (optional).

Serving temperature

Champagne Rosé de Saignée Dry Duval-Leroy: 10°C (50°F).

Neusiedlersee Schilfwein The Red One 1999, Weingut Gerhard Nekowitsch: 12°C (53°F).

Rosé Champagne

As well as white wines, the region of Champagne also produces rosés by one of two techniques – bleeding and *cuvée* blending. The first, which is only legally authorized in the Champagne area, involves starting the red winemaking process and then stopping fermentation on the skins when the desired colour has been obtained. The second is much more widespread and involves blending white and red Champagnes made from Pinot Noir or Pinot Meunier – before the base wine is bottled and fermented – in proportions specific to each Champagne house. The *dosage* of a Champagne depends on the amount of *liqueur d'expédition*, composed of old Champagne and sugar, added after disgorging (*i.e.* the expulsion of the sediment in the wine). This dosage varies according to European wine legislation, *i.e.* six grams per litre for *extra-brut* Champagne, six to fifteen grams for *brut*, twelve to twenty grams for extra dry, seventeen to thirty-five grams for dry, thirty-

five to fifty grams for *demi-sec*, and over fifty grams for sweet Champagne. While Champagne tends to be drunk on special occasions and to celebrate a particular event, it is unfortunately often matched with desserts. In fact, only extra-dry, dry, *demi-sec*, and sweet Champagnes make suitable dessert wines. Even so, many *cuvées* produced in these categories often fall short of the mark because the base wines used for the production of sweeter Champagnes are rarely good quality.

CHAMPAGNE ROSE DE SAIGNEE DRY DUVAL-LEROY

Owned by Carole Duval-Leroy, a dynamic and determined wine-grower, this Champagne house in Vertus produces some 550,000 cases a year. The vineyard is quite large and the quality of the blends, produced under the watchful eye of dedicated cellar master Hervé Jestin, is extremely interesting. This *cuvée*, made entirely from Pinot Noir, was produced by bleeding. The colour is bright, the nose intense and the whole pure and fresh. It has a creamy frothiness and fine, regular bubbles. The Champagne was aged for two years on lees before being disgorged and dosed as a "dry" with twenty-

two grams of sugar per litre. The end product is deliciously coherent and fresh.

Neusiedlersee Schilfwein

This wine area in Burgenland covers an area of almost 11,000 hectares in Eastern Austria, on the eastern shores of Lake Neusiedl. The vines grow on soils that are predominately loess, silt, and sand. The production of high-quality botrytized wines is favoured by the damp, warm conditions. Strobwein and Schilfwein, in the Prädikatswein class, are quite simply wines made from desiccated grapes – the term *schilf* (reed) is a reference to the racks on which the grapes are dried for a statutory minimum period of three months before pressing.

NEUSIEDLERSEE SCHILFWEIN THE RED ONE 1999, WEINGUT GERHARD NEKOWITSCH

This tiny four-hectare vineyard produces wines made from desiccated grapes. The grapes are harvested in mid-September and laid out to dry for ten weeks on reed mats before being pressed very slowly. The small quantity of juice extracted explains the incredible concentration of acidity and sugars. The Red One 1999, made from a blend of raisined Blaufrankisch and Zweigelt grapes, has 260g of residual sugar per litre and over six grams of tartaric acid.

Figs Baked in Collioure Wine

(Figues rôties au vin de Collioure)

In this simple and delicious dessert, the figs and wine conjure up images of ancient Rome, Homeric Greece, and biblical lands. Who could resist the temptation to try and match these elements with wines that are not only steeped in tradition and history, but are also of Mediterranean descent? The Commandaria from Cyprus is one of the oldest wines in the world. Made from raisined grapes, it is slightly fortified after fermentation and aged using the solera system. Its deep amber colour is echoed by an extremely complex array of candied aromas – fruit paste, quince jelly, oranges, and cocoa. The Banyuls shares the same Mediterranean heritage and aromatic associations – a sweetness that echoes the syrupiness of the dessert, the aromas of figs, dried fruit, cocoa, caramelized almonds, and ground nut kernels, with just a hint of *rancio* and an underlying affinity with the red Collioure wine.

SERVES 8

Preparation time: 20 minutes

Cooking time: 30 minutes

Infusion: 4–5 hours

FOR THE FIGS

16 well-ripened figs

80g (3oz) butter

100g (3¾oz) granulated sugar

FOR THE SPICY WINE INFUSION

500ml (18fl oz) red Collioure wine

1½ tablespoons blackcurrant liqueur

2 cinnamon sticks

2 vanilla pods, split lengthways

1 thinly sliced orange

1 thinly sliced lemon

Preparing the spicy wine infusion

Pour the measured wine into a saucepan and bring to the boil. Add the blackcurrant liqueur, cinnamon sticks, vanilla pods, and sliced orange and lemon.

Remove from the heat and leave to infuse for 4–5 hours. Strain through a sieve and put to one side.

Preparing the baked figs

Cut the figs into quarters from the stalk end but leave them attached at the base. Gently heat the butter and sugar in a non-stick pan. Add the figs and cook over a low heat, spooning the cooking syrup over them at regular intervals. As you cook the figs, gradually add the Collioure wine infusion and continue to cook until the liquid has a syrupy consistency.

Finishing

Place two figs in each dish, drizzle with the syrup and decorate with a piece of vanilla pod or cinnamon stick. Can be served with vanilla ice-cream.

Serving temperature

Banyuls L'Oublée, Domaine de la Rectorie, Marc and Thierry Parcé: 10°C (50°F).

Commandaria Saint John, Keo: 12°C (53°F).

Banyuls

This appellation, created in 1936, incorporates the villages of Port-Vendres, Cerbère, Collioure, and Banyuls. The terraced vineyards lie on steep hillsides overlooking the Mediterranean. According to European wine legislation, oxidized Banyuls wines (i.e. aged for a long time in wood) have to contain a minimum fifty per cent Grenache Noir, while the *grands crus* have to contain a minimum of seventy-five per cent. Like all *vins doux naturels*, they are fortified in one of two ways. If the grapes undergo a "short maceration", fermentation is limited to about three days, the wine is fortified after de-vatting and only involves the must. These wines are often slightly lacking in colour and tannin. If the grapes are macerated under alcohol, a process that lasts for three weeks, the wine is fortified before pressing, i.e. the alcohol is poured directly onto the grapes during fermentation.

These wines are much richer in colour and tannin. The density of residual sugar varies depending on the sugar content of the grapes and the point at which the wine is fortified. There are therefore dry Banyuls with forty-five to fifty grams of sugar per litre, semi-dry Banyuls with fifty to eighty grams, and sweeter versions with over eighty grams of sugar per litre.

BANYULS L'OUBLEE, DOMAINE DE LA RECTORIE, MARC ET THIERRY PARCE

The Parcé family runs an eighteen-hectare vineyard near the village of Banyuls. At twenty hectolitres per hectare, the yield is low. Although they specialize in vintage Banyuls, they also produce some excellent Collioure wines from a different vine stock grown on clearly differentiated plots. As its name suggests, this *cuvée* represents the contents of a barrel that had lain forgotten (*oubliée*) in a corner of the yard. It is a very old vintage produced from old Grenache Gris vines, fortified on the juice and aged traditionally, i.e. in barrels exposed to the sun for several years without being topped up. Ageing in oxidative conditions is always fairly unpredictable and the contents of this *cuvée* are therefore an unknown quantity.

COMMANDARIA SAINT JOHN, KEO

The writings of the eighth century Greek poet Hesiod attest to the fact that "Cyprus nama" – a sweet wine made from raisined grapes well-matured in oak barrels – was being made thousands of years ago. It acquired its present name in the twelfth century, during the time of the Hospitallers of St John of Jerusalem. In 1993, Commandaria became the first AOC wine to be geographically protected. It is produced in fourteen villages scattered across the Troodos Mountains, about thirty kilometres (eighteen miles) north of Limassol. It is made from the red Mavro and white Xynisteri grape varieties which are harvested in mid-September. When harvested, the grapes must have a minimum sugar content of 212g and 258g per litre respectively. They are then left to dry (raisin) in the sun for at least a week. After raisining, the sugar content has increased to 390g per litre for the Mavro variety and 450g for the Xynisteri. The grapes are fermented in the area of production and must have a minimum alcohol content of ten degrees. After fermentation, the wine is taken down to wineries in Limassol, where it is fortified by the addition of pure wine alcohol and aged in oak barrels for at least two years. Some Commandaria wines are aged in three stages using the *solera* system.

Yoghurt Cakes with Red Fruit Filling

(Gâteaux au yaourt fourrés aux fruits rouges)

These deliciously moist cakes filled with red fruit are equal to a wine with strength and volume. The Floc de Gascogne Rosé complements both the flavour and colour of the dessert – its strength offsets the creamy smoothness of the yoghurt while its colour echoes that of the bilberries and redcurrants. Far from being superficial, this reflection of colour is expressed in a very real affinity of flavour between the wine and the fruit. The Tan'nage de Madiran is a relatively new wine, based on the idea of making a dessert wine from the Tannat grape variety. The result is an unqualified success – an excellent red wine that combines the flavours of red fruit (especially redcurrant) with notes of liquorice. Its deep-purple colour is a perfect match for the redcurrants and bilberries, while a slight touch of astringency echoes the flavour of their seeds.

SERVES 8

Preparation time: 25 minutes

Cooking time: 25 minutes

Maceration: 1 hour

FOR THE YOGHURT CAKES

220g (8oz) flour + 30g (1oz)
  for the moulds

2 teaspoons baking powder

30g (1oz) butter for the moulds

3 eggs

250g (9oz) granulated sugar

125g (4½oz) plain yoghurt

grated zest of 1 lemon

FOR THE FILLING

100g (3¾oz) bilberries

100g (3¾oz) redcurrants

1 tablespoon granulated sugar

juice of half a lemon

1 tablespoon icing sugar

Preparing the fruit

Mix the bilberries and redcurrants together in a large mixing bowl, add the granulated sugar and lemon juice.

Leave to macerate in the refrigerator for at least 1 hour.

Making the cakes

Sieve the flour and baking powder. Grease and flour the small *manqué* moulds.

Beat the eggs and sugar in a food processor or using a balloon, rotary, or electric hand whisk. When the mixture turns white and acquires a creamy texture, carefully incorporate the yoghurt and lemon zest, and then the flour and baking powder. Divide the mixture between the moulds.

Sprinkle the surface with bilberries and redcurrants and bake in a preheated oven – 170°C (325°F), Gas Mark 3 – for about 25 minutes.

Finishing

Take the cakes out of the oven, remove from the moulds and leave to cool on a wire cake rack.

When completely cool, dust with icing sugar.

Serving temperature

Floc de Gascogne Rosé, Château de Tariquet: 10–11°C (50–52°F).

Maydie or Tan'nage Château d'Aydie 2000, Laplace: 14°C (57°F).

Floc de Gascogne AOC

Floc de Gascogne is a dessert wine that obtained AOC status in 1990. Its area of production corresponds to the geographical region of the Armagnac, Ténarèze and Haut-Armagnac appellations. The officially approved grape varieties used in the production of this AOC rosé are Cabernet Franc, Cabernet Sauvignon, Cot, Fer Servadou, Merlot, and up to fifty per cent Tannat. Wine legislation requires the sugar content of the grape must to be equal to 170g per litre before it is fortified (muté) with armagnac. The brandy must have a minimum alcohol content of fifty-two degrees and come from the same estate that produces the floc. It must be added to the grape must before fermentation and the mixture be allowed to rest for a minimum of nine months. The final alcohol content is between sixteen and eighteen degrees. These wines cannot leave the cellar before September 1 of the year following the grape harvest.

FLOC DE GASCOGNE ROSE, CHATEAU DE TARIQUET

As well as producing some very good Côtes de Gascogne Vins de Pays, the Château de Tariquet also excels in the art of distilling and boasts some equally good Armagnacs. The vineyard, situated at Eauze, in the heart of the Bas-Armagnac region, is run by the Crassa family who produce some well-structured Flocs de Gascogne. This rosé is made from fifty per cent Merlot and fifty per cent Cabernet Franc, and fortified with Folle Blanche brandy. It reveals hints of red fruit – cherries, Morello cherries, blackcurrants – and notes of mild spices. The palate is round and full, and the richness well-balanced. The whole is extremely harmonious, and the alcohol well-controlled.

MAYDIE OR TAN'NAGE CHATEAU D'AYDIE 2000, LAPLACE

This is a wine without an appellation. It is made from Tannat and comes from the Madiran region. In the past, wine-growers in the Pays de l'Adour region of southwestern France offered guests and friends a rich, smooth mistelle (grape juice with added spirits). With this in mind, the Laplace family decided to produce a dessert wine from a beautifully rich Tannat vintage. When harvested, the hand-picked grapes had a natural sugar content of 250–300g per litre. They were macerated cold before being fermented, fortified before pressing with pure wine alcohol (96.4 degrees) to bring out the aromas and colours, and then macerated for a month under alcohol before the wine was run off into 400-litre barrels where it was left for eighteen months. Because it wasn't filtered, the wine has an intense, deep-purple colour and is pervaded by aromas of liquorice, blackcurrants, and blackberries. The mouth is round and sweet, and the alcohol well-balanced. Above all, there is a beautiful tannic contrast that offsets the sweetness of the wine.

Yoghurt Ice-cream with Wild Strawberries

(Glace au yaourt et fraises des bois)

It is always fascinating to try and match sparkling wines with an ice-cream because they have to be fairly acidic, yet relatively sweet, in order to complement the dessert. In the case of the slightly sparkling Bugey-Cerdon Rosé, the association is based on lightness – the sparkling exuberance of this low-alcohol wine has light aromatic undertones of red fruit, strawberries and grenadine syrup; while the harmony between the frothiness of the wine and the creamy texture of the ice-cream is also reinforced by the mutual flavour of red fruit. The Austrian wine places more emphasis on acidic notes, which complement the citrus flavour of the ice-cream, and create a combination based primarily on the citrus element of the dessert.

SERVES 8
Preparation time: 45 minutes
Cooking time: 45 minutes

FOR THE YOGHURT ICE-CREAM
450g (1lb) plain yoghurt
150ml (¼ pint) single cream
150g (5¼oz) granulated sugar
grated zest of 1 lime

FOR THE STRAWBERRY JUICE
250g (9oz) strawberries, washed and hulled
1 tablespoon granulated sugar
juice of half a lemon

TO FINISH
500g (1lb 2oz) wild strawberries, washed and hulled

Making the yoghurt ice-cream

Use a balloon, rotary, or electric hand whisk to mix the yoghurt, single cream, sugar and grated lime zest together in a large mixing bowl.

Pour into an ice-cream maker and leave to churn for 25–30 minutes. Pour into a container with an airtight lid and put in the freezer.

Making the strawberry juice

Cut the strawberries into pieces, place in a large mixing bowl, and add the granulated sugar and lemon juice. Stand the bowl in a simmering bain-marie, cover and leave to cook for 45 minutes. Strain the juice through a sieve into a saucepan and simmer to reduce by half.

Finishing

Warm the strawberry juice, remove from the heat and add the wild strawberries.

Divide the mixture between individual bowls, add a scoop of yoghurt ice-cream, and serve immediately.

Serving temperature-

Bugey-Cerdon Rosé Pétillant, Alain Renardat-Fache: 8°C (47°F).

Wachau Trockenbeerenauslese 2000, Freie Weingartner: 10°C (50°F).

Vin du Bugey-Cerdon VDQS

The VDQS region of Bugey, situated in the French *département* of Ain, offers an extensive choice of local wines known as Vins du Bugey. The Bugey-Cerdon appellation incorporates sixty-three villages, characterized by a wide variety of soils, exposures, climates, and altitudes, near the Jura Mountains. The sparkling and slightly sparkling white, red, and rosé wines produced by the appellation are mainly consumed within the region. Cerdon, the best-known, is made in eight villages to the southeast of Bourg-en-Bresse, the departmental capital. Although there are a few non-sparkling red and white Cerdon wines, the appellation produces mainly sparkling and slightly sparkling wines according to the Champagne or traditional methods. The vine stock for these wines comprises the Pinot Noir, Pinot Gris, Gamay Noir à Jus Blanc, and Poulsard varieties, with sparkling rosés representing the greater part of production. The sugar content of this wine before fermentation is 136g of sugar per litre.

BUGEY-CERDON ROSE PETILLANT, ALAIN RENARDAT-FACHE

Alain Renardat-Fache produces an extremely agreeable, full-flavoured semi-sparkling rosé according to traditional methods. This involves bottling the wine before it has finished fermenting. It continues to ferment partially, producing effervescence and also leaving a certain amount of residual sugar, which avoids the need to add a *liqueur de tirage* to the base wine. This rosé is produced from eighty-five per cent Gamay and fifteen per cent Poulsard, and its pink colour is obtained by direct pressing and partial maceration on the skins. It is bottled immediately and continues to ferment in the bottle, at a cellar temperature of 10°C (50°F). After two months, the fermentation process is completed by a *dégorgement* that involves filtering the wine from bottle to bottle. The results are superb. The wine has a deep pink colour, the nose is marked by the aroma of red berries and grenadine syrup, the palate is light and agreeable, and the whole extremely fresh. Its alcohol content is a modest 7.5 degrees. The mousse is fine and well-integrated into the overall balance of the wine, while the mouth finishes with a sensation of sweetness and acidity. In short, this slightly sparkling rosé is an unqualified success.

Wachau

This Austrian wine region has one of the best Riesling vineyards in the world and produces sweet or botrytized wines, depending on the vintage year. This is because the climate in this part of Niederösterreich (Lower Austria), on the banks of the Danube, is more unpredictable than in regions like Burgenland, which makes it more difficult to produce wines in the TBA class. To achieve this standard, the grapes affected by botrytis must have a minimum of 156 oechsle, *i.e.* 22.1 degrees potential alcohol. The main difference between TBA wines from the Wachau region and those produced in Burgenland lies primarily in the perception of their acidity – TBA wines from Wachau tend to be slightly weaker.

WACHAU TROCKENBEERENAUSLESE 2000, FREIE WEINGARTNER

This golden, amber-yellow TBA 2000 was made from a blend of grapes harvested on different plots with silica, basalt, and mica soils. In 2000, the grapes were harvested on November 16 with yields of fourteen hectolitres per hectare. This wine is a blend of forty per cent Müller-Thurgau, thirty per cent Riesling, fifteen per cent Pinot Blanc, and fifteen per cent Chardonnay. Given the sugar-rich medium, fermentation occurred naturally. The wine, which was aged in oak for seven months, has 108g of residual sugar per litre.

Cakes with Black-cherry Filling

(Gâteaux fourrés aux cerises noires)

This dessert, a variation on the classic Gâteau Basque (a cake filled with rich pastry cream and cherry preserves), lends itself to sweet, fairly rich wines whose sweetness will be absorbed by the cake. At the same time, it is important to choose wines that highlight the aromatic note of cooked cherries. In the Pineau Rosé, a strong but agreeable dessert wine, the flavour of cherries is very much in evidence. Early fortification, at the start of the fermentation process, preserves the colour and fragrance of the wine with its strong overtones of Montmorency cherries and Morello cherries in eau-de-vie. The intensely coloured Terra Alta is a slightly fortified *vin doux naturel* made from Grenache grapes. Its aromas of red fruit, Morello cherries, and spices, and lower alcohol content make it a much more delicate accompaniment than the Pineau Rosé.

SERVES 10

Preparation time: 40 minutes

Cooking time: about 1 hour

Chilling: 1 hour

FOR THE CAKES

370g (13oz) wholemeal flour

1 teaspoon baking powder

300g (10oz) softened butter + 20g (¾oz) for the cake tins

310g (11oz) granulated sugar

1½ teaspoons vanilla sugar

pinch table salt

1 egg + 1 egg yolk + 1 beaten egg for the glaze

2 teaspoons rum

2 teaspoons aniseed liqueur

FOR THE BLACK-CHERRY FILLING

250g (9oz) black-cherries, washed and stoned

80g (3oz) soft brown sugar

freshly milled black pepper

Making the cake mixture

Sieve the flour and baking powder. Mix the softened butter with the granulated sugar, vanilla sugar, and salt. Then add the egg and egg yolk, stirring briskly with a wooden spoon. Incorporate the flour and baking powder, and then add the rum and aniseed liqueur.

Bring the mixture together in an evenly textured ball and chill for 1 hour.

Making the black-cherry filling

Put the cherries and brown sugar in a saucepan and cook for about 8 minutes over a moderate heat. When the cooking juices have completely evaporated and the cherries have a firm consistency, remove from the heat, add 2–3 twists of black pepper and leave to cool.

Baking the cakes

Grease ten small cake tins – 5cm (2 inches) in diameter x 5cm (2 inches) deep – with the 20g (¾oz) of butter.

Halve the ball of cake mixture and part-fill the tins with mixture from the first half. Top with a layer of cold cherries and cover with mixture from the second half, pressing down the edges to seal in the filling. Brush the top of the cakes with beaten egg before scoring with the prongs of a fork.

Bake in a preheated oven – 170°C (325°F), Gas Mark 3 – for 25 minutes. Leave to cool in the tins and then turn out onto a serving dish.

Serving temperature

Pineau des Charentes Rosé Raymond Raynaud: 11°C (52°F).

Terra Alta Tinto Dulce con Crianza, Millennium 2000: 14°C (57°F).

Pineau des Charentes

The appellation of this dessert wine, which obtained AOC status in 1945, lies in the French *départements* of Charente and Charente-Maritime. According to European wine legislation, only white dessert wines made from the must of Ugni Blanc, Folle Blanche, Colombard, Blanc Rosé, Jurançon Blanc, Montils, Sémillon, Sauvignon Blanc, and Merlot Blanc are entitled to use this label. The rosés have to be made from the must of Cabernet Franc, Cabernet Sauvignon, Malbec, and Merlot Rouge. These grape musts are required to have a minimum sugar content of 170g per litre, *i.e.* ten degrees' potential alcohol. The cognac used to fortify them must be the product of an earlier distillation, have been aged in wood and have a minimum alcohol content of sixty degrees. The mixture of must and brandy has to remain in the barrels until at least October 1 of the year following fortification. The acquired alcohol content must be between sixteen degrees and twenty-two degrees.

PINEAU DES CHARENTES ROSE RAYMOND RAYNAUD

This fine wine house, situated in Ambleville, produces some excellent Grande Champagne cognacs and quality Pineaux des Charentes. This rosé was made from eighty-five per cent Cabernet Sauvignon and fifteen per cent Merlot Noir. Its colour is obtained by maceration. The wine is fortified with cognacs that are at least one year old and the fortified wine is aged for three years in wood. The balance is seventeen degrees alcohol for 125g of residual sugar per litre. This dessert wine is pervaded by aromas of cherries, Kirsch, and even red peppers. The palate is full, generous, luscious and extremely harmonious.

Terra Alta DO (Spain)

This Denominación de Origen is situated in the southernmost part of Catalonia, near Priorat. The vines, the highest the region, are grown at an average altitude of 400–800 metres (1,312–2,624 feet) on steep, predominately limestone slopes. The continental climate means that the vineyard enjoys maximum hours of sunshine, while its elevated situation prevents it from being overwhelmed by the blistering summer heat. Garnatxa (Grenache), the dominant grape variety, accounts for more than seventy per cent of the vine stock in the form of Garnatxa Negra (Grenache Noir) and Garnatxa Peluda (Hairy-leaved Grenache), and there is also a small amount of Carinenya (Carignan). This wine area also produces white wines based on the alcohol-rich and relatively unrefined Viura and Garnatxa Blanca (Grenache Blanc) varieties. As in the Priorat region, there is an old tradition of sweet and dry *rancios* – the *seco* must have a minimum alcohol content of fifteen degrees and be aged in wood for a minimum of five years, while the smooth and pleasant *abocado* also has an alcohol content of fifteen degrees but is only aged in wood for two years.

TERRA ALTA TINTO DULCE CON CRIANZA, MILLENNIUM 2000

Based on the Garnatxa Negra, Millennium 2000 is a rich ruby-red wine with deep-purple reflections. It has an intense and beautifully complex nose redolent of blackcurrants, blackberries, and mild spices, with a mellowness added by the wood. The mouth is luscious and well-balanced, with a good tannic structure that provides contrast and sweetness. The wine, fortified at the end of the fermentation process, is aged in wood for three months.

Morello Cherries with Lemon Thyme and Black Pepper

(Griottes au thym citron et au poivre noir)

Red fruit is the dominant flavour, with the lightly cooked cherries preserving a freshness and crunchiness that is further enhanced by the creaminess of the freshly churned ice-cream. *Vins doux naturels* of character, from sunny, southern regions to echo the flavour of the thyme, are a delicious and perfectly rational choice. The Maury 2000, produced in non-oxidative conditions, has retained its rich, ruby-red colour. The nose is pervaded by the aroma of spices (especially pepper which echoes the pepper and thyme of the dessert), dark-red and black fruit, and candied Morello cherries. The Primitivo di Manduria 1997 is also a rich, unfortified wine whose sweetness is balanced by an interesting tannic structure. Its fragrance is strongly reminiscent of red fruit and it would go equally well with a strawberry or raspberry dessert. In this instance, it provides an wonderful complement for the freshness, juiciness, and flavour of the cherries.

SERVES 6

Preparation time: 30 minutes
Cooking time: 15 minutes
Maceration: 1 hour

FOR THE PAN-FRIED MORELLO CHERRIES

600g (1lb 5oz) really ripe Morello (Bigarreau or Burlat) cherries, stoned

80g (3oz) granulated sugar

2 teaspoons Cherry Marnier liqueur

FOR THE VANILLA THINS

1 vanilla pod, split lengthways

60g (2oz) softened butter

60g (2oz) icing sugar

2 egg whites

60g (2oz) flour

SERVING

2 lemon thyme sprigs

freshly milled black pepper

500ml (18fl oz) vanilla ice-cream

Making the vanilla thins

Scrape the seeds from the inside of the vanilla pod with the point of a knife. Cream the butter and icing sugar and then use a balloon, rotary, or electric hand whisk to mix in the egg whites, vanilla seeds, and flour. Place spoonfuls of the mixture on a greased baking sheet, shaping them into wafer-thin ovals.

Bake in a preheated oven – 160°C (320°F), Gas Mark 2–3 – for 10 minutes.

Remove the thins from the oven and use the blade of a knife to detach them from the baking sheet. Keep in a dry place.

Preparing the pan-fried Morello cherries

Mix the Morello cherries carefully with the granulated sugar. Leave to macerate for 1 hour at room temperature and then transfer the cherries and sugar syrup into a frying pan.

Cook over a moderate heat, removing the pan from the heat as soon as the mixture begins to bubble. Strain off the liquid, keep the cherries to one side and return the juice to the heat.

Add the Cherry Marnier and reduce for about 2 minutes, until the liquid acquires a syrupy consistency. Return the cherries to the pan and mix well.

Finishing

Divide the cherries between individual dishes, sprinkle with lemon thyme leaves and add a twist or two of freshly milled black pepper.

Add a scoop of vanilla ice-cream, decorate with the vanilla thins, and serve immediately.

Serving temperature

Maury 2000, Domaine Pouderoux: 14–15°C (57–59°F).

Primitivo di Manduria Dolce Il Madrigale 1997, Consorzio Produttori Vini: 14°C (57°F).

Maury AOC

This appellation incorporates five villages, including the village of Tautavel, in the French *département* of Pyrénées-Orientales, in the heart of the Agly valley. The vineyards lie on rugged hillsides of black schist and cover a total area of 1,700 hectares. As in the case of Banyuls and Rivesaltes, they produce two main types of wine: vintage, with its deep-purple colour and dominant red fruit, and oxidative, with its notes of dried plums, coffee, and caramel. The classic vine stock includes all the grape varieties authorized by the wine legislation covering *vins doux naturels*. Grenache Noir must represent at least seventy-five per cent, with ten per cent of additional grape varieties – Carignan, Cinsault, Syrah, and Listan. The wine must also undergo a compulsory ageing period of twenty-four months, from September 1 of the year of harvest. Some eighty-five per cent of the appellation's wine is produced by the Maury wine-growers' cooperative, which has 227 members. Among the independent vineyards, the Domaines du Mas-Amiel, des Pléiades, and Pouderoux produce some attractive wines.

MAURY 2000, DOMAINE POUDEROUX

This vineyard covers ten hectares in the heart of the appellation. Established in 1909, it is now run by the founder's grandson, Robert Pouderoux. This 2000 vintage was made entirely from Grenache Noir, selectively picked from each plot. The grapes are hand-picked into *bacs* (tubs), destalked, fortified before pressing, and subjected to a lengthy maceration of twenty-seven days. The wine is then aged in bottle. This Maury 2000 has an extraordinary fruity concentration – Burlat cherries, blackberries and blackcurrants – with notes of mild spice adding complexity. On the palate, there is a superb balance between sweetness, alcohol, and tannic structure.

Primitivo di Manduria Dolce (Italy)

The Primitivo di Manduria appellation covers the local area of Manduria and incorporates a number of villages in the southern provinces of Tarento and Brindisi. It makes some excellent sweet wines (*dolce*). The Primitivo grape variety can develop an exceptionally high sugar content that favours the production of some truly excellent, naturally sweet wines. These include a Dolce Naturale with an alcohol content of sixteen degrees that has to be aged for nine months, a Liquoroso Dolce Naturale with an alcohol content of 17.5 degrees that is aged for a minimum of two years, and a Liquoroso Secco with a minimum alcohol content of eighteen degrees and a compulsory ageing period of two years.

PRIMITIVO DI MANDURIA DOLCE IL MADRIGALE 1997, CONSORZIO PRODUTTORI VINI

The Consorzio Produttori Vini is a wine-growers' cooperative with a mission – to obtain official certification for the local wine and, above all, to demonstrate that the Primitivo grape variety can produce quality dessert wines. Conditions in 1997 made this an exceptionally good year for wine-growers throughout Italy. The Dolce Il Madrigale 1997 has an intense ruby-red colour, a complex nose – cherry preserve, sugared strawberries and mild spices – and a pleasant, well-balanced palate. The sweetness is superbly well-controlled, while the contrast provided by the tannic density creates an unusually tactile sensation.

Strawberry Semolina

(Semoule aux fraises)

This delicate dessert, in which a touch of balsamic vinegar adds fragrance to the creamy sweetness of milky semolina, has inspired the choice of two wines that have an excellent balance between sugar, acidity, and alcohol. The Loupiac is a rich, nobly rotted wine whose alcohol is balanced by its acidity. Hints of cream caramel echo the milky flavour of the semolina, while notes of well-ripened yellow fruit make it a perfect complement for the dessert. The golden, amber-yellow San Leonardo from Slovenia is based on raisined Rebula grapes fermented entirely in wood. Its nose is dominated by wonderfully exotic aromas, notes of dried fruit, stewed fruit and fruit compote, while its sugar and acidity provide a perfect balance for the alcohol.

SERVES 8

Preparation time: 35 minutes

Cooking time: 15 minutes

Chilling: at least 2 hours

FOR THE RED FRUIT

300g (10oz) strawberries, washed and hulled

30g (1oz) caster sugar

juice of half a lemon

FOR THE VANILLA SEMOLINA

250ml (9fl oz) milk

1 vanilla pod, split lengthways

30g (1oz) fine semolina

30g (1oz) granulated sugar

grated zest of 1 lemon

1 egg yolk

FOR THE CARAMEL

50ml (2fl oz) single cream

100g (3¾oz) granulated sugar

50ml (2fl oz) water

2 teaspoons balsamic vinegar

Preparing the strawberries

Cut the strawberries in half and mix with the sugar and lemon juice in a large mixing bowl. Chill for 30 minutes.

Making the vanilla semolina

Place the measured milk and vanilla pod in a saucepan and bring to the boil.

Sprinkle in the semolina and stir gently with a balloon whisk for 1 minute. Add the sugar and lemon zest, remove from the heat and beat in the egg yolk.

Pour into a large mixing bowl and leave to cool.

Making the caramel

Bring the single cream to the boil and remove from the heat.

Make a light brown caramel with the sugar and measured water.

Remove from the heat and add the warm cream to lower the cooking temperature and give the caramel the correct consistency.

Leave to cool. Add the balsamic vinegar and put to one side.

Finishing

Divide the strawberries between individual glass bowls, cover with semolina, and chill in the refrigerator for 1 hour.

Just before serving, cover the semolina with the caramel. Decorate with extra fruit.

Serving temperature

Loupiac Château du Cros 1988, Michel Boyer: 10°C (50°F).

Slovenia San Leonardo 1999, Edvin Simcic: 10°C (50°F).

Loupiac

This appellation is situated on the right bank of the River Garonne, opposite the Barsac and between the Cadillac and Sainte-Croix-du-Mont appellations. Loupiac produces sweet white wines that are botrytized in exceptional years. However, the appearance of botrytis is becoming increasingly rare and, as a general rule, the wines are potentially less rich than those of Sauternes and Barsac. In spite of this, several Loupiac vineyards have demonstrated their ability to produce some excellent wines that are also extremely good value. Like the other appellations on the right bank of the Garonne, these vineyards occupy a much hillier site than those on the opposite side of the river. The soil is clay and chalk and the grape varieties are typical of those used for the production of sweet Bordeaux wines. The best producers are Château du Cros, Château Loupiac-Gaudiet, Haut-Loupiac, and Clos-Jean.

LOUPIAC CHATEAU DU CROS 1998, MICHEL BOYER

The Château du Cros is one of the flagships of the Loupiac appellation. Michel Boyer and his son Henri, operate a policy of quality in both the vineyard and winery, and do not hesitate to abandon production in bad years. The estate has forty hectares of vines with an average age of forty years, and one plot of 100-year-old vines. The clay-and-chalk soil is typical of the region and the vine stock is primarily Sémillon, with some Sauvignon, and a small proportion of Muscadelle. This 1998 vintage is a brilliant golden-yellow colour. The nose has hints of yellow fruit, with a touch of honeyed exoticism and undertones of caramel added by the wood. The palate is full and pleasant, with a perfect balance between sugar, acidity, and alcohol. Compared with 1989 and 1990, this vintage is not one of the estate's most concentrated and candied wines, but it is certainly one of the most elegant.

Primorski

Slovenia is divided into three major wine regions. Primorski (Primorje), on the borders of Italy, is the most productive and accounts for one-third of the country's vineyards. Also known as the Littoral, Primorski is an extension of the Collio hills in the Italian regione of Friuli-Venezia Giulia and has a typically Italian vine stock of white and red grape varieties – Malvasia Istriana, Ribolla Gialla, Tocai Friulano, and Pinot Bianco (known locally as Malvazija, Rebula, Frilanski Tokaj, and Beli Pinot) for the whites, and Merlot, Refosco del Peduncolo Rosso (Teran), Barbera, and Cabernet Sauvignon for the reds. The Primorski region is divided into four sub-regions. In the north, the wine-growing hills of Brda produce mainly white and rosé wines. The Vipava region, wedged between Brda and the Karst vineyards, produces mainly white wines from the indigenous Zelen and Pinela varieties, while the chalky Karst region specializes in red wines based on Teran. Further south, near the Istrian Peninsula, the warmer Koper region, on the shores of the Adriatic, produces mainly red wines based on Teran, Merlot, Cabernet, and Barbera.

SAN LEONARDO 1999, EDVIN SIMCIC

Along with Ales Kristancic and Stogan Scunek, Edvin Simcic is one of the top producers in the Brda region. They represent a younger generation of growers who are revitalizing this region. Edvin Simcic produces two fine sweet wines by raisining – Edijev Izbor, a blend of the Rebula (the Italian Ribolla Gialla), Verduzzo, Chardonnay, and Sauvignon Blanc varieties, and San Leonardo, made entirely from raisined Rebula grapes. This old variety, which originated in the Friuli region and has been cultivated since the thirteenth century, is thought to be related to Robola, the white variety from the Greek island of Cephalonia. Aromatic, floral, and spicy, this is a wine with real potential that should be drunk relatively young. This 1999 vintage, fermented in wood, has a nose redolent of candied oranges and red peaches, a concentrated and well-balanced mouth, and an agreeable persistence. It is a beautifully harmonious wine.

Exotic and
Citrus Fruit

Chocolate Lime Dacquoise

(Douceur lactée au citron vert)

This dessert is characterized by notes of milk chocolate and the light crispness of meringue and, above all, by the tang of citrus that pervades the chocolate-lime cream. These delicate yet complex flavours call for the fineness of aromatic expression found in botrytized wines. The Amigne du Valais has remarkable flavours of white fruit and citrus peel, while its great elegance in the mouth balances the piquancy of the lime zest. The Rheingau Eiswein is a well-balanced botrytized wine, rich in sugar but pleasantly lively and fresh. A final note of clear acidity provides a superb complement for the lime and creates an undeniably harmonious partnership.

SERVES 10

Preparation time: 40 minutes

Cooking time: 25 minutes

Chilling: 2 hours

FOR THE MERINGUE

40g (1½oz) ground hazelnuts

40g (1½oz) ground almonds

125g (4½oz) icing sugar

3 egg whites

30g (1oz) granulated sugar

FOR THE CHOCOLATE LIME CREAM

finely grated zest of 2 limes

150ml (¼ pint) single cream

300g (10½oz) milk chocolate, finely chopped

150g (5¼oz) whipped cream

SERVING

20g (¾oz) cocoa powder

Making the meringue

Mix the ground hazelnuts and almonds with 80g (3oz) of the icing sugar.

Use a balloon, rotary, or electric hand whisk to beat the egg whites and granulated sugar until they form stiff peaks. Incorporate the ground nuts and icing sugar, stirring carefully with a wooden spoon, and then transfer the mixture onto a greased baking sheet covered with greaseproof paper.

Spread out the meringue mixture to a thickness of 2cm (¾ inch) and dust with the rest of the icing sugar.

Bake in a preheated oven – 200°C (400°F), Gas Mark 6 – for 18 minutes and then leave to cool.

Use a 5-cm (2-inch) pastry cutter to cut twenty rounds out of the baked meringue and keep to one side.

Preparing the chocolate lime cream

Add the grated lime zest to the single cream and bring to the boil.

Pour onto the finely chopped milk chocolate and mix with a balloon, rotary, or electric hand whisk to obtain a smooth creamy texture.

Leave to cool before incorporating the whipped cream with a wooden spoon.

Finishing

Divide the mixture between ten individual glass dishes, with alternate layers of cream and meringue.

Chill in the refrigerator for 1 hour.

Serve well chilled with a dusting of cocoa powder.

Serving temperature

Weingut Franz Künstler Hochheimer Kirchenstück Eiswein 2001: 10°C (50°F).

Amigne Grains Nobles 1999, Fabienne Cottagnoud: 10°C (50°F).

Rheingau

Together, Mosel-Saar-Ruwer and Rheingau constitute Germany's leading wine-growing region where Rieslings can reach the peak of perfection. The Rheingau vineyards cover a total area of 3,181 hectares and produce mainly white (90.8 per cent) and some red (9.2 per cent) wines. They stretch along the right bank of the river Rhine, between Lorchhausen, on the southern boundary of the state of Rhineland-Palatinate, and Hochheim, which lies slightly apart, to the east, on the banks of the river Main. The Riesling grape variety has been grown here since 1435. Today, it reigns supreme, regardless of its level of maturity. The main vineyard area lies on gently sloping, south-facing slopes, a situation that hastens ripening and favours the production of very mature grapes. In the vineyards located at higher altitudes, the grapes ripen later, which makes the logistics of harvesting much easier. The main wine style is Spätlese, a late-picked, slightly sweet wine. The type of soil varies, from more schistose soils in the west, to clay, sand and gravel in the east, around Hochheim.

WEINGUT FRANZ KUNSTLER HOCHHEIMER KIRCHENSTUCK 2001

The Franz Künstler estate lies near Hochheim, in the eastern part of the Rheingau, overlooking the river Main. Part of the vine stock is planted in the sand- and gravel-rich soil of the beautiful Kirchenstück and Hölle vineyards. For owner Gunther Künstler, the secret of quality lies mainly in the purity of the wines he produces. German wine legislation requires these wines to have a minimum natural maturity of 110–128 Oechsle, *i.e.* a minimum of 15.3–18.1 degrees potential alcohol. This Eiswein 2001 is a beautiful pale golden colour, with a nose redolent of citrus fruit and lime zest. The palate has a syrupy sweetness and an attractive candied flavour relieved by a wonderful underlying acidity. It has only 6.5 degrees of fermented alcohol and over 200g of residual sugar per litre.

Les Grains Nobles Valais AOC

In 1996, new wine legislation governing the Grains Nobles AOC appellation was introduced in the Valais region of Switzerland. It took the form of a ten-point charter – the "Charte Grain Noble Confidentiel" – that laid down the conditions and principles for the production of authentic, top-quality wines. These wines must come from vines grown on the region's best slopes and the vine stock must be at least fifteen years old. The choice of grape variety is limited to Arvine, Ermitage (the Swiss name for Marsanne Blanche), Johannisberg, Malvoisie (Pinot Gris), and Amigne. The wine must be produced from grapes overripened on the vine, with a minimum natural maturity of 130 Oechsle. Chaptalization is forbidden. Producers undertake to observe a minimum ageing period of twelve months in wooden barrels or large oak barrels (*foudres*) and to produce only nobly rotted grapes in suitable years, *i.e.* when the climatic conditions favour the development of botrytis.

AMIGNE GRAINS NOBLES 1999, FABIENNE COTTAGNOUD

Amigne is a rare old grape variety indigenous to the Valais region. It represents a modest vine stock of eighteen hectares and is well-suited to the production of sweet and botrytized wines. When raisined or botrytized, the wines have an extremely good balance between alcohol, sugar and acidity. The village of Vétroz specializes in this grape variety and type of wine. With this Amigne 1999, Fabienne Cottagnoud has produced an exceptional wine whose purity and cleanness are the result of a top-quality selection process. The wine has great aromatic precision, with fragrances of mandarins and candied lemons, and is beautifully fresh. The harmonious palate is characterized by great delicacy and an attractive freshness.

Lemon Meringue Shortcrust Tart

(Tarte sablée au citron meringuée)

This lemon meringue tart, with its concentrated flavours of citrus and lemon zest, calls for a simple accompaniment. The *cédratine* is a classic and absolutely delicious choice. This bright, greenish-yellow Corsican lemon liqueur releases both fresh and candied aromas, reminiscent of lemon drops and lemon marmalade, with notes of citronella and candied citron. The second choice, the Malvasia de Lipari, complements the mouth-feel of the dessert – sweetness, minerality, and acidity reminiscent of lime. As the wine ages, it develops aromas of candied lemon and lemon zest, with a noticeable citrus tang. This powerful aromatic expression is a natural progression, even the final acidity reveals the lingering persistence of lemon tart. This is more than an accompaniment, it is a natural alliance.

SERVES 8

Preparation time: 40 minutes

Cooking time: 16 minutes

Chilling: 1 hour

FOR THE LEMON TART

250g (9oz) Sweetened Shortcrust Pastry (see page 26)

160g (5¾oz) butter + 30g (1oz) for greasing

150ml (¼ pint) lemon juice

200g (7oz) caster sugar

finely grated zest of 3 lemons

4 eggs

FOR THE MERINGUE

3 egg whites

60g (2oz) granulated sugar

10g (¼oz) flaked almonds

20g (¾oz) icing sugar

Preparing the pastry case

Roll out the shortcrust pastry to a thickness of 3mm (⅛ inch) and use it to line a lightly greased, 20-cm (8-inch) flan ring.

Leave to stand for at least 1 hour in the refrigerator.

Preparing the cream and baking the tart

Put the lemon juice, butter, caster sugar, and grated lemon zest in a saucepan and bring to the boil. Remove from the heat and beat in the eggs one at a time. Reheat the mixture until it simmers, leave to cool, and then chill in the refrigerator.

Bake the pastry case for 12–14 minutes in a preheated oven – 180°C (350°F), Gas Mark 4 – until it begins to turn a light golden colour.

Remove from the oven and leave to cool. Fill with lemon cream to 5mm (¼inch) below the rim. Keep to one side.

Preparing the meringue and finishing the dessert

Use a balloon, rotary, or electric hand whisk to beat the egg whites, gradually adding the granulated sugar, until you obtain a firm, shiny meringue.

Use some of the meringue to cover the lemon cream and spoon the rest into a piping bag.

Pipe a circle of meringue around the edge of the tart, sprinkle the centre with almonds and then dust the tart with icing sugar.

Bake for 2 minutes in a preheated oven – 210°C (410°F), Gas Mark 6–7 – so that the meringue turns a light golden colour.

Remove from the oven and leave to cool on a wire cake rack. Chill in the refrigerator until serving.

Serving temperature

Liqueur Cédratine Mattei: 7–8°C (45–47°F).

Malvasia Passito di Lipari 1999, Pietro Colosi: 10°C (50°F).

LIQUEUR CEDRATINE MATTEI IN 1872, LOUIS-NAPOLEON

Mattei, founder of the Mattei wine house, created the wine-based aperitif known as Cap Corse. This family wine house subsequently produced an entire range of flavoured spirits – an excellent myrtle liqueur obtained by distilling the berries whose scent pervades the Corsican *maquis* (scrub), Castagnica made from sweet chestnuts, the mandarin-flavoured Bonapartine, and Cédratine, the lemon liqueur with an alcohol content of twenty-four to thirty-five degrees. Cédratine is produced from best-quality citrons, a large lemon-like but non-acidic citrus fruit whose thick, bumpy skin has a superb aromatic palette of candied citrus fruit, lime, and lemon zest. The liqueur has a sweet, pleasant palate whose sweetness is controlled by a wonderful acidity, with long, lingering persistence. An attractive freshness highlights the expression of flavours but should be enhanced by the serving temperature. This liqueur is best served chilled.

Malvasia Passito di Lipari

This DOC appellation is located in the Aeolian Islands in the Tyrrhenian Sea, mainly on the islands of Salina, Panarea, Filicudi, Stromboli, Vulcano, and Lipari. The warm Mediterranean climate and acid soil of this volcanic group is ideally suited to the Malvasia (Malvoisie) and, to a lesser extent, Corinto Nero grape varieties. The Malvasia grape originated in the Peloponnese and its name is wrongly applied to a number of Italian and French varieties as a synonym for Pinot Gris in the Loire region, Savoy, and Switzerland. The appellation produces several styles of Malvasia, all more or less sweet, depending on their level of natural maturity and degree of raisining. The Malvasia Passito di Lipari has a minimum alcohol content of eighteen degrees after raisining, with six per cent residual sugar. The wine must be aged for at least nine months before it is marketed. The even sweeter Malvasia Passito Liquoroso has a minimum alcohol content of twenty degrees, with six per cent residual sugar, and is aged for six months. Tasting a Malvasia di Lipari is a truly amazing experience; it is a sweet wine with a great deal of character – its sweetness, minerality, and acidity give it an intensely pleasurable mouth-feel.

MALVASIA PASSITO DI LIPARI 1999, PIETRO COLOSI

The Colosi family produces what is undoubtedly the purest expression of the appellation. This Malvasia Passito 1999, which has 120g of residual sugar per litre, is produced from vines grown on terraced vineyards, using ninety-five per cent Malvasia and five per cent Corinto Nero. The grapes are raisined for several days on the rocks before being fermented in thermoregulated stainless-steel vats where the wine is aged for twelve months.

Lemon Mousse with Red Fruit

(Mousse citronnée aux fruit rouges)

This dessert is dominated by the flavour of lemon rather than red fruit. The choice of accompanying wines must therefore be based on their notes of citrus and lemony acidity. The Austrian Welschriesling certainly fits the bill since, when affected by botrytis, it becomes more concentrated in sugar and acidity. Its sugar therefore provides a perfect complement for the lemon mousse, while its acidity offsets the sweetness of the dessert. The La Palma Malvasia is an entirely different proposition. This old grape variety from the Canary Islands, grown and raisined on volcanic soil, has complex and concentrated aromas, with wonderfully acid notes reminiscent of lime. The first combination is based on acidity and freshness, while the second is dominated by the tang of citrus peel.

SERVES 8

Preparation time: 35 minutes

Chilling: at least 1 hour

FOR THE LEMON CREAM

3 eggs
1 gelatine leaf
60g (2oz) butter
110ml (4fl oz) lemon juice
110 g (4oz) granulated sugar
1 teaspoon cornflour
grated zest of 1 lime
300ml (½ pint) whipped cream

FOR THE RED FRUIT

100g (3¾oz) strawberries
100g (3¾oz) wild strawberries
100g (3¾oz) raspberries
1 tablespoon strawberry syrup

Preparing the lemon cream

Use a balloon, rotary, or electric hand whisk to beat the eggs. Soak the gelatine in cold water to soften it.

Quickly melt the butter in a saucepan. Add the lemon juice, sugar, and cornflour and bring to the boil stirring continuously. Add the beaten eggs, stirring briskly with a whisk to obtain a smooth creamy texture, taking care not to let the mixture boil. Remove from the heat.

Drain the gelatine and incorporate into the lemon cream along with the grated lime zest. Stir until dissolved. Leave to cool and then incorporate the whipped cream. Spoon the mixture into a piping bag.

Finishing

Rinse the red fruit, drain carefully, and hull the strawberries. Keep eight pieces of fruit aside for the decoration.

Mix half the raspberries with the strawberry syrup and push the mixture through a sieve. Add the rest of the red fruit to the strained syrup and half fill eight individual glass dishes.

Top with lemon cream and decorate with a piece of reserved red fruit.

Chill in the refrigerator for 1 hour before serving.

Serving temperature

Welschriesling TBA 1998 Neusiedlersee-Hügelland, Gunther Schönberger: 10°C (50°F).

La Palma Malvasia Dulce 1999, Bodegas Teneguia: 10°C (50°F).

Neusiedlersee-Hügelland

Neusiedlersee is one of the four sub-regions of the Austrian wine area of Burgenland. In terms of vineyard area, it is the second largest with 3,910 hectares of vines planted on gently sloping hillsides overlooking Lake Neusiedl, to the southeast of Vienna. It produces dry white wines based on Pinot Blanc (Weissburgunder), Chardonnay, Sauvignon Blanc, and Welschriesling, and, in the St Margarethen area, some fine red wines based on the Blaufränkisch, Zwiegelt, and Saint-Laurent grape varieties. The continental climate, with its hot summers and warm, late autumns, and the ambient humidity due to the proximity of the lake favour the development of botrytis. The vines grow on variously coloured, silt-laden, and sandy soils. Under these conditions, the lakeside villages are able to produce fine sweet wines, the best known being the famous Ruster Aubrusch from the village of Rust. In this region, you will find every level of sweetness and maturity laid down by Austrian wine legislation, including some particularly good Beerenauslese and TBA wines. In this last category, the minimum natural maturity of the grapes before fermentation must be 156 oechsle, i.e. 22.1 degrees' potential alcohol. The richness and concentration of the region's TBA wines are truly remarkable.

WELSCHRIESLING TBA 1998 NEUSIEDLERSEE-HUGELLAND, GUNTHER SCHONBERGER

Gunther Schönberger runs a vineyard near the village of Morbich, at the southern end of Lake Neusiedl, near the Hungarian border. This dedicated wine-grower is a professional musician who took up wine-growing relatively late in life with, it has to be said, some amazing results – the quality of his wines is truly sensational. His vineyard is cultivated according to biodynamic methods which involves taking account of the grape variety, the selective picking of botrytized grapes and low yields. In his Morbich vineyard, every effort is made to produce top-quality wines. The vines are grown on acid soils consisting of slate and mica, sand and gneiss. The Welschriesling TBA 1998 is produced from thirty-year-old vines. When harvested, the botrytized grapes are pressed, fermented and then aged for thirty months in new wooden barrels. The perfect harmony of this wine, with 144g of residual sugar per litre, is simply amazing.

La Palma

The Canary Islands, off the coast of Morocco, have eleven appellations divided between the islands of Hierro, Gomera, Tenerife, Lanzarote, La Palma, and Gran Canaria. On the volcanic island of La Palma, the vines are planted at an altitude of between 200 and 1,200 metres (656–3,937 feet). The appellation is divided into three areas – Hoyo de Mazo, Fuencaliente and La Palma. It produces white and red wines, as well as the sweet Malvasia Dulce which is legally required to have an alcohol content of between fifteen and twenty-two degrees and a minimum residual sugar of forty-five grams per litre.

LA PALMA MALVASIA DULCE 1999, BODEGAS TENEGUIA

The Malvasia grape variety reigns supreme in The Canaries. It reached the islands in 1676, after being introduced to Madeira in 1424. The Bodegas Teneguia produce this Malvasia Dulce in the Fuencaliente wine area of La Palma. It is a naturally sweet wine, made from sixty-year-old Malvasia vines cultivated at an altitude of between 300 and 500 metres (984–1,640 feet). The grapes are harvested late, raisined on the vine, fermented in stainless-steel vats and bottle aged for twelve months before being marketed. With a natural maturity of twenty degrees potential alcohol, it was fermented to 14.5 degrees and has 110g of residual sugar per litre. This Malvasia Dulce is expressed on hints of citrus fruit, lime and honey. The mouth is rich, full, and supple with a wonderful sweetness balanced by fine touches of acidity.

Coconut Petits Fours and Passion-fruit Mousse

(Noix de coco et fruit de la passion)

In this dessert, the passion-fruit calls for extremely fragrant wines that create a harmonious complement based on delicate and exotic notes. A floral nose, with the scent of irises, scented geraniums, exotic fruit, and lychees, makes the Gewurztraminer a perfect aromatic match. It is an ideal and extremely delicate accompaniment. The Muscat of Samos has a very different structure. It is a naturally sweet wine produced from raisined grapes and its aromas are more reminiscent of fruit than flowers – candied and sugared yellow fruit, with an underlying touch of controlled oxidation. An element of candied orange peel, late-ripening peaches and a concentration of extremely ripe, yellow-fruit highlights the flavour of the passion-fruit mousse.

SERVES 12

Preparation time: 30 minutes

Cooking time: 20 minutes

Chilling: 5 hours

FOR THE COCONUT PETITS FOURS

75g (2½oz) granulated sugar

100g (3¾oz) grated coconut

2 egg whites

40g (1½oz) butter

FOR THE PASSION-FRUIT MOUSSE

4 gelatine leaves

250ml (9fl oz) passion-fruit juice

60g (2oz) granulated sugar

250g (9oz) whipped cream

SERVING

200ml (7fl oz) raspberry coulis (see page 119)

Making the coconut petits fours

Mix the granulated sugar and grated coconut, add the egg whites and then 20g (¾oz) of melted butter. Mix well and leave to harden for 1 hour in the refrigerator.

Use a fork to shape petits fours, 6cm (2½ inches) in diameter, from the hardened mixture and place on a buttered baking sheet.

Bake in a preheated oven – 170°C (325°F), Gas Mark 3 – for 10 minutes and then remove from the baking sheet and leave to cool. Keep in a dry place.

Preparing the passion-fruit mousse

Soak the gelatine leaves in cold water.

Heat the passion-fruit juice, taking care not to let it boil, add the softened gelatine and stir until it has dissolved.

Add the granulated sugar and leave the mixture to cool to 20°C (68°F).

Incorporate the whipped cream, stirring gently with a whisk.

Finishing

Divide the passion-fruit mousse between twelve individual glass dishes.

Chill for at least 4 hours in the refrigerator.

Serve with raspberry coulis and the petits fours.

Serving temperature

Gewurztraminer SGN 1994, Trimbach Wines: 10°C (50°F).

Samos Nectar, Samos Wine-growers' Cooperative: 10°C (50°F).

Gewurztraminer SGN

Gewurztraminer is an aromatic grape variety that expresses a wide range of exotic aromas – lychees, mangoes, and passion-fruit – especially when affected by botrytis. When harvested at the nobly rotted stage, the grapes give the wine both delicacy and complexity. Gewurztraminer in fact often produces intoxicating, exuberant wines with rather unsubtle aromas, whereas well-botrytized grapes add delicacy. The SGN designation was introduced on March 1, 1984. However, it has been recently revised and standards have become even more exacting. Gewurztraminer, like Pinot Gris, must have a natural sugar content of 306g per litre without any form of added sugar, *i.e.* 18.2 degrees' potential alcohol. It is self evident that, at this level of maturity, the yield is low and the concentration extremely high.

GEWURZTRAMINER SGN 1994, TRIMBACH WINES

This SGN 1994 is a top-quality wine. In Alsace, 1994 was a good year for botrytis and the wines from this vintage are concentrated, clean, extremely delicate, and have a good aptitude for ageing. With this Gewurztraminer, Trimbach Wines has produced a full, dense wine with an aromatic array of roses, lychees, mild spices, and an attractive note of candied fruit melting into exotic and citrus fruits. The mouth is full and dense, superbly structured, with a good balance between sugar and alcohol.

Muscat of Samos

The Muscats of Samos and Lemnos are two wines named after islands in the Aegean Sea. The Muscat de Lemnos appellation, which also includes a dry white wine, is based on the Muscat of Alexandria grape variety. The mountainous island of Samos lies in the eastern Aegean about 1.5 kilometres (one mile) off the Turkish coast and is separated from it by the narrow Samos Strait. Its name derives from the Phoenician word *sama* meaning "altitude", most probably a reference to its two principal mountains, Mount Kerketeus in the west and Mount Ambelos in the north, which rise to 1,430 metres

(4,692 feet) and 1,150 metres (3,773 feet) respectively. The vineyards cover an area of 2,300 hectares, mainly along the island's northern shore, rising from sea level to an altitude of 800 metres (2,625 feet). The harvest begins in the second week of August at sea level and finishes in the mountains at the end of October. Muscat of Samos, based on Muscat à Petits Grains, can have several levels of concentration – sweet Muscat, fortified with the most ordinary type of alcohol, sweet Samos Grand Cru, produced from a lower yield, also fortified with alcohol but noticeably more concentrated, and Samos Nectar, a naturally sweet wine produced from raisined grapes.

SAMOS NECTAR, SAMOS WINE-GROWERS' COOPERATIVE

Samos Nectar is a naturally sweet, raisined wine, produced from the best high-altitude terraced vineyards. After being harvested, the grapes are laid out to dry in the sun on reed mats for at least a week. The desiccated (raisined) grapes are then pressed and the must fermented in stainless-steel vats at low temperatures. After being fortified, the wine is barrel aged for three months. This "nectar" has an alcohol content of fourteen degrees and 151g of residual sugar per litre. It is a rich, complex wine with exotic aromas of candied oranges, pine, menthol, and a touch of honey. The palate is rich and concentrated with a lingering finish.

Caramelized Bananas and Traditional French Doughnuts

(Bananes caramelisées et merveilles)

This dessert requires a wine to complement the crisp sweetness of the doughnuts and creamy smoothness of the caramel, while the banana allows for wines that are slightly rustic in character. The Arbois Vin de Paille is sweet and well-rounded, rich in sugar but low in acidity and nervosity. The crispness of the doughnuts absorbs the wine's sugary sweet energy and gives it relief, while the caramelized smoothness of the bananas is strongly reminiscent of rum – qualities echoed by the raisined aromas and rich, exotic alcohol content of the *vin de paille*. The Moscatel de Lanzarote 1975, with its hints of lime and orange peel, offers slightly acidic notes that balance the smooth sweetness of the dessert, while touches of fruit jam complement the flavour of the bananas. Although there is an element of old wine about this well-developed Moscatel, its aromatic nature adds a touch of freshness to the density of fragrances and flavours.

SERVES 6

Preparation time: 25 minutes
Cooking time: about 15 minutes
Chilling: 1 hour

FOR THE DOUGHNUTS

250g (9oz) flour
half teaspoon table salt
half teaspoon baking powder
1 egg + 1 egg yolk
60g (2oz) butter, melted
2 teaspoons orange-flower water
1 litre (1¾ pints) groundnut oil
 (for frying)
50g (1¾oz) icing sugar

FOR THE CARAMELIZED
BANANAS

50g (1¾oz) soft brown sugar
50g (1¾oz) butter
2 vanilla pods, split lengthways
12 small bananas, peeled
juice of 1 lemon
30g (1oz) white grapes
100ml (3½fl oz) brown rum

SERVING

750ml (1¼ pints) vanilla
 ice-cream

Making the doughnuts

Mix the flour, salt, 30g (1oz) of icing sugar, and the baking powder together in a large mixing bowl. Then mix and add the egg and egg yolk, melted butter, and orange-flower water. Bring the dough together in a smooth, evenly textured ball and chill for 1 hour in the refrigerator.

Roll out the dough as thinly as possible and cut out rectangular shapes with a pastry wheel.

Fry in the preheated oil – 180°C (350°F) – until the doughnuts are crisp and golden and then drain on absorbent kitchen paper.

Dust with icing sugar and keep to one side.

Preparing the caramelized bananas

Melt the soft brown sugar and butter in a non-stick pan and add the split vanilla pods and peeled bananas. Cook for about 10 minutes, turning the bananas to ensure they are evenly browned.

Add the lemon juice, grapes, and rum, burn off the alcohol and reduce the cooking syrup by half.

Finishing

Place two caramelized bananas on each plate, add a little of the cooking syrup and a few grapes.

Serve with the doughnuts and a scoop of vanilla ice-cream.

Serving temperature

Arbois Vin de Paille 1995, Domaine Rolet: 12°C (53°F).

Moscatel de Lanzarote 1972, Solera Mozzagua: 12°C (53°F).

Arbois Vin de Paille

Created in 1936, the Arbois appellation – which incorporates twelve villages, including Arbois, in the French region of Jura – was one of the first to receive AOC status. As well as white, red and yellow (*vin jaune*) wines, it also produces *vins de paille*, wines made from semi-dried grapes according to an old local tradition. Today, European wine legislation requires this type of wine to be produced according to a strict set of regulations. The grapes must be harvested when well-ripened and have a natural sugar content of 306g per litre of must – and therefore an acquired alcohol content of no less than 14.5 degrees and no more than eighteen degrees – when pressed. The yield is limited to twenty hectolitres per hectare. Once harvested, the red, rosé, and white grapes are laid out to dry for at least six weeks on layers of straw or on racks before being pressed. The concentration of natural sugars by raisining under natural conditions is compulsory. *Vins de paille* are aged for thirty-six months from the date of pressing, including eighteen months in oak. The "Vin de Paille" designation can be legally used in the Jura by the Côtes du Jura, Arbois, and L'Étoile appellations, and, in the Rhône Valley, by L'Hermitage.

ARBOIS VIN DE PAILLE 1995, DOMAINE ROLET

The Rolet family believe that, when it comes to *vins de paille*, the condition of the grapes is more important than the concept of terroir. For raisining to be successful, the grapes must be impeccable. Arbois Vin de Paille 1995 is made from sixty per cent Savagnin, twenty per cent Poulsard, and twenty per cent Chardonnay. After harvesting, the grapes have to undergo the slow, three-month desiccation process that gives them the required level of raisining. The wine is fermented to sixteen degrees of alcohol and retains ninety-six grams of residual sugar per litre. This is an attractive *vin de paille*, sweet and delicate, with aromas of dried fruit, fruit jellies, and candied fruit. The palate is rich and full, with a controlled sweetness and an excellent balance.

Lanzarote DO

The volcanic island of Lanzarote, in the Canary archipelago, has its own appellation. It specializes in the production of classic Malvasia, which has an alcohol content of fifteen to twenty-two degrees, and sweet wines based on Moscatel. The classic sweet wines must have at least forty-five grams of residual sugar per litre.

MOSCATEL DE LANZAROTE 1972, SOLERA MOZZAGUA

This superb Moscatel 1972 is a beautiful golden-amber colour. It has a candied nose, with hints of apricot, fruit preserve, orange peel, and mandarin. The note of complexity imparted by the *solera* system adds touches of quinine and orange wine. The mouth is smooth, with an attractive syrupy sweetness balanced by the underlying alcohol. This particular vintage proves that Muscat à Petits Grains is well-suited to ageing. It has a freshness of flavour and slightly acid notes that offset the sweetness in the mouth, and a wonderful lingering finish.

Pineapple Sorbet with Hibiscus Syrup

(Coupe glacée à l'ananas et jus d'hibiscus)

This dessert calls for wines that reinforce its fruity aromas. When overripened, Petit Manseng (the dominant grape variety in Pacherenc wines) acquires sweet, slightly candied aromas of pineapple, with an underlying acidity typical of this type of wine. The fragrances of exotic fruit are very much in evidence. Although a little less aromatic than the first wine, the Romanian Muscat Ottonel, made from botrytized grapes, develops a certain delicacy. In the mouth, there is a burst of yellow-fruit flavours, strong notes of overripened pineapple, and candied oranges, but with a slight touch of menthol and resin, and a fresh sensation of crisp, crunchy grapes that make this a truly remarkable wine – a perfect match for the pineapple sorbet.

SERVES 6

Preparation time: 50 minutes

Freezing: 30 minutes

FOR THE PINEAPPLE SORBET

500g (1lb 2oz) fresh pineapple pulp

100g (3¾oz) icing sugar

juice of 1 lime

2 fresh mint leaves, finely shredded

FOR THE HIBISCUS SYRUP

grated zest of 1 small orange

15g (½oz) dried hibiscus flowers

150ml (¼ pint) water

40g (1½oz) granulated sugar

SERVING

300g (10oz) fresh pineapple

Preparing the pineapple sorbet

Mix the pineapple pulp and icing sugar and add the lime juice. When the sugar has dissolved, pour the mixture into an ice-cream maker and churn.

Add the shredded mint leaves when the mixture begins to set. Continue to churn until you obtain the right texture.

Transfer the sorbet to an airtight container and put in the freezer for 30 minutes.

Preparing the hibiscus syrup

Add the orange zest and hibiscus flowers to the measured water and bring to the boil. Remove from the heat, cover, and leave to infuse for 10 minutes.

Strain through a sieve, add the sugar and reduce for 8 minutes over a moderate heat until you have a smooth syrup. Leave to cool.

Finishing

Use a spoon to incorporate the cold hibiscus syrup into the pineapple sorbet. Then use an ice-cream scoop to make sorbet balls.

Place a few balls in individual glass dishes and serve with pieces of fresh pineapple.

Serving temperature

Pacherenc du Vic-Bilh Passion de Frimaire 1995, Alain Brumont: 10°C (50°F).

Murfatlar, Muscat Ottonel VSOC, CIB 1984: 10°C (50°F).

Pacherenc du Vic-Bilh

The area of this AOC wine region is the same as the Madiran appellation. It covers some 1,300 hectares and incorporates thirty-seven villages in the French *département* of Gers, six in the Hautes-Pyrénées and three in the Pyrénées-Atlantiques. The region has hot summers, mild autumns (ideal for raisining), and harsh winters. The appellation, with its predominantly clay and silica soils, specializes in the production of dry and sweet white wines. Its name comes from an expression in the old local dialect meaning "trellis post in the Pays du Vic-Bilh", a reference to the fact that the vines used to be grown in trellis rows. Wines using this AOC label must be made from the Arrufiac, Courbu, Petit Manseng, Gros Manseng, Sauvignon Blanc or Sémillon varieties. Petit Manseng is the dominant variety, and is even used on its own in the production of sweet wines when it is raisined in the same way as for the Jurançon appellation. The maximum yield is forty hectolitres per hectare for Pacherenc and sixty hectolitres per hectare for dry white wines.

PACHERENC DU VIC-BILH PASSION DE FRIMAIRE 1995, ALAIN BRUMONT

Alain Brumont, widely acclaimed as one of the region's top producers and a pioneer of the Madiran revival, also produces some top-quality Pacherenc wines. This Passion de Frimaire 1995 was harvested on December 16, 1995. When the Petit Manseng grapes were raisined, they contained twenty-five degrees' potential alcohol. After a slow pressing, the must was fermented in new wood. This golden, straw-coloured vintage has a complex and intense nose of mango and well-ripened pineapple, with exotic hints of passion-fruit and a touch of cream caramel added by the wood. The mouth is pleasant, full, and beautifully concentrated. The balance of flavours is perfect and the finish is characterized by flavours of baked mango.

Dobroudja

Romania is one of the world's great producers of quality sweet and botrytized wines. The Dobroudja region, situated in the southeast of the country, near the Black Sea, is particularly important since it has a microclimate that favours the development of noble rot. With 300 days' sunshine and no more than 150–200mm (6–8 inches) of rain per year, the region is relatively dry, while the winds and breezes blowing off the Black Sea ensure successful raisining. Romanian wine classifications, established in 1972, define several categories of wine according to the ripeness of the grapes. DOC (*denumire de origine controlata*) and DOCC (*vinuri de calitate superioara cu denumire de origine controlata si trepte de calitate*) wines are produced in a demarcated region. DOCC wines are of a higher quality – they must be made from a *Vitis vinifera* variety and have a minimum level of maturity. The CIB category (*cules le inobilarea boabelor*) corresponds, in terms of sweetness, to wines of a well-developed Beerenauslese level, with a minimum of 240g of sugar per litre. The CSB category (*cules la stafidirea boabelor*) is even sweeter and corresponds to the level of TBA.

MURFATLAR, MUSCAT OTTONEL VSOC, CIB 1984

The Murfatlar appellation, that lies near the Black Sea port of Constanta, has a hot, continental climate modified by the proximity of the sea. Murfatlar is the Turkish name for the ancient Greek city of Tomis. This Muscat Ottonel, an old-established grape variety in Central and Eastern Europe, is harvested by the selective picking of botrytized grapes. This vintage had 18.5 degrees' potential alcohol when harvested, 13.5 degrees' fermented alcohol and eighty degrees of residual sugar per litre. The wine has a wonderful golden colour and a complex nose of well-ripened yellow fruit, apricot, fruit jellies, and orange peel, with an underlying touch of menthol and resin typical of Muscat at this level of maturity. The palate is harmonious, with well-balanced sweetness, well-integrated alcohol, and good length.

Exotic Fruit Compote with Vanilla Ice-cream

(Compote des fruits exotiques vanillée)

This delicious compote, with its exotic fruit flavours, delicate touch of vanilla and sharp tang of lime, is well-matched by the choice of wines. Made from top-quality Muscat à Petits Grains that has been meticulously raisined, they both provide an interesting match in terms of flavour and aroma. Their fragrances of mandarin, candied orange and mango make them ideally suited to the exotic fruit – mango, papaya, banana, pineapple – and mild vanilla flavours of the dessert. The young Alicante Moscatel has aromas of fresh fruit – especially peaches – candied apricots, stewed fruit, and citrus peel. A pleasant touch of acidity adds freshness and makes this an extremely drinkable wine. Both wines are an ideal accompaniment for the dessert.

SERVES 8

Preparation time: 50 minutes

Cooking time: 25 minutes

FOR THE VANILLA ICE-CREAM

1 vanilla pod, split lengthways

1 crushed coffee bean

500ml (18fl oz) milk

200ml (7fl oz) single cream

5 egg yolks

180g (6¼oz) granulated sugar

FOR THE FRUIT COMPOTE

4 kiwi fruit

1 large mango

1 large papaya

250g (9oz) fresh pineapple

2 bananas

juice of 2 limes

60g (2oz) butter

80g (2¾oz) soft brown sugar

50ml (2fl oz) Mandarine Imperiale or Grand Marnier

100ml (3½fl oz) orange juice

2 vanilla pods, split lengthways

Preparing the ice-cream

Add the split vanilla pod and crushed coffee bean to the milk and single cream and bring to the boil. Remove from the heat, cover, and leave to infuse for 20 minutes.

Use a balloon, rotary or electric hand whisk to beat the egg yolks and sugar until the mixture turns white. Continue beating and gradually add the boiling milk.

Transfer the mixture to a saucepan and cook over a low heat, stirring with a wooden spoon, until the cream thickens.

Strain into a large mixing bowl and stand the bowl on a bed of ice so the cream cools rapidly.

Pour into an ice-cream maker and leave to churn for 15 minutes.

Transfer the ice-cream into an airtight container and put into the freezer.

Preparing the fruit compote

Wash and peel the fruit and cut into large pieces, using a sharp knife to obtain a clean cut. Add the lime juice.

Lightly brown the butter in a non-stick pan and add the soft brown sugar. Mix the butter and sugar, add the orange juice and split vanilla pods, and reduce the liquid by half. Add the fruit pieces, stirring gently with a wooden spoon.

Remove the fruit from the pan and keep to one side. Turn up the heat and continue to reduce the liquid. When it becomes syrupy, add the Mandarine Impériale or Grand Marnier and fruit pieces, and mix rapidly.

Finishing

Divide the fruit and syrup between individual dessert dishes, add a scoop of vanilla ice-cream and decorate with a small piece of vanilla pod.

Serving temperature

Alicante Vino Dulce de Moscatel Casta Diva 2001, Gutierrez de la Vega: 10°C (50°F).

Moscato Passito 1999 La Spinatta, Giorgio Rivetti: 10° (50°F).

Alicante DO

This appellation, which comprises the Valencia and Utiel-Requena DOs, is situated in the hot and arid province of Valencia, in eastern Spain, where the climate is tempered by the proximity of the Mediterranean. It is divided into two sub-regions – La Marina and Alicante. The first of these lies nearest the sea and has alluvial, sandy soil. It mainly produces attractive Muscat wines based on Moscatel de Alejandria (Muscat of Alexandria), including some delicious Vinos de Licor Moscatel. The chalky soil of Alicante is better suited to red wines based on Monastrell, Bobal and Garnacha, as well as a dessert wine known as Fondillon.

ALICANTE VINO DULCE DE MOSCATEL CASTA DIVA 2001, GUTIERREZ DE LA VEGA

The vineyard, founded in 1978, is run by Felipe Gutierrez de la Vega. Although it produces a number of red, rosé and white wines, the property excels in the production of dessert wines – modern-style Fondillons, characterized by a rich fruitiness and much less oxidative in nature than most of the rest of the appellation. The superb Vino Dulce de Moscatel is produced from two hectares of vines planted on the Ribera del Rio Gorgos, in the village of Jaya, in the Marina Alta region. Four types of Moscatel are produced here, each the result of different soils or different winemaking processes and different levels of sweetness. The Casta Diva 2001 is made from well-ripened Moscatel de Alejandria (Muscat of Alexandria). It has a superb orangey-yellow colour, is fermented naturally and has a fermented alcohol content of just two degrees. The nose is redolent of mandarins, candied oranges, and exotic fruit. The balance of flavours is remarkable, the alcohol well-integrated, with a final touch of citrus in the mouth.

MOSCATO PASSITO 1999 LA SPINATTA, GIORGIO RIVETTI

This wine, made from Muscat à Petits Grains, comes from the Asti appellation in Italy. Giorgio Rivetti is one of the top producers in Piedmont and makes the best Barbaresco and Moscato d'Asti wines. In 1998, he extended his range by producing his first Moscato Passito – the term *passito* means that the wine is made from raisined grapes. The grapes are grown on chalky soil, harvested when well-ripened, and then left to dry on racks for several weeks. During this time, they lose water and weight, becoming dehydrated and more concentrated in sugars. After the drying stage, they are pressed and fermented in barrels. Fermentation stops naturally and the wine remains in the barrel for twenty-four months. It is then bottle-aged for twelve months before being marketed. Although this Moscato Passito has 220g of residual sugar per litre, the sweetness is well-controlled. The wine is rich, concentrated, aromatic, and truly delicious.

Mascarpone Cream with Hibiscus Jelly

(Crème de mascarpone en gelée d'hibiscus)

The mascarpone gives this dessert a note of smooth creaminess that calls for wines with enough acidity to highlight the combination of textures and flavours. With their controlled sweetness and richness, the Gaillac Doux and Recioto di Soave both make an extremely elegant accompaniment. Their fine balance between sugar and acidity allows them to complement the contrasting flavours of the dessert, including the slightly acid note of the hibiscus jelly, while their vivacity offsets the rich creaminess of the mascarpone. The wonderfully syrupy structure of the Gaillac is balanced by an equally wonderful acidity that provides an immediate contrast with the cream. The old *gaillacois* variety, Len de l'El, with its extremely delicate aroma of flowers and citrus fruit, provides a perfect match for the subtle flavours of the dessert. The Soave does much the same with its notes of yellow fruit and its well-balanced richness.

SERVES 8
Preparation time: 40 minutes
Chilling: 2 hours

FOR THE HIBISCUS JELLY
1 gelatine leaf
50g (1¾oz) granulated sugar
250ml (9fl oz) water
20g (¾oz) dried hibiscus flowers
30 ripe raspberries

FOR THE MASCARPONE CREAM
1 gelatine leaf
3 egg yolks
35g (1¼oz) granulated sugar
125g (4½oz) mascarpone cheese
125g (4½oz) whipped cream

SERVING
8 untreated rose petals

Preparing the hibiscus jelly

Soak the gelatine leaf in cold water. Add the sugar to the measured water, bring to the boil and add the dried hibiscus flowers. Remove from the heat, leave to infuse for 20 minutes, and then strain through a sieve. Drain off the gelatine leaf and dissolve in the hibiscus infusion.

Mix well and divide the jelly between individual glass dessert dishes.

Add the raspberries and chill for 1 hour in the refrigerator.

Preparing the mascarpone cream

Soak the gelatine leaf in cold water. Use a balloon, rotary or electric hand whisk to beat the egg yolks and granulated sugar in a large mixing bowl until the mixture turns white.

Dissolve the gelatine in a bain-marie and add to the mixture. Stir well and then incorporate the mascarpone and whipped cream.

Divide the mixture between the glass dishes, covering the layer of the hibiscus jelly.

Chill for at least 2 hours in the refrigerator and decorate with a rose petal before serving.

Serving temperature

Gaillac Doux Cuvée Renaissance 1999, Domaine Rotier: 10°C (50°F).

Recioto di Soave Col Foscarin 1997, Claudio e Sandro Gini: 10°C (50°F).

Gaillac Doux

Gaillac obtained AOC status for its white wines in 1938, but had to wait until October 23, 1970 for the reds to be included in the appellation. The Gallo-Romans were already cultivating vines in the area in the first century AD, which makes this one of the oldest French wine regions. The Gaillac vineyards cover a vast area, incorporating seventy villages in the French *département* of Tarn, and produce a wide variety of different wines. The soils are varied, with a mixture of clay and chalk on the right bank of the River Tarn, sand and gravel on the left bank. There are also a number of indigenous grape varieties – Mauzac, Ondenc, and Len de l'El ("far from the eye", so called because the bunches have a long fruit stalk) for the whites and Duras for the reds – combined with other, better-known varieties from southwestern France. To qualify for the Gaillac Doux appellation, white wines must have a minimum acquired alcohol content of eight degrees and a minimum residual sugar of forty-five grams per litre, while the maximum yield must not exceed forty-five hectolitres per hectare. The best grape varieties for this type of wine are Mauzac, Len de l'El, Ondenc, Muscadelle, Sémillon, and Sauvignon Blanc.

GAILLAC DOUX CUVEE RENAISSANCE 1999, DOMAINE ROTIER

The Domaine Rotier, situated in the district of Cadalen, produces seventy per cent red and thirty per cent white wines. The Cuvée Renaissance is one of the vineyard's top-quality wines. This 1999 vintage was made entirely from the Len de l'El grape variety grown on gravel soil, in a year that favoured the development of noble rot. The grapes were harvested in three selective pickings, between October 6–15, and fermented in oak barrels. When harvested, the grape must had twenty degrees' potential alcohol and the wine has a residual sugar content of 125g per litre. This is a really luscious wine in which the sweetness is brilliantly offset by a wonderful acidity on the finish.

Recioto di Soave DOCG

Recioto di Soave has just been granted DOCG status. The wines come from the area around Soave, an attractive town nestling at the foot of a medieval castle in the Italian province of Verona. The wine is made from the Garganega grape variety, combined with Pinot Bianco, Chardonnay, and Trebbiano di Soave. The grapes are raisined and the wine must have a minimum alcohol content of fourteen degrees.

RECIOTO DI SOAVE COL FOSCARIN 1997, CLAUDIO E. SANDRO GINI

This Col Foscarin 1997 comes from the village of Monteforte d'Alpone, where it is produced on the chalk and basalt soil of a small vineyard plot – 1.5 hectares – cultivated according to biodynamic methods. The vine stock comprises ninety per cent Garganega and ten per cent Chardonnay. After harvesting, the grapes are raisined on racks for between five and six months, pressed, and then fermented slowly in oak barrels with a proportion of fifty per cent new wood. It is aged in the same oak barrels and then bottle aged for eight months before being sold. It has 170g of residual sugar per litre.

Saffron Shortcrust Biscuits and Mangoes in Orange Sauce

(Sablés au safran et mangues à l'orange)

The harmony of flavours in this dessert is dominated by two ingredients with pronounced personalities – mango and saffron. The choice of accompaniment should tend towards well-developed, preferably botrytized, wines that have lost their primary aromas and are able to bring out the spiciness of these two elements. The Sainte-Croix-du-Mont 1985 certainly fits the bill since it is pervaded by aromas of mango, passion-fruit, papaya, and a touch of vanilla. The Tokaji Aszú 5 Puttonyos, with its fine balance between sugar and acidity, also makes an ideal partner for the exotic flavours of the saffron biscuits and mangoes. This modern-style wine with its beautiful colour and clean purity is the product of extremely successful raisining.

SERVES 8

Preparation time: 40 minutes
Cooking time: 30 minutes
Chilling: 1 hour

FOR THE SAFFRON BISCUITS

50g (1¾oz) softened butter
100g (3¾oz) icing sugar
100g (¾oz) flour
25g (1oz) ground almonds
pinch table salt
3 saffron strands, powdered
2 egg yolks

FOR THE MANGOES IN
ORANGE SAUCE

4 mangoes
150g (5¼oz) granulated sugar
1 vanilla pod, split lengthways
200ml (7fl oz) orange juice
juice of half a lemon

SERVING

1 litre exotic fruit sorbet
  (mango, passion-fruit,
  pineapple)

Making the saffron biscuits

Mix the creamed butter with the icing sugar, salt, and saffron. Then add the ground almonds and flour, and mix the ingredients with your fingertips until you have a fine, crumbly texture. Incorporate the egg yolks and bring the dough together in an evenly textured ball. Chill in the refrigerator for 1 hour.

Roll out the pastry to a thickness of 3mm (⅛ inch) and then cut out circles with a round pastry cutter. Place the circles on a greased baking sheet and bake in a preheated oven – 170°C (325°F), Gas Mark 3 – for 12 minutes.

Preparing the mangoes in orange sauce

Peel the mangoes and cut the flesh into strips. Add the sugar and split vanilla pod to the orange juice and bring to the boil. Add the mangoes and bring back to the boil.

Remove from the heat and leave to cool. When the mangoes are completely cold, strain off the fruit (reserving the liquid) and arrange evenly on the saffron biscuits.

Finishing

Reduce the liquid for 8 minutes until you have a syrupy consistency, adding the lemon juice at the last moment.

Pour the syrup over the biscuits and serve immediately, accompanied by exotic fruit sorbet.

Serving temperature

Sainte-Croix-du-Mont, Château Loubens 1985: 10°C (50°F).

Tokaji Aszú 5 Puttonyos 1993, Disnókó: 10°C (50°F).

Sainte-Croix-du-Mont

The geographical area of Sainte-Croix-du-Mont lies on the right bank of the River Garonne, opposite the Cérons and Sauternes appellations. It acquired AOC status in 1936 and, without detracting from the quality of the neighbouring Loupiac and Cadillac appellations, is incontestably the top producer of sweet wines on this side of the river. Sainte-Croix-du-Mont has a greater potential and greater aptitude for developing noble rot and, thanks to such vineyards as Château Loubens, Château La Rame and Château Le Mont, the quality of its wines are fairly consistent. To aspire to the Sainte-Croix-du-Mont appellation, wines must be produced from grapes cultivated in this commune, with the exception of the *terres de palus* (recent alluvial deposits). The vine stock comprises the classic varieties used in sweet Gironde wines – Sémillon, Sauvignon Blanc, Muscadelle – with a maximum yield of forty hectolitres per hectare. It goes without saying that, to obtain quality Gironde wines suitable

for ageing, the yield must be reduced. The grapes, which have to be overripened or nobly rotted, must be harvested by selective picking. The minimum acquired sugar content before fermentation is 221g per litre.

SAINTE-CROIX-DU-MONT, CHATEAU LOUBENS 1985

This twenty-three-hectare vineyard is the flagship of the Sainte-Croix-du-Mont appellation. Its owner, Arnaud de Sèze, operates a policy of quality and is continually striving to achieve balance based on the consistency of his vintages, the quality of his wines, their concentration and delicacy. This is reflected in the quality of the wines he produces. The vine stock comprises ninety-five per cent Sémillon and five per cent Sauvignon Blanc.

Tokaji Aszú

Today, the Tokaji vineyards of Hungary cover some 5,500 hectares, with only twenty-eight villages entitled to use the appellation. The clay soil and microclimate of this volcanic wine area, on the south- to southeast-facing slopes of Mount Tokaj and near the Tisza and Bodrog rivers, favour the development of noble rot. Over the centuries, Tokaji wines have been enjoyed by people of rank

and distinction. In 1703, it was introduced to the French court when Ferenc Rakoczi II, Prince of Transylvania, presented a bottle of Tokaji to Louis XIV. It subsequently became a favourite with Peter the Great and Catherine the Great of Russia, Frederick II of Prussia, the French and German writers Voltaire and Goethe, and the Austrian composer Schubert. Tokaji 5 Puttonyos must have a minimum of 120g of residual sugar per litre and has one of the finest balances between sugar, acidity, and alcohol. It is aged for a minimum of three years, two of which must be in wood.

TOKAJI ASZU 5 PUTTONYOS 1993, DISNOKO

The Disnókó vineyard became part of the Axa Insurance group in the early 1990s. Situated between the towns of Mad and Tarcal, its 130 hectares of vines are today run by Laszlo Meszaros. Investment has been poured into the vines and wineries, and the style of the vineyard's Tokaji wines – the quality of the selection process, the delicacy and balance of the wines – is exemplary. This Tokaji Aszú 5 Puttonyos 1993 was produced in one of the greatest vintage years for two decades, and its concentration, balance and freshness are truly superb. It has a candied nose pervaded by aromas of apricots and oranges, and an interesting strength. The whole is harmonious, complex and extremely elegant.

Cream Caramel with Lime

(Crème renversée au caramel et au citron vert)

In this dessert, the acidity of the lime juice and zest contrasts with the creamy smoothness and natural sweetness of the vanilla cream. By its very lightness, the caramel doesn't affect this complex and delicate balance of flavours pervaded by lime. The choice of less sugary wines, sweet but with mineral and acid tones, complements the notes of citrus and highlights the lime element of the cream caramel. The late-harvest Riesling certainly has these qualities – sweetness, acidity, and sharpness – and makes a perfect match as it echoes the aromatic register of the dessert. The Riesling Ice Wine from Ontario, made from grapes frozen naturally before they reach full maturity, is both sweeter and more acid. In this wine, the concentration of aromas comes from frosts rather than raisining or noble rot, giving it a clear affinity with the lime.

SERVES 10

Preparation time: 30 minutes

Cooking time: 20 minutes

Chilling: 2 hours

FOR THE LIME CREAM

7 eggs

260g (9oz) granulated sugar

juice of 2 limes

zest of 2 limes

500ml (18fl oz) water

FOR THE LIME CARAMEL

300g (10½oz) granulated sugar

juice of 2–3 limes

100ml (3½fl oz) water

Preparing the lime caramel

Put the sugar and measured water in a heavy-bottomed saucepan and cook for about 10 minutes over a moderate heat until you obtain a light-brown caramel.

Remove from the heat, add the lime juice and divide the caramel between ten individual ramekins. Keep to one side.

Preparing the lime cream

Put half the measured water, lime juice, 100g (3¾oz) of the granulated sugar, and the grated lime zest in a saucepan and bring to the boil. Remove from the heat and leave to infuse for 3 minutes.

Use a balloon, rotary, or electric hand whisk to beat the eggs with the rest of the granulated sugar and measured water. Add the egg mixture to the infusion, beating briskly, and then divide between the ramekins containing the caramel.

Place the ramekins in a bain-marie in a preheated oven – 150°C (300°F), Gas Mark 2. Cook for about 20 minutes, until the cream has set. Remove from the oven and leave to cool.

Chill in the refrigerator for at least 2 hours .

Serving temperature

Riesling Grand Cru Altenberg de Bergheim 1998 Vendange Tardive, Domaine Marcel Deiss: 10°C (50°F).

Riesling Ice Wine Inniskillin Silver, Niagara Peninsula 1989: 10°C (50°F).

Riesling Vendange Tardive (Late Harvest)

Riesling is one of the noblest and most complex white grape varieties in the world. It is incredibly aromatic and produces dry, sweet, and botrytized wines that are extremely pure and have a wonderfully delicate balance of flavours. Few grape varieties have such a strong affinity with the soil in which they are grown and reflect the local wine area and climate with such honesty, precision and accuracy. The Vendange Tardive – designation has been officially recognized since March 1, 1984 and its wines, which are excellent for laying down, are produced according to a strict set of regulations. They must be made from a single grape variety, harvested by hand, and the grape variety and vintage year must appear on the label. Rieslings are legally obliged to have a minimum natural maturity of 235g of residual sugar per litre, have undergone no chaptalization and have been the subject of a prior declaration of harvest to the authorities. The wines must subsequently be presented, tasted, and approved at the analytical examination and official tasting for their particular designation at least eighteen months after the harvest.

RIESLING GRAND CRU ALTENBERG DE BERGHEIM 1998 VENDANGE TARDIVE, DOMAINE MARCEL DEISS

Altenberg de Bergheim is a truly extraordinary *grand cru* produced in an area whose sandstone, clay, and chalk soils are rich in fossils. The hot and dry, almost overexposed, microclimate enables the grapes to reach an exceptional level of maturity, often enhanced by the development of noble rot. This 1998 vintage is a beautiful golden colour. A touch of citronella and an underlying minerality give it fullness. The whole is fresh and complex, the palate ample and beautifully rich.

Riesling Ice Wine, Niagara Peninsula

Eighty-five per cent of Canada's vineyards, which cover a total area of 7,000 hectares, are in Ontario. The province has three wine areas – Niagara Peninsula, Pelee Island, and Lake Erie – at a similar latitude to the wine regions of Alsace, Oregon, and Germany. The production method for Ice Wine involves leaving the grapes on the vine during December and January. The continual frosts and thaws of this winter period desiccate the ripe grapes, which are then harvested individually, by hand, at temperatures of between 10°C (14°F) and 13°C (8.6°F) and usually at night. The grapes are pressed in extremely cold temperatures and, because the freezing point of water is different from that of sugar, only very small amounts of the sweet, concentrated juice are collected. An Ice Wine must come from an officially designated wine area and be made from Riesling or Vidal, a hybrid grape variety derived from Trebbiano and which can only be used in varietal wines. The wine must have an alcohol content of between 8.5 degrees and 14.9 degrees and a minimum acidity of 6.5g per litre. When harvested, the grapes must have a minimum sugar content of thirty-five brix (the unit of measurement used in Canada) and chaptalization is forbidden. The wine must have a minimum level of residual sugar of 125g per litre.

RIESLING ICE WINE INNISKILLIN SILVER, NIAGARA PENINSULA 1999

The Inniskillin vineyard was founded by Karl Kaiser and Donald Zinaldo, winners of the "Grand Prix d'Honneur" (1991) and "Best Sweet Wine" (2003) awards at Vinexpo in France. Today, they are the top producers of Canadian Ice Wine. In 1975, their vineyard obtained the first winemaking permit issued in Ontario since 1929. This Inniskillin Silver was harvested between December 30, 1998 and January 17, 1999. It has an alcohol content of 10.5 degrees and twenty per cent residual sugar. The wine expresses notes of exotic fruit – mangoes and pineapple – while a touch of grapefruit and lemon adds freshness. On the palate, it is rich and full, relieved by an underlying acidity that gives it a lingering finish.

Candied Fruit, Dried Fruit, and Fruit in Alcohol

Mediterranean Fruit Cake

(Gâteau aux fruits confits de Méditerranée)

The mild fruitiness of this cake is brought out by a dash of Grand Marnier that creates a moist texture and adds candied citrus flavours. This cake is not too sweet, so it can absorb the sugars of a rich, sweet wine. Made from late-harvest, nobly rotten grapes, the Vin Noble du Minervois is rich and full-bodied with overtones of sweet, candied fruit and a light oxidative note that adds hints of almond, hazelnut, toasted almond, and walnut. It is also an apt geographical pairing because this Mediterranean white goes very well with candied fruit from the same area, as does the Vin Santo. Just as rich in sugar, this Italian wine has a complex aromatic palate with hints of fruit drops and candied fruit which make it a perfect match for the fruit cake. The flavours linger in the mouth for a remarkably long time.

SERVES 12

Preparation time: 25 minutes
Cooking time: 40 minutes
Standing: 3–4 days

FOR THE FRUIT CAKE

125g (4½oz) softened butter + 10g (¼oz) for the cake tin

190g (6½oz) sifted flour + 20g (¾oz) for the cake tin

120g (4¼oz) icing sugar

pinch table salt

2 eggs

1 teaspoon baking powder

grated zest of 1 orange

grated zest of 1 lemon

60g (2¼oz) currants

60g (2¼oz) sultanas

60g (2¼oz) finely diced candied orange peel

100g (3½oz) glacé cherries

10g (¼oz) split almonds

FOR THE GRAND MARNIER SYRUP

50g (1¾oz) caster sugar

50ml (2fl oz) water

20ml (¾fl oz) Grand Marnier

Making the fruit cake

Grease a 14-cm (5½-inch) cake tin and dredge with flour.

Beat the icing sugar, softened butter and salt vigorously.

Add the eggs one at a time, followed by the flour and baking powder. Add the grated orange and lemon zest, currants, sultanas, candied orange peel, and whole glacé cherries and mix together until the fruit is evenly distributed.

Pour the cake mixture into the tin, sprinkle with split almonds and cook for about 40 minutes in a preheated oven – 160°C (320°F), Gas Mark 2–3.

Preparing the syrup and decorating the fruit cake

Add the sugar to the measured water and bring to the boil. Remove from the heat, add the Grand Marnier and cover with a plate to keep the aromas from escaping.

A knife inserted into the centre of the fruit cake will come out clean when the cake is fully cooked.

Take the cake out of the oven and drizzle with Grand Marnier syrup.

When completely cool, cover with clingfilm. Keep in a cool place for three or four days before eating to let the flavours develop.

Serving temperature

Vin Noble du Minervois, Cuvée 1998, Domaine Tour-Boisée, Jean-Louis Poudou: 10°C (50°F).

Vin Santo Nobile di Montepulciano 1990, Avignonesi: 12°C (53°F).

Vin Noble du Minervois

The production of dry white wines made from ancient grape varieties which have been raisined or infected with noble rot is an age-old tradition in Minervois. However, when this area obtained an AOC in 1985, no mention was made of this legitimate method of wine production. Things have changed over the past few years though, and certain producers have been working towards the establishment of a wine category called "Vin Noble du Minervois". A statute covering approved standards for grape varieties, minimum alcohol content and sugar levels has already been drawn up and will soon be officially released.

VIN NOBLE DU MINERVOIS, CUVEE 1998, DOMAINE TOUR-BOISEE, JEAN-LOUIS POUDOU

Jean-Louis Poudou runs the superb Château Tour-Boisée vineyard in the heart of the Minervois region. This vast estate extends over eighty hectares and produces exquisite wines of all colours. The 1998 vintage was made from late-harvested Chardonnay grapes, picked in whole bunches. These contain grapes at different stages of ripeness – nobly rotten, overripened, raisined – which determine the wine's levels of sweetness and acidity. The wine is pressed in traditional vertical wooden wine presses then transferred immediately to barrels for fermentation. This is a perfectly balanced wine with 160g per litre of residual sugar for 14.5 degrees of fermented alcohol. Chardonnay grapes are not usually used when overripened or nobly rotted, since this vine variety can be susceptible to disease if left until late harvest.

Vin Santo di Montepulciano

Vin Santo di Montepulciano comes from the region of the Vino Nobile di Montepulciano in the Italian province of Sienna. This wine is produced from Malvasia Blanco, Grechetto, and Trebbiano Toscano grapes grown on a sand and clay soil. The grapes are pressed between December 1 of the harvest year and February 28 of the following year. The minimum ageing period is three years in *caratelli* (small topped-up barrels) and four years for *riserva*. The minimum alcohol level is seventeen degrees and there is a variety known as *occhio di pernice* ("partridge eye") which has a deeper, reddish hue. This latter must be made from at least fifty per cent Prugnolo Gentile with other local grape varieties making up the rest.

VIN SANTO NOBILE DI MONTEPULCIANO 1990, AVIGNONESI

This is one of the oldest wineries in Italy, dating back to the fourteenth century. It has been owned by the Flavo brothers since 1974. The winery has 205 hectares of vines divided into four separate vineyards: Poggetti, La Selva, Le Capezzine, and La Lamborda. This 1990 Vin Santo comes from the La Selva vineyard, situated at an altitude of 300 metres (984 feet), and was made from Grechetto, Malvasia Toscano, and Trebbiano Toscano grapes. It was wood-aged in *caratelli* for eight years and bottle-aged for six months before appearing on the market. This full-bodied wine has an alcoholic content of 16.5 degrees. It is amber in hue and its nose has notes of figs, dates, vanilla, and sweet spices.

Iced Nougat with Raspberry Coulis

(Nougat glacé au coulis de framboises)

Sweetened with honey and pepped up with the subtle orangey tang of Grand Marnier, this iced nougat needs wines to complement dried, candied-fruit flavours. The Muscat de Saint-Jean-de-Minervois has the necessary aromatic sweetness and crispness: this lively wine, with its notes of yellow fruit, is the perfect match for the myriad flavours of this dessert. The amber-coloured Breganze Torcolato is a naturally raisined wine that pays particular tribute to candied fruit and nougatine: its smell encapsulates all the fun of the fair with aromas of candyfloss, marshmallow, and fruit drops. The bouquet with its medley of candied fruit is the ideal accompaniment for this dessert, and the harmonious blend of candy sugar, honey, and sweet-fruit lingers in the mouth.

SERVES 10

Preparation time: 30 minutes

Freezing: 5 hours

FOR THE NOUGAT

500ml (18fl oz) water

40g (1½oz) sultanas

50g (1¾oz) finely chopped glacé cherries

30g (1oz) finely chopped candied orange peel

1 dessertspoon Grand Marnier

4 egg whites

30g (1oz) caster sugar

125g (4½oz) all-flowers honey

400g (14oz) whipped cream

40g (1½oz) crushed roasted hazelnuts

FOR THE RASPBERRY COULIS

15g (½oz) icing sugar

200g (7oz) fresh raspberries

juice of half a lemon

FOR THE DECORATION

fresh red fruit (strawberries, raspberries, redcurrants, etc.)

Preparing the coulis

Mix the raspberries with the icing sugar and lemon juice.

Push through a sieve and chill in the refrigerator.

Making the nougat

Bring the water to the boil. Add the sultanas and boil them for 30 seconds, then strain and cool in cold water. Drain. Add them to the glacé cherries and candied orange peel, drench with Grand Marnier and chill in the refrigerator.

Using an electric mixer if possible, beat the egg whites vigorously, gradually adding the caster sugar as they begin to form stiff peaks. Continue beating the mixture until it is dense and shiny.

Pour the honey into a saucepan and boil for exactly 2 minutes. Pour it over the meringue in a thin trickle, whisking continuously, then beat the egg whites steadily until the meringue is completely cold.

Put into a large container, fold in the whipped cream, and add the macerated candied fruits and crushed hazelnuts.

Divide the mixture between ten small circular rings, 5–8cm (2–3¼ inches) high, and leave in the freezer for 4–5 hours.

Finishing

Pour a little raspberry coulis into some glass dishes and carefully place an iced nougat, removed from its ring, in each one.

Decorate with red fruits before serving.

Serving temperature

Muscat de Saint-Jean-de-Minervois Domaine de Barroubio, Raymond Miquel: 10°C (50°F).

Breganze Torcolato 1998, Fausto Maculan: 10°C (50°F).

Muscat de Saint-Jean-de-Minervois AOC

This *vin doux naturel*, that benefits from its own AOC in the northeast of the Minervois region, is produced in the commune of Saint-Jean-de-Minervois. The clay and chalk soil is fairly dense and slate-based in the north and production is limited. The situation of the vineyard at an altitude of 300 metres (984 feet) is largely responsible for the finesse and balance of these wines. The Muscat de Saint-Jean-de-Minervois has an undeniable freshness and elegance when compared with other Muscats produced in the Hérault region.

MUSCAT DE SAINT-JEAN-DE-MINERVOIS, DOMAINE DE BARROUBIO, RAYMOND MIQUEL

The Domaine de Barroubio has belonged to the Miquel family since the fifteenth century. It was given a new lease of life in 1976 by Jean Miquel, who restructured production by removing his Muscats from the Saint-Jean-de-Minervois cooperative cellar in order to bottle the wine on his estate. After his death, in 1985, his wife created a crisper, more pleasing style of Muscat. Since 2000, Raymond Miquel has devoted himself to running the twenty-five hectares of vineyards, that include sixteen hectares dedicated to the production of AOC Muscat de Saint-Jean-de-Minervois. The south-facing winery is situated at an altitude of 300 metres (984 feet) and the soil is chalky mixed with over seventy per cent scree. The 2001 vintage boasts fruity and floral notes. The aromatic palette is characterized by late-ripening peach, apricot, and citrus fruit. The palate is rich and flavoursome with a delicious, refreshing fruity taste and lingering persistence.

Breganze Torcolato

The Italian DOC Breganze is situated in the Vicentine hills, an area stretching between Brenta and Astico, and includes the village of Breganze. The appellation applies to several types of wine: dry white, fruity red, a more robust red, and several raisined wines made from Vespaiolo grapes. The natural raisining process produces a top-quality wine that is a dessert in itself with its aromas of fruit drops, candy floss, and bergamot orange. The minimum alcohol content of Torcolato must be fourteen degrees and the minimum ageing period is two years from November 1 of the harvest year.

BREGANZE TORCOLATO 1998, FAUSTO MACULAN

Fausto Maculan is the best producer of this appellation. His Torcolato is made from three grape varieties: eighty-five per cent Vespaiolo, ten per cent Tocai Friulano, and five per cent Garganega. With some vintages, you can taste the effect of the noble rot. The grape is raisined for between four and five months, fermented in stainless-steel vats then aged in new barrels. Fausto Maculan also makes another sensational wine called Acininobili.

Crunchy Hazelnut Meringue

(Croquant aux noisettes)

A simple fusion of flavours with undertones of dried fruit (praline and roasted nuts) and chocolate (roasted coffee bean, iced coffee, and mocha) is needed to preserve the delicate aromatic structure of this nutty dessert. The Rivesaltes Ambré 1991 goes perfectly with hazelnut and cocoa. This "winter wine" conjures up the flavours of traditional Yuletide desserts. Controlled oxidation has added a slightly bitter edge to the overall sweetness, which works wonders with the sharp tang of dried fruit. Although not as sweet, the oloroso sherry is also a good pairing. It is unusually supple for this type of dry wine, offering an array of sugary, cocoa-infused aromas, reminiscent of dried fruit – hazelnut, almond, date, and dried fig – that complement this dessert perfectly.

SERVES 10

Preparation time: 50 minutes

Cooking time: 20 minutes

FOR THE HAZELNUT MERINGUE

90g (3¼oz) icing sugar

90g (3¼oz) ground almonds

4 egg whites

30g (1oz) caster sugar

50g (1¾oz) crushed roasted hazelnuts

FOR THE CHOCOLATE CREAM

3 egg yolks

30g (1oz) caster sugar

250ml (9fl oz) single cream

250g (9oz) milk chocolate, broken into small pieces

FOR THE PRALINE CRUNCH

25g (1oz) plain chocolate

100g (3½oz) pralines

90g (3¼oz) thin crumbled pancakes

FOR THE FILLING

220g (8oz) milk chocolate

220g (8oz) whipped cream

Making the meringue

Sift the icing sugar and ground almonds together.

Beat the egg whites with the sugar and, as soon as they begin to form stiff peaks, fold into the previous mixture, followed by the hazelnuts.

Spread the mixture over a baking sheet lined with greaseproof paper and sprinkle with sugar.

Cook for 16 minutes in a preheated oven – 180°C (350°F), Gas Mark 4. Put to one side.

Making the chocolate cream

Beat the egg yolks with the sugar until the mixture whitens. Bring the cream to the boil and stir in. Pour over the chocolate, mix, and put to one side.

Preparing the praline crunch

Melt the chocolate in a bain-marie, making sure there are no lumps.

Blend in the praline to form a paste. Add the chocolate and crumbled pancakes.

Spread a 3-mm (⅛-inch) layer of this mixture between two sheets of greaseproof paper. Chill in the refrigerator.

Making the filling and decoration

Melt 150g (5¼oz) of the milk chocolate in a bain-marie, spread thinly over a sheet of clingfilm and leave to set in the freezer. Cut into two rectangles.

Melt the rest of the chocolate in the bain-marie. Fold the cream into the melted chocolate when cool.

Pour this mixture into a piping bag with a plain nozzle.

Finishing and serving

Spread the meringue with chocolate cream, then add the praline crunch. Place a rectangle of chocolate on top, cover with whipped cream and finish off with another rectangle of chocolate.

Serving temperature

Rivesaltes Ambré 1991, Domaine Cazes: 14°C (57°F).

Jerez Oloroso: 14°C (57°F).

Rivesaltes AOC

The Pyrénées-Orientales region produces the greatest variety of AOC Vins Doux Naturels in France. The region also produces the largest volume of these wines, nearly half of which come from Rivesaltes. There are different types of Rivesaltes. Deep purple Rivesaltes Vintage is intensely fruity. Wine legislation states that Rivesaltes Ambré must be made from ripe white grapes, and Rivesaltes Tuilé must be made from red grape varieties. They are all, including the *rancios*, aged in the winery for extended periods in oxidative conditions until at least September 1 in the second year of maturing. These wines have glorious colours, ranging from topaz to mahogany, and are dominated by notes of coffee, cocoa, and praline.

RIVESALTES AMBRE 1991, DOMAINE CAZES

Quality is a priority for the Cazes family, which operates a superb vineyard and has produced the best naturally sweet wines in the region for several generations. Bernard and André, along with their respective offspring, are continuing the family tradition. They produce an impressive range of *vins doux naturels,* from vintage wines to *rancios,* including the Muscat de Rivesaltes. These wines boast a well-balanced mouth, aromatic complexity, and unusual flavours. Sampling a Rivesaltes Aimé Cazes 1963 or 1973 is a truly memorable experience.

Jerez

The sherry vineyard in south-west Andalusia extends over a triangular area bounded by three towns: Puerto de Santa Maria, Sanlucar de Barrameda, and Jerez de la Frontera. The climate is warm and dry, tempered by the nearby ocean, and a white chalky soil called *albariza* covers eighty per cent of the territory, which is visited by two main winds: the Levante, from the east, and the moist Ponante, ushered in by the Atlantic. Sherry was originally a fortified dry white wine which now comes in a wide range of styles, from dry to extremely sweet and from very pale to very dark. The grape varieties used are Palomino Fino, Palomino de Jerez, Pedro-Ximénez, and Moscatel. The production of Jerez essentially revolves around the practice of blending wines from different casks and of different ages (the *solera* system). The grapes are harvested in September and taken to the wine press where the must is allowed to ferment naturally. At this stage, the wine has an alcohol level of 13.5 degrees. The wine is then funnelled into 500-litre barrels and stored in the wine cellars. The surface of the wine then becomes covered by *flor* (a Spanish word that literally means "flower"), a gauzy layer of yeast that protects the wine from oxidation and confers a distinctive taste. The complexity, finesse and range of aromatics vary from barrel to barrel, each of which forms a different environment. The wines are subsequently categorized depending on the thickness of their *flor* layer. The best are used to make fino or amontillado sherries. Wines without *flor* growth are classified as *rayas*. Their fermentation is stopped immediately and they are used to make olorosos.

JEREZ OLOROSO

This type of Jerez never develops a layer of *flor* because the wine is fortified at the start of the ageing process to an alcoholic strength of eighteen degrees (*flor* will not grow on wines with an alcohol content higher than sixteen per cent). It is then aged using the *solera* system (an annual blending process based on the rotation of younger and older wines) and may attain an even higher alcoholic strength. True olorosos have a rich, concentrated, dry flavour. Sweeter varieties are obtained by adding Pedro-Ximénez.

Apricot Financiers

(Financiers aux abricots)

Small pieces of apricot bring out the flavour of these melt-in-the-mouth sponge cakes, which are not too sugary. Their moist, delicate texture calls for a smooth, mellow wine with controlled sweetness. Made from Chenin Blanc, the Coteaux du Layon from Claude Papin is a well-balanced wine. Its sugar and acidity were concentrated by the noble rot of 1997. This superb wine offers notes of yellow and white fruit and has great finesse and purity of expression. The bouquet of the Sélection de Grains Nobles from Domaine Rouvinez 1999, made from Marsanne and Pinot Gris, owes more to the fact that the grapes were left to dry naturally on the vine than to infection by noble rot: this Swiss wine is not as rich as the Coteaux du Layon and, although it has controlled sweetness, it lacks the tart undertones provided by the Chenin Blanc. As this wine is not as sweet as the former, however, the balance is similar and the taste is just as harmonious.

SERVES 10

Preparation time: 30 minutes

Cooking time: 20 minutes

FOR THE FINANCIER MIXTURE

130g (4¾oz) ground almonds

30g (1oz) ground pistachios

50g (1¾oz) plain flour

2 teaspoons all-flowers honey

1 teaspoon vanilla sugar

220g (8oz) icing sugar

125g (4½oz) butter +
    20g (¾oz) for the tins

5 egg whites

10 apricot halves in syrup

1 dessertspoon caster sugar

FOR THE SYRUP

100ml (3½fl oz) water

1 dessertspoon rum

30g (1oz) caster sugar

Preparing the cake mixture

Mix the ground almonds, pistachios, flour, honey, vanilla sugar, and icing sugar in a large mixing bowl.

Cut the butter into small pieces and heat gently in a saucepan until it has turned a light nut-brown.

Remove immediately from the heat and pour into a container. Once cooled, add the melted butter to the cake mixture, whisking vigorously.

Beat the egg whites to stiff peaks, then gently fold into the mixture.

When the mixture is nice and smooth, chill in the refrigerator for 20 minutes.

Preparing the syrup

Add the measured water to the sugar and bring to the boil.

Leave to cool and add the rum.

Cooking and finishing

Grease ten small individual cake tins and divide the mixture between them.

Put an apricot half on top of each cake then sprinkle with caster sugar.

Cook for about 20 minutes in a preheated oven –170°C (325°F), Gas Mark 3.

Take the cakes from the oven and drizzle with the syrup. Serve warm or cold.

Serving temperature

Coteaux du Layon Beaulieu-Les Rouannières 1997, Claude Papin: 10°C (50°F).

Sélection de Grains Nobles 1999, Domaine Rouvinez: 10°C (50°F).

Coteaux du Layon-Villages

Coteaux du Layon, an appellation obtained in 1950, is a smooth, well-rounded wine produced on the banks of the River Layon. This appellation applies to twenty-five communes in Maine-et-Loire. The mild weather conditions, the humidity generated by the river and the warm temperatures in late autumn encourage the growth of noble rot. Each vintage is distinctive – the key factor is the quality of the selective harvesting that creates a harmonious balance between sugar, acidity, and alcohol. In good years, this area can produce some sensational wines. Unfortunately, poor selection often undermines quality. Many producers resort to chaptalization or sugaring, which results in heavy, heady and characterless wines. The Coteaux du Layon-Villages appellation is produced in six villages (Faye-d'Anjou, Rablay-sur-Layon, Rochefort-sur-Loire, Saint-Aubin-de-Luigné, Saint-Lambert-du-Lattay, and Beaulieu-sur-Layon) plus the hamlet of Chaume. The wines must have a minimum sugar content of 234g per litre and the maximum yield is thirty-five hectolitres per hectare.

COTEAUX DU LAYON BEAULIEU-LES ROUANNIERES 1997, CLAUDE PAPIN

Claude and Joëlle Papin run an estate in Beaulieu-sur-Layon with their children. This vineyard has fifty-five hectares of vines planted on different soils. Les Rouannières is a plot of five hectares planted on rocky spilite soil of volcanic origin. Although this type of soil is not very fertile, the vineyard benefits from ideal exposure to sun and wind. The excellent 1997 vintage was given an added boost by noble rot while a hint of raisining provided crispness. The balance is perfect: 12.5 degrees fermented alcohol and two grams per litre of residual sugar. The wine has an exquisite nose of candied white fruit with a touch of quince, rhubarb and plum, and is incredibly rich and full-bodied with a classy bouquet.

The Valais

The Valais is the largest wine-producing region in Switzerland with nearly 5,300 hectares of vineyards, bordering the Rhône from Viège to Martigny. These are situated at an altitude of between 400 metres (1,312 feet) and 800 metres (2,624 feet) at the foot of the hills and on the slopes and are influenced by the continental climate. The Valais produces many types of wines – dry white, rosé, red, and sweet white. The sweet, sometimes syrupy, white wines can be made from a wide range of grape varieties. Marsanne, Gros Rhin which is actually Riesling, Petite Arvine, and Amigne produce some superb results, as does Pinot Gris.

SELECTION DE GRAINS NOBLES 1999, DOMAINE ROUVINEZ

This vintage is made from fifty-year-old vines dotted over the entire estate. The soil is mainly chalk and silica and the grapes are overripened on the vine and harvested in mid-December – eighty per cent of the grapes are raisined and twenty per cent are infected by noble rot. This wine is made from seventy per cent Marsanne and thirty per cent Pinot Gris. It is fermented in new oak barrels, then aged for twelve months. The nose is candied, with creamy, caramel undertones. The palate is well-balanced, mellow, and robust, while a welcome hint of acidity adds crispness and creates a pleasing suppleness. This wine has 140g of residual sugar per litre.

Peanut Ice-cream Profiteroles

(Profiteroles glacées aux cacahuètes)

This classic pairing of choux pastry and ice-cream is dominated by the roasted flavour of peanuts and the bitterness of plain chocolate. The distinctive taste of the walnut liqueur made by the Maison Denoix in Brive is the perfect partner to this dessert. It is not too sweet and its strong walnut flavour takes prominence over other tastes. Barrel ageing brings out its woody bite which combines with notes of cocoa and praline and a slight astringency to bring out the flavour of the peanuts and chocolate used in this dessert. The cream sherry is a sweet, oxidative type of sherry. Its notes of cocoa, coffee and mocha linger in the mouth and it is not as naturally sweet as the liqueur. Both drinks complement the aromatic qualities and taste of these ice-cream profiteroles.

SERVES 8

Preparation time: 45 minutes

Cooking time: 25 minutes

Freezing: 30 minutes

FOR THE SESAME CHOUX BUNS

10g (¼oz) toasted sesame
  seeds

400g (14oz) choux pastry
  (see page 166)

1 beaten egg for the glaze

30g (1oz) icing sugar

FOR THE PEANUT ICE-CREAM

500ml (18fl oz) milk

30g (1oz) butter

110g (4oz) caster sugar

60g (2oz) peanut butter

FOR THE CHOCOLATE SAUCE

200g (7oz) plain chocolate

200ml (7fl oz) water

20g (¾oz) butter

Making the sesame choux buns

Mix the toasted sesame seeds with the choux pastry and transfer to a piping bag with a plain 10-mm (½-inch) nozzle.

Pipe out balls of dough the size of walnuts onto a baking sheet and brush with beaten egg.

Cook in a preheated oven – 180°C (350°F), Gas Mark 4 – for about 25 minutes without opening the oven door as this may cause the choux pastry to collapse.

Take the choux buns out of the oven and put to one side on a wire rack.

Preparing the peanut ice-cream

Bring the milk to the boil. Remove from the heat and add the other ingredients. Mix them together in a blender and leave until completely cool.

Churn this mixture in an ice-cream maker for 15 minutes, or pour into a freezerproof container and freeze until firm.

Finishing and preparing the sauce

Split the profiteroles, fill with ice-cream, and put them back together. Sprinkle with icing sugar and freeze for 30 minutes.

Crush the plain chocolate and add to the boiling measured water in a small pan. Bring back to the boil, remove from the heat and add the butter. Whisk vigorously and put the pan in a bain-marie to keep warm.

Arrange the profiteroles in a dish or on individual plates, coat them with hot chocolate sauce and serve immediately.

Serving temperature

Liqueur Suprême de Noix, Maison Denoix/Brive: 15–16°C (59–61°F).

Elegante Cream Sherry, Gonzalez Byass, Jerez: 14°C (57°F).

Liqueurs

Liqueurs can be divided into various categories, such as fruit, herbal, nut, and seed. Although liqueurs made from fruit kernels come under the category of "fruit liqueurs", they deserve to be treated separately because they involve a special production process. Liqueurs are made with fruit, plants, herbs, or peel, as well as eau-de-vie or neutral alcohol – Cognac or Armagnac – sugar and water. The process is simple: the fruit is macerated in alcohol for extended periods of time, then distilled at least once. The quality of a liqueur depends on the quality, ripeness, and freshness of the fruit used. According to European wine laws, the minimum sugar content of a liqueur must be 100g per litre. There are a few exceptions: gentian liqueur must have eighty grams of sugar per litre. Cherry liqueurs, whose ethyl alcohol consists entirely of cherry eau-de-vie with a minimum sugar content of 250g per litre, must have seventy grams per litre. Crème de Cassis must have at least 400g of sugar per litre.

LIQUEUR SUPREME DE NOIX, MAISON DENOIX/BRIVE

Suprême de Noix is a superb thirty per cent proof walnut liqueur offering flavours of dried fruit, walnut, caramel, a hint of coffee, and a light woody note that adds complexity. It is made from green walnuts picked between June 24 (Midsummer's Day) and July 22. The Maison Denoix, a small family distillery, was founded in Brive-la-Gaillarde in 1889. The Denoix family make their liqueurs exclusively with appellation Cognac and Armagnac eaux-de-vie. The alcoholic base is obtained using a small boiler, then the syrups are heated in cauldrons and the liqueurs aged in oak barrels in Limousin.

Cream Sherry

Sherry-type wines can be divided into two basic families. The first includes finos, manzanillas, and amontillados, and is characterized by the development of flor. This |yeast grows in moist, cool surroundings, forming a gauzy layer over the surface of the wine ageing in the cask. This covering gradually hardens, protecting it from the air and preserving its freshness for long periods of time. The second family comprises the olorosos (from the Spanish word for "fragrant"), that have hardly any *flor* growth in the barrels. The wines are fortified with wine alcohol to an alcoholic strength of 17.5 per cent, then aged. Richer in colour, more robust and stronger than the former, olorosos are mellow and velvety in flavour, but usually dry. Cream sherry is produced by adding wine made from Pedro-Ximénez grapes to an oloroso, which contributes a touch of sweetness and mellowness. The deeper colour is obtained by adding *vino dulce*.

ELEGANTE CREAM SHERRY, GONZALEZ BYASS, JEREZ

Gonzalez Byass is one of the leading wine producers in Spain. Situated in Jerez de la Frontera, the company, once English, is now wholly Spanish-owned. It is famous for two wines: Tio Pepe Fino and La Concha Amontillado, which are the best-known and most widely consumed sherries in the world. In Jerez, the Byass company has some very old *soleras*, dating back to the nineteenth century, and is famous for its Oloroso Dulce and Oloroso Seco. Its cream sherry is a sweet oloroso. The Elegante is a fairly dark wine with rich mahogany highlights. The nose has prominent notes of sesame, pine nut, toast, brioche, and poppy seed, with the roasted, slightly creamy overtones of coffee, caramel, and cappuccino. Although the palate is robust and sweet, this sophisticated wine maintains an exquisite balance between alcohol and sugar levels. This is an elegant blend, worthy of its name.

Paris-Brest with Praline Cream

(Paris-Brest à la crème pralinée)

This ring-shaped choux cake with its low-fat whipped cream filling is deliciously light. It calls for slightly oxidized wines with aromas that complement the praline cream. The two selected wines are well-aged and bursting with the flavours of praline, coffee, and dried fruit. Their sugar content has been reduced by the maturing process. The aromas of the Verdelho Madeira are oxidative rather than fruity. This wine has great aromatic complexity, mingling smoky, and mineral aromas – and a hint of incense – with dried fruit and praline, while its colour and taste have a slightly faded quality. The Montilla-Moriles 1972 is a well-matured, unfortified wine. Smooth and oily in the glass, it is rich brown in colour and its aromas are reminiscent of dried fruit, praline, and cocoa.

SERVES 8

Preparation time: 35 minutes

Cooking time: 25 minutes

Chilling: 2 hours

FOR THE CHOUX PASTRY

300g (10oz) Choux Pastry (see page 166)

1 egg

30g (1oz) split almonds

20g (¾oz) icing sugar

FOR THE PRALINE BUTTER CREAM

50g (1¾oz) ground praline

250g (9oz) Butter Cream (see page 177)

Making the choux cakes

Transfer the choux pastry to a piping bag with a fluted nozzle and pipe out two rings, 18cm (7 inches) in diameter, making one thinner than the other.

Beat the egg and brush over the thicker ring. Sprinkle the split almonds over the surface of this ring.

Bake the two rings for about 25 minutes in a preheated oven – 180°C (350°F), Gas Mark 4 – without opening the door as this may cause the choux pastry to collapse.

Leave to cool on a wire rack.

Preparing the praline butter cream

If the ground praline is not fine enough, crush more finely or process in a liquidizer.

Whisk vigorously into the butter cream and pour the mixture into a piping bag with a fluted nozzle.

Decorating the dessert

Cut the choux rings in half horizontally with a serrated knife and put the lower half of the fatter ring on a plate.

Fill with praline cream and place the lower half of the thinner ring on top, cut side up.

Fill this with cream and cover with the upper half of the small ring.

Fill this with cream and top with the almond-decorated upper half of the large ring, cut side down.

Dust the Paris-Brest with icing sugar and leave in the refrigerator for 2 hours. Serve well chilled.

Serving temperature

Madeira Verdelho 1933, Barbeto: 14°C (57°F).

Montilla-Moriles Don Pedro 1972, Toro Albala: 12°C (53°F).

Madeira

The volcanic island of Madeira lies in the Atlantic Ocean and has been a Portuguese colony since 1418. Due to its strategic position, the island served as a port of call and supply station for the merchant fleet and the English set up trading posts there. This sparked off a growing interest in Madeira wines, which were loaded onto boats and sent to ports all over the world. As this cargo was not always sold, the wine sometimes arrived back at its port of departure, considerably altered by the hot temperatures and tropical climate. This led to the practice of heating the wine in ovens, a process known as *estufagem* (derived from the Portuguese word *estufa* for "oven"). It involves heating the wines to temperatures of 40–46°C (104–115°F) for six months which gives them their burnt, toasted aromas. Madeira is a *vinho generoso*: it can be dry (fortified after fermentation) or sweet (fortified before fermentation). There are several types of Madeira which vary according to their level of sweetness. Sercial, a noble grape variety, is the driest. This is followed by Verdelho, which is semi-dry, then Bual, semi-sweet, and Malmsey, which is the sweetest. Other less important grape varieties like Tinta Negra Mole are also used in the

appellation. The basic yield is eighty hectolitres per hectare. The alcohol content ranges between 17.5 per cent and twenty-two per cent. The minimum ageing period is thirty-six months after the final stage of *mutage*. According to Portuguese wine laws, the label "Reserva" is used for five-year-old Madeiras, "Reserva Especial" for ten-year-old Madeiras and "Reserva Extra" for fifteen-year-old Madeiras (which must contain at least eighty-five per cent of a noble grape variety). The highest quality *colheita* (vintage) must be made from a single grape variety and have been aged for a minimum of twenty years in the cask and two years in the bottle.

MADEIRA VERDELHO 1933, BARBETO

Founded in 1946, Barbeto is unusual in Madeira because it has no vineyards and purchases its grapes from wineries within the appellation area. It was also lucky enough to acquire stocks of old casks when it was founded. Verdelho 1933 is part of that stock. This semi-dry wine owes its sweetness and aromatic complexity to its age, since it would have been impossible to create such a harmonious blend with a younger wine. Aged in old oak casks, it has changed and acquired complexity. Its aromatic nose is characterized by creamy notes of sesame, toast, pine nut, and coffee. Its colour is a distinctive cloudy or hazy amber. The palate is slightly sweet with a hint of oiliness provided by

its underlying structure. It has remarkable aromatic persistency, with final notes reminiscent of balsamic vinegar.

Montilla-Moriles (Spain)

The rolling hills of Montilla to the north of Malaga, in the province of Cordoba, are home to 10,500 hectares of vineyards. The area known as *Superior Calidad* (superior quality) is situated largely in the Sierra de Montilla and the Moriles Altos area, near Moriles. The main difference between this wine and sherry is the grape variety used: Pedro-Ximénez accounts for ninety per cent of this wine although it is only used to make oloroso and cream sherry in Jerez. Pedro-Ximénez is better at withstanding hot temperatures. It produces much more sugar and consequently more alcohol: as a result, *flor* wines in Montilla-Moriles are never fortified, while the sherries made from the Palomino grape are nearly always fortified. Wines must be aged for at least two years using the *solera* system. In addition to Pedro-Ximenez, the white grape varieties used in this appellation are Lairen, Baladi, Torrontes, and Moscatel.

MONTILLA-MORILES DON PEDRO 1972, TORO ALBALA

This bodega, or winery, founded in 1844 was given a new lease of life by José Maria Toro Albala. The 1972 vintage has spent twenty-five years in American oak barrels. The wine is dark black, and syrupy, giving off notes of coffee, chocolate, dried fruit, date, and fig. It offers a remarkable concentration of aromas.

Rum Babas with Vanilla Cream

(Babas au rhum à la crème vanillée)

It is always hard to recommend a wine that will not clash with the strong alcoholic flavour of a sponge cake steeped in spirits. Just enough rum has been used in this dessert to moisten the texture of the cake without drowning its flavour. As a result, although the wines selected must have enough character to hold their own, they must also be sufficiently mellow and robust to bring out the smooth, delicate taste of the vanilla cream. The idea was not to choose wines that created a contrast with this dessert, but ones that enhanced its subtle array of flavours. The Saussignac has vanilla-flavoured, creamy caramel notes that go perfectly with this dessert. Its mellow bouquet complements the smooth taste of the cream and its sweetness is absorbed by the light sponge. The Noble One creates a similar harmony of flavours, with greater emphasis on vanilla-woody overtones.

SERVES 10

Preparation time: 35 minutes

Cooking time: 25 minutes

Standing: 30 minutes

Chilling: 2 hours

FOR THE BABA

100ml (3½fl oz) milk

10g (¼oz) dried yeast

220g (8oz) flour

20g (¾oz) caster sugar

1 teaspoon table salt

3 eggs, beaten

50g (1¾oz) softened butter

50g (1¾oz) apricot jam

FOR THE SYRUP

250g (9oz) caster sugar

500ml (18fl oz) water

zest of 1 orange

1 tablespoon dark rum

1 tablespoon Grand Marnier

FOR THE FILLING

250g (9oz) Confectioner's Custard (see page 177)

150ml (¼ pint) whipped cream, flavoured with vanilla

Making the baba

Gently warm the milk and, off the heat, whisk in the dried yeast so that it dissolves. Add flour, sugar, salt, and eggs and knead until the dough stands away from the sides of the bowl. Add the creamed butter and knead for a further 5 minutes.

Pour the cake mixture into ten greased savarin moulds and leave in a warm place for about 30 minutes until doubled in size.

Cook for 20 minutes in a preheated oven – 180°C (350°F), Gas Mark 4.

Turn out onto a rack and leave to cool.

Preparing the syrup and finishing

Add the sugar and orange zest to the measured water and bring to the boil. When cooled to 50°C (122°F), add the dark rum and Grand Marnier. Soak the babas in this warm syrup for several minutes, then put on a plate.

Top with the gently warmed apricot jam and leave until completely cold.

Mix the confectioner's custard with the vanilla whipped cream in a large mixing bowl and pour most of it into the centre of the babas.

Use a piping bag with a fluted nozzle to decorate the top of the baba with the remainder of the cream.

Chill in the refrigerator for 2 hours.

Serving temperature

Saussignac Château des Essarts, Cuvée Flavie 1997: 10°C (50°F).

Noble One Botrytis Semillon 1996, De Bortoli: 10°C (50°F).

Saussignac AOC

Saussignac, formerly called Côtes de Saussignac, obtained an *Appellation d'Origine Contrôlée* in 1982. The vineyard borders that of Monbazillac and the appellation applies to only five villages in the Dordogne: Gageac, Rouillac, Monestier, Razac-de-Saussignac, and Saussignac. This region produces sweet, sometimes syrupy, wines in good years. Due to its low yield, the appellation maintains a modest profile on the national market, although it produces some surprisingly good wines. Most of the white wines are crisp, well-balanced, and sweet with an interesting yet harmonious combination of flavours. They have a minimum residual sugar content of eighteen grams per litre and the basic yield is fifty hectolitres per hectare. Although both Saussignac and Monbazillac are produced using Sémillon, Sauvignon Blanc, and Muscadelle, the former appellation, which established its planted vine stock in 1973, also uses Chenin Blanc, which gives the wine a slightly acidic edge. As a result, the aromatic balance of a good Saussignac is not dissimilar to that of a good Monbazillac.

SAUSSIGNAC CHATEAU DES ESSARTS, CUVEE FLAVIE 1997

The reputation of Monbazillac wines has plummeted since the 1950s because they have been unable to maintain a steady level of high-quality production. However, certain estates, which conform to current constraints relating to low yield in Sauternes, produce excellent wines. The same holds true for Saussignac, an appellation that has found it even harder to produce some really good dessert wines. With the exception of a few excellent years, these wineries rarely produce anything other than sweet wines. However, there can be no doubt that 1997 was a great vintage. The Cuvée Flavie boasts a botrytized Sauvignon-Sémillon base and the typically botrytic aromas of apricot and ripe, citrusy, yellow fruit. This is a great wine, full of character.

New South Wales

Australian wine began its rise to fame in New South Wales, one of the leading wine-producing regions in Australia. This area has a very varied climate: it can be scorching hot and oppressive in the north, while the vineyards benefit from cooler locations near the coast and in the mountains of the Australian Cordillera. The wine industry depends on successful irrigation. Hunter Valley, the best-known wine-producing zone, planted in 1820, is home to the main vineyards. The estate that produces the Noble One is near Griffith, in Riverina, 400 kilometres (249 miles) north of Melbourne.

NOBLE ONE BOTRYTIS SEMILLON 1996, DE BORTOLI

The vineyard was founded in 1928 in Bilbul, near Griffith, by Vittorio de Bortoli, who emigrated from Italy in 1924. This large company operates 350 hectares of vines and owns another winery in the Yarra Valley (in the south of the State of Victoria). The first Semillon vintage was produced in 1982 (Australians do not apply the é in Semillon). This wine, regarded as one of Australia's best dessert wines, was created by Darren de Bortoli (Vittorio's grandson). It is fermented in vats, then aged for twelve months in French oak barrels. The percentage of new barrels used increases each year. The wine is bottle-aged for twelve months before being sold. In such a hot, dry climate, natural botrytis does not develop easily, so this nobly rotted Semillon vintage represents a huge achievement.

The 1996 vintage has a yellowish, pale-golden robe. The nose is pleasing with undertones of yellow fruit, apricot, pineapple, a hint of mango, and candied citrus fruit. This wine has a delicately woody appeal and a rich, full-bodied mouth. The crisp acidity relieves the sweetness of this rich, sophisticated dessert wine which is strong and well-balanced with 11.5 per cent fermented alcohol and 125g per litre of residual sugar. The only thing this wine lacks is an underlying acidity, which is unavoidable due to its production in a very hot climate.

Praline Floating Islands

(Les flottantes aux pralines)

The Coteaux du Layon-Villages from Vincent Ogereau goes marvellously with the vanilla custard and delicate praline aromas of the floating islands. Aged in new oak barrels, this 1997 vintage – a good year for noble rot – has milky, vanilla overtones. The acidity of the Chenin Blanc balances the sweetness of this dessert and the praline provides a delicious hint of nuttiness that offsets the mellowness of the wine. The MEL is a sweet wine from Italy, whose flavour owes more to raisining than noble rot. It is also aged in new barrels, although it does not taste as sweet as the first wine. It has slightly acid notes of fruit drop, liquorice, and milk caramel that make it a perfect match for the praline.

SERVES 6

Preparation time: 25 minutes

Cooking time: 20 minutes

Chilling: 1 hour

FOR THE PRALINE FLOATING ISLANDS

30g (1oz) butter

100g (3¾oz) caster sugar + 30g (1oz) for the ramekins

6 egg whites

1 teaspoon vanilla sugar

50g (1¾oz) finely ground pralines

FOR THE VANILLA CUSTARD

1 vanilla pod, split lengthways

300ml (½ pint) milk

60g (2oz) caster sugar

3 egg yolks

Preparing the praline floating islands

Butter six ramekins and sprinkle with caster sugar.

Beat the egg whites with the caster sugar and vanilla sugar until stiff, then add the ground pink pralines and fold in gently until well-blended.

Pour this mixture into the ramekins and place in a bain-marie.

Cook for 15 minutes in a preheated oven – 150°C (300°F), Gas Mark 2.

Remove the ramekins from the bain-marie and leave to cool at room temperature before chilling for 1 hour in the refrigerator.

Preparing the vanilla custard

Add the split vanilla pod to the milk and bring to the boil.

Whisk the caster sugar and egg yolks in a large mixing bowl. Add the boiling milk gradually, whisking constantly, and pour the mixture into the saucepan.

Stir over a low heat until the custard thickens a little.

Pour into a mixing bowl and cool immediately on a bed of ice.

Put through a fine sieve and chill in the refrigerator.

Finishing

Run a knife round the edges of the ramekins and turn out the floating islands onto a dish or soup dishes. Surround with the vanilla custard.

Serving temperature

Coteaux du Layon-Villages, Clos des Bonnes-Blanches 1997, Vincent Ogereau: 10°C (50°F).

MEL 2000, Antonio Gaggiano: 10°C (50°F).

Coteaux du Layon-Villages

More restrictive than the Coteaux du Layon appellation, Coteaux du Layon-Villages is restricted to six villages on the left bank of the River Layon, including Saint-Lambert-du-Lattay. This village is now characterized by the large number of committed wine-growers, like Vincent Ogereau, Robineau, and Jo Pithon, whose vineyards produce top-quality wines. The soil is slate-based and the exposure conducive to growing *vins de terroir*. Minimum natural sugar content is 221g per litre at harvest, with a minimum of thirty-four grams per litre of residual sugar after fermentation, and the yield is thirty-five hectolitres per hectare.

COTEAUX DU LAYON-VILLAGES, CLOS DES BONNES-BLANCHES 1997, VINCENT OGEREAU

Catherine and Vincent Ogereau operate a twelve-hectare vineyard in the commune of Saint-Lambert-du-Lattay.

This couple, who rank among the finest producers in the Loire valley, are renowned for their precision, passion, and planning. It is unusual to come across such a homogenous cellar containing highly concentrated, well-balanced wines that are packed with fruit. The grapes are cultivated with care and the wines of all colours are made with precision. The village's leading vintage is Clos des Bonnes-Blanches and Vincent Ogereau has devoted two hectares to its production. The soil comprises two different geological layers: sandy, silt-laden topsoil to a depth of fifty centimetres (twenty inches) with green schists underneath to a depth of two metres (6.5 feet). The 1997 vintage is one of the area's top-quality wines. The grapes were selectively harvested throughout October at different stages of ripeness: raisined, botrytized, or overripened. The wine was then fermented for at least six months in new half-hogshead casks and bottled in early September 1998. The end result is a concentrated, mature wine which is not too heavy: a superb nectar with 195g per litre of residual sugar. This wine, which has a pleasing underlying acidity, can be cellared and could well be a future 1947.

Campania

Campania, which extends around the Italian city of Naples, is a major wine-producing area. It hugs the Tyrrhenian sea from Latium to the Basilicata and extends deep inland where it borders the Molise region and Apulia. The region is characterized by numerous plains alternating with mountains and volcanic hills. Although only a limited area in Campania is devoted to wine-growing, it is the ninth largest wine region in Italy and the ninth most productive. Weather conditions are affected by the proximity of the sea and the area enjoys mild winters and very hot summers. Many renowned appellations, including Taurasi, Fiano di Avellino, and Peninsula Sorrentina, are found at altitudes of between 500 and 600 metres (1,641 and 1,969 feet), a situation that also favours the production of well-balanced wines.

MEL 2000, ANTONIO GAGGIANO

This vintage is made from raisined grapes grown on volcanic soil. This is a surprisingly densely planted vineyard, given the climate – 8,000 vines per hectare. The wine is made from seventy per cent Fiano, a very common white grape variety in this region, and thirty per cent Greco. After raisining for several weeks, the grapes are fermented in new wood, then aged for twelve months in oak casks. The level of residual sugar is 150g per litre.

Grape Cream Parcels

(Crème croustillante aux raisins blonds)

This dessert is dominated by the flavours of sweet white grapes and caramel, offset by the tart fruitiness of the accompanying rhubarb compote. The wines should complement the crunchy texture of the filo pastry wrapped around the cream and reveal the influence of raisined and nobly rotted fruit. Montlouis is a great Loire vintage that is rich but well-balanced. This well-blended, mellow wine offers intermingled aromas of raisin and nobly rotted Chenin grapes with strong overtones of candied and crystallized fruit. The wonderful Tokaji Eszencia has an even more pronounced candied flavour with notes of citrus zest, honey, and raisin. These two wines go perfectly with this sweet, creamy dessert.

SERVES 8

Preparation time: 40 minutes

Cooking time: 40 minutes

Freezing: 1 hour

FOR THE RHUBARB COMPOTE

200ml (7fl oz) red wine

1 vanilla pod, split lengthways

50g (1¾oz) caster sugar

250g (9oz) washed, diced rhubarb

FOR THE GRAPE CREAM

3 egg yolks

80g (3oz) brown sugar

130ml (4½fl oz) milk

375ml (13fl oz) single cream

50g (1¾oz) white grapes

8 sheets filo pastry

1 beaten egg white

TO SERVE

1 litre vegetable oil for frying

2 fresh mint sprigs

50g (1¾oz) icing sugar

Preparing the rhubarb compote

Reduce the wine by two-thirds in a saucepan, then add the split vanilla pod, sugar and rhubarb.

Cover and cook for 10 minutes on a low heat, then put somewhere cool.

Preparing the grape cream

Beat the egg yolks and brown sugar until the mixture whitens, then mix in the milk and single cream.

Divide the white grapes between small individual tins, 4cm (1½ inches) in diameter, and pour the mixture over them.

Cook for 30 minutes in a bain-marie in a preheated oven – 110°C (225°F), Gas Mark ¼. Make sure the creams have completely cooled before putting in the freezer for 2 hours.

Turn out the creams.

Heat a deep fat fryer to 180°C (350°F).

Cut 24 × 10-cm (4-inch) squares of filo pastry and brush with beaten egg white.

Place a frozen cream at the centre of each square and fold the sides over to form a parcel.

Fry the parcels in hot oil for 2 minutes, drain and sprinkle with icing sugar.

Serving

Place a spoonful of rhubarb compote in the centre of each plate, arrange three cream parcels around it in a star pattern and decorate with a mint leaf. Serve immediately.

Serving temperature

Montlouis Moelleux Cuvée Romulus 1997, Jacky Blot: 10°C (50°F).

Tokaji Aszú Eszencia 1983, Oremus: 10°C (50°F).

Montlouis AOC

Montlouis is an AOC dating from 1938. The vineyard, on the south bank of the Loire, produces dry, semi-dry, sweet, and sparkling white wines as well as dessert wines in good years. The production area is restricted to three villages: Montlouis, Lusseau, and Saint-Martin-Le-Beau. There are two main types of soil: the first, known locally as *perruches*, that is predominantly clay and silica; and *aubuis*, which is clay and limestone. Montlouis, like Vouvray, its neighbour on the north bank, produces wines from Chenin Blanc. At their best, these wines are pure and clean and acquire even more character when cellared. This appellation, which is a little overshadowed by Vouvray, deserves to be better-known, particularly since the area boasts committed wine-growers like François Chidaine, Jacky Blot, Thierry Chaput, and Olivier Delétang, who respect the soil and produce some excellent wines.

MONTLOUIS MOELLEUX CUVEE ROMULUS 1997, JACKY BLOT

Jacky Blot has fourteen hectares of vines in Montlouis and Vouvray and, since 1989, has been operating a winery in Montlouis. He is now one of the leading producers of appellation wines and has achieved a great deal in a very short space of time in his quest for perfection. The Cuvée Romulus 1997 is a magnificent wine, ideal for laying down.

Highly concentrated, well-balanced and refined, it is made from seventy-year-old Chenin vines, planted on south-facing clay and silica slopes. The grapes are successively harvested in the last two weeks of October. The noble rot was of high quality in 1997. The remarkable fruit purity and aromatic clarity of this wine are largely due to the quality of the grape selection. It was fermented in barrels, without yeasting, and boasts an extraordinarily well-balanced array of flavours with a residual sugar content of 170g per litre. The keynotes of this first-class dessert wine are freshness and finesse.

Tokaji Aszú Eszencia

The Tokaji appellation is found in the northeastern part of northern Hungary, near the Slovakian and Ukrainian borders, and applies to 5,400 hectares of vines grown on predominantly volcanic loess and clay soil. The climate is continental with cold winters and hot, dry summers. Created accidentally by Chaplain Máté Szepsi Laczkó in 1630, this wine was a great favourite with the Tsars as well as with King Louis XIV of France. The grapes are harvested between and November 1–15 and are measured by *puttony* or basket which contains twenty-five kilos (fifty-five pounds) of aszú grapes. The number of *puttonyos* used, which can vary between three and six, determines the sweetness and strength of the

Tokaji. Tokaji Aszú Eszencia, which is extremely rich, uses the equivalent of seven *puttonyos*. This highly concentrated wine has a minimum of 180g per litre residual sugar. It must be aged for at least five years, including three years in the barrel. This type of concentrated vintage naturally requires sufficient ageing to ensure its balance and harmony.

TOKAJI ASZU ESZENCIA 1983, OREMUS

Built between the thirteenth and eighteenth centuries, the superb Oremus cellar in Tolcsva is hollowed out of the mountainside. Andras Bacso, its director, is a talented winemaker who has produced some marvellous wines. In the early 1990s, the winery was bought by Bodegas Vega Sicilia, owned by the Spanish Alvarez family. The winery has gone from strength to strength as a result of the Spanish owner's qualitative policy and investment programme. The amazingly concentrated Tokaji Aszú Eszencia 1983 is made from Furmint and Harslevelu grapes. The aromas of dried fruit, candied orange and apricot, and the honeyed, well-balanced and flavoursome mouth make this exceptional wine a delicious and unusual treat.

Pancakes with Chestnut Cream in Chocolate Sauce

(Aumônières de marrons glacés au chocolat)

The sweet chestnuts and chestnut flour pancakes used in this *aumônière* recipe inevitably bring to mind the rugged landscapes of Corsica. The first wine, a fortified Rappu, was selected for its regional affinities. With its high alcohol content, it counterbalances the dense taste of the marron glacé, cutting through its oiliness, while the aromas of controlled oxidation work wonders with the chocolate sauce. The Pedro-Ximénez is another good pairing for similar reasons. This wine, blended from the *solera* and aged in cask for twelve years since, complements the cocoa and chestnut flavours with notes of mocha, iced coffee, sesame, dried fig, and date. The rich sugary taste of these wines is absorbed by the pancakes. Both go beautifully with this dessert.

SERVES 8

Preparation time: 35 minutes

Cooking time: about 25 minutes

Chilling: 1 hour

FOR THE PANCAKE BATTER

430ml (15fl oz) milk

100g (3½oz) flour

75g (2½oz) chestnut flour

3 eggs

40g (1½oz) melted butter

50ml (2fl oz) vegetable oil

30g (1oz) caster sugar

1 tablespoon whisky

1 pinch salt

FOR THE CHESTNUT CREAM

8 finely diced marrons glacés

150g (5½oz) whipped cream flavoured with vanilla

150g (5¼oz) whipped cream

FOR THE PLAIN CHOCOLATE SAUCE

200g (7oz) plain chocolate

20g (¾oz) butter

150ml (¼ pint) water

Making the pancakes

Mix the milk and both types of flour in the bowl of a food processor. Add the other ingredients and mix until you obtain a smooth batter.

Chill for 1 hour in the refrigerator.

Make some medium-sized pancakes in a lightly oiled frying pan, allowing two per person. Put in a cool place.

Preparing the chestnut cream

Add the diced marrons glacés to the chestnut cream.

Fold in the whipped cream and mix with a spatula.

Chill in the refrigerator.

Preparing the chocolate sauce

Break the plain chocolate into pieces.

Add the butter to the measured water, bring to the boil, then add the chocolate and simmer until melted.

Stand in a warm place.

Finishing

Spread some chestnut cream over the pancakes and fashion them into little pouches.

Put two pancakes on each plate or arrange on a serving dish and drizzle with chocolate sauce.

Serving temperature

Rappu Domaine Gentile: 14°C (57°F).

Jerez Pedro-Ximénez El Candado Valdespino: 14°C (57°F).

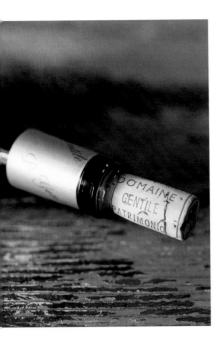

Rappu

Rappu is an ancestral Corsican tradition. Since every winemaker's Rappu is different, it is hard to describe the process in detail. Broadly speaking, though, Rappu is a dessert wine which can be made from a variety of grapes. This passe-tout-grains style of wine is made from Muscat, Grenache, Aleatico, and Nielluccio grapes. It is fortified with wine alcohol then wood aged for as long as required.

RAPPU DOMAINE GENTILE

The Gentile winery, in the Patrimonio appellation, extends over thirty-four hectares of vineyards and Rappu is one of its specialities. The cellar is at Saint-Florent. Jean-Paul Gentile has slightly modified his father's recipe for Rappu: the wine is now made from Muscat à Petits Grains blended with Nielluccio. It is fortified with neutral alcohol and its alcohol level can vary between sixteen and eighteen degrees. It is aged for a year in stainless-steel vats then for two years in old oak barrels. This wine is not necessarily topped up. Controlled oxidation and the presence of *rancio*, coffee, and chocolate aromas are considered far more desirable qualities during this ageing period. This is a generous wine, tempered by sixty grams per litre of residual sugar.

Jerez

There are many quality dessert wines in Andalusia, including the sherry appellation that occupies a key place in this category. All basic sherries belonging to the family of dessert wines that are not aged under *flor* – certain olorosos, pale cream, cream, brown cream, East India – are fortified to a strength of about eighteen degrees' alcohol, since this yeast layer will not grow above sixteen degrees. They are then sweetened with natural sweeteners made from grapes such as Moscatel or the sugar-rich Pedro-Ximénez. Like all sherries, they are aged using the *solera* system which gives them greater complexity. Wine legislation states that sherry must be wood aged for a minimum of three years.

JEREZ PEDRO-XIMENEZ EL CANDADO VALDESPINO

Pedro-Ximénez, or Pedro-Ximen, is one of the four grape varieties authorized for use in the original sherry label. This varietal is either used on its own, as in this case, or in a blend, adding sweetness, mellowness, and smoothness. In this warm climate, this grape variety has produced some extremely rich wines. It is picked when overripe, then sun-dried on mats spread on the ground, which concentrates the sugars and aromas. It is pressed, fortified with alcohol, then aged using the *solera* system. This tawny El Candado vintage is an old Pedro-Ximénez which has been aged for twelve years in cask. The nose reveals hints of dried fig, chocolate, an aromatic woodiness, and a hint of iced coffee and cappuccino. The mouth is intensely rich and concentrated, with a total of 450g of sugar per litre.

Spices, Honey, Cream, and Caramel

Gingerbread with Orange-blossom Honey

(Pain d'épice au miel d'oranger)

Although this gingerbread has prominent candied, honeyed flavours, the aromatic spices and caramelized honey add a slight bitterness that needs to be offset by the sweetness of the wines. The botrytic character of these wines is very important since noble rot complements the subtle flavours of honey and cinnamon, and the high level of residual sugar brings out the taste and texture of the gingerbread. Château d'Yquem 1990 is a superbly botrytized vintage with abundant aromas of candied citrus fruit and mandarin that work well with the orange-blossom honey. The Tokaji Aszú 6 Puttonyos 1972 Oremus is also a particularly rich, sweet wine that makes a good pairing for this dessert. The gingerbread tempers the high sugar content of the wine and enhances its flavours of orange, citrus peel, plum, and lemon.

SERVES 8

Preparation time: 20 minutes

Cooking time: 40 minutes

Standing: several days

250g (9oz) wholemeal flour

1 egg

1½ teaspoons baking powder

1 teaspoon bicarbonate of soda

½ teaspoon ground cinnamon

½ teaspoon ground ginger

½ teaspoon ground anise

150ml (¼ pint) milk

325g (11½oz) orange-blossom honey

1 pinch table salt

Preparing the dough

Mix the flour, baking powder, bicarbonate of soda and ground spices together.

Bring the milk to the boil.

Remove from the heat, add the honey and salt and pour over the flour mixture.

Add the egg and whisk vigorously.

Cooking the gingerbread

Pour the mixture into a 7 × 14cm (2¾ × 5½ inch) cake tin lined with greaseproof paper.

Cook in a preheated oven – 170°C (325°F), Gas Mark 3 for about 40 minutes. A knife inserted into the centre of the gingerbread will come out clean when it is fully cooked.

Turn the gingerbread out and leave to cool completely before wrapping in clingfilm. Chill for several days before eating. The gingerbread will keep for two weeks on the bottom shelf of your refrigerator.

Serving temperature

Sauternes Château d'Yquem 1990, Lur-Saluces: 11° C (52° F).

Tokaji Aszú 6 Puttonyos 1972, Oremus: 11–12° C (52–53° F).

Sauternes

One of the finest appellations in the world, Sauternes can produce outstanding sweet syrupy wines in good years. The area covers the communes of Sauternes, Fargues, Bommes, Preignac and Barsac and has gravelly, clay soil which becomes more chalky in Barsac. Autumn mists rising off the River Ciron, a tributary of the Garonne that flows through the appellation area, are an important factor in the development of noble rot. The maximum yield permitted by the INAO (French National Institute for AOC and AOVDQS) is twenty-five hectolitres per hectare, but the most successful results are achieved with yields between eleven and fifteen hectolitres per hectare. The minimum sugar content is 221g per litre before fermentation. In good years, potential alcohol levels vary between twenty and twenty-four degrees, enabling producers to obtain wines fermented to a strength of fifteen degrees. The rest of the sugar remains in the wine as residual sweetness. Sémillon, Sauvignon Blanc, and Muscadelle are the authorized grape varieties, although only a small percentage of the latter is used. The dominant grape is Sémillon; it has a thin skin that is highly susceptible to noble rot and therefore provides richness and sweetness. Sauvignon Blanc grapes are less hardy and particularly vulnerable to bad rot. However, when harvested successfully, they provide complexity and underlying acidity.

CHATEAU D'YQUEM 1990, LUR-SALUCES

The name Château d'Yquem has become virtually synonymous with the Sauternes appellation. Its consistently high performance is clear proof of its greatness. Until its recent buyout by the French LVMH group, the 103-hectare winery had been owned for generations by the Lur-Saluces family and Alexandre de Lur-Saluces is still the company's director. Château d'Yquem has set the benchmark for the wine industry: very low yields, painstaking selection of top-quality grapes, meticulous winemaking processes and long ageing periods (nearly always over three years) in oak barrels. The vine stock is eighty per cent Sémillon and twenty per cent Sauvignon Blanc. Perfect for cellaring, this wine is renowned for its complexity, finesse, and balance. 1990 was a star vintage: rich and luscious, with remarkable ageing potential.

Tokaji Aszú

Tokaji is produced in northeast Hungary, around the town of Tokaj, near the Slovakian and Ukrainian borders. It applies to 5,400 hectares of vines grown on predominantly volcanic loess and clay soil in a continental climate. This wine was a great favourite with the tsars as well as with King Louis XIV of France who called it "the wine of kings, the king of wines". The grapes are harvested between November 1–15 and are measured by *puttony* (basket). Each basket contains twenty-five kilos (fifty-five pounds) of aszú grape paste. The number of *puttonyos* used, which can vary between three and six, determines the sweetness and strength of the wine. Tokaji 6 Puttonyos is a remarkably well-balanced wine with a pleasing level of sweetness. It has a minimum residual sugar content of 150g per litre and must be aged for at least three years, including two in the barrel.

TOKAJI ASZU 6 PUTTONYOS 1972, OREMUS

The fifty-one-hectare vineyard extends over the southern slopes of Mount Zemplen. Situated in Tolcsva, the vaulted, candlelit cellar was hollowed out of the rock between the thirteenth and eighteenth centuries. Its director, András Bacso, is a walking dictionary of Tokaji wines. The winery produces excellent wines and recent vintages are impressive: 1972 is true nectar. Bottled in 1991, it spent almost nineteen years in barrel. Amber and dark topaz in colour, it has a complex nose: gingerbread, dried fruit, candied fruit, apricot, mandarin, and fruit paste. The robust yet smooth mouth boasts a remarkable balance between sugar and acidity and the wine has an exceptional finish.

Fruit Salad in Citronella Syrup

(Nage de fruits à la citronelle)

This medley of fruit in a subtly spiced syrup calls for wines that complement the freshness and simplicity of the dessert. Citronella has a delicate, lingering fragrance that requires a wine with good length. The Cadillac was chosen for its classic fruity undertones. It is a crisp wine, perfect for this dessert, with lush yellow fruit aromas – pineapple, citron, grapefruit – combining sweetness and acidity. This is a wine bursting with fresh fruit flavours. The Californian Vin de Glacière is outstanding for several reasons. It has a particularly prominent flavour of crunchy grape coupled with yellow and white fruit and its acid concentration goes perfectly with the fresh, lemony aromas of the fruit salad.

SERVES 8
Preparation time: 20 minutes
Chilling: 2 hours

FOR THE FRUIT SALAD

1 large mango
2 green apples
300g (10oz) peeled pineapple
200g (7oz) peeled papaya
200g (7oz) strawberries
10 mint leaves

FOR THE CITRONELLA SYRUP

2 fresh passion fruits
2 citronella stalks
1 lime
80g (3oz) granulated sugar
250ml (9fl oz) water
1 vanilla pod, split lengthways
1 stick cinnamon

Preparing the citronella syrup

Halve the passion fruits, scoop out the pulp and put through a sieve to extract the juice.

Slice the lime into thin rounds and cut the citronella stalks into large pieces.

Put the sugar and measured water in a saucepan and bring to the boil.

Remove from the heat, add the passion fruit juice, sliced lime, cinnamon stick, split vanilla pod, and citronella.

Cover and leave to infuse in the refrigerator for 1 hour.

Preparing the fruit salad

Wash the fruit and slice into medium-sized chunks.

Pour the citronella syrup over the fruit and macerate for 1 hour in the refrigerator.

Serve in individual bowls, decorated with a mint leaf.

Serving temperature

Cadillac Château Reynon 1998, Denis and Florence Dubourdieu: 10°C (50°F).

Vin de Glacière Muscat Canelli Bonny Doon 1999, Randall Graham: 10°C (50°F).

Cadillac

The Cadillac appellation stretches along the right bank of the river Garonne. The villages at the northern end of this area qualify for the Premières-Côtes-de-Bordeaux appellation that applies to red wines. Cadillac, however, only produces sweet, sometimes syrupy, white wines. The Cadillac appellation is currently struggling to retain its identity due to overgenerous yields and the low incidence of noble rot, resulting more often than not in an unexciting style of sweet wine. As a result, inexpensive sweet wines are stealing the march on more concentrated wines. However, a handful of top-ranking winemakers are paving the way for a brighter future by producing delicious rich wines that are more complex and display a refreshing sugar-alcohol balance. These wines are made from Sémillon, Sauvignon Blanc, and Muscatelle grapes planted on the hillsides. The soils vary from silt-laden to clayey and chalky. The maximum yield is set at forty hectolitres per hectare and the minimum percentage of residual sugar must be eighteen grams per litre.

CHATEAU REYNON 1998, DENIS AND FLORENCE DUBOURDIEU

Château Reynon is a fine vineyard run by Denis and Florence Dubourdieu in the commune of Béguey. Denis Dubourdieu has succeeded in his goal of restoring the former glory of Cadillac. Five vintages have been produced since 1996. The superb Cadillac 1998 is made from sixty per cent Sauvignon Blanc and forty per cent Sémillon. The wine has a wonderful crisp, candied flavour with a smooth, well-balanced palate. The grapes were harvested at twenty degrees potential alcohol from yields of fifteen hectolitres per hectare. This beautifully balanced wine boasts a residual sugar content of 102g per litre.

VIN DE GLACIERE MUSCAT CANELLI BONNY DOON 1999, RANDALL GRAHAM

Randall Graham, who lives in Santa Cruz County, is the most eccentric producer in California. He is passionate about Riesling and Rhône Valley grape varieties, both red and white, and buys grapes all along the Central Coast: Livermore Valley, Contra Costa, Paso Robles and Salinas Valley. He produces some wonderful vintages, each more unexpected than the last. The Muscat Canelli 1999 is not actually 100 per cent Muscat: small amounts of Malvasia have been added. The grapes, that come from Salinas Valley, are harvested when very ripe and pressed when frozen, a process known as cryoextraction. This produces a superb wine with aromas of lemony citrus fruit and candied orange. The mouth is well-balanced, with a wonderful level of acidity.

Assam Tea Crème Brûlée

(Crème brûlée au thé d'Assam)

This creamy dessert is infused with the grassy, vegetable aromas of the tea, whose slightly bitter taste provides a delicious counterbalance to the smooth, sweet cream and light crunchy caramel topping. Although the natural exuberance of the Condrieu Vendange Tardive is tempered by noble rot, it is still lively enough to complement the astringent aromas of the tea. The Moscatel de Setubal, one of the finest Muscat-based *vins doux naturels* in the world, is amazingly complex and rich. This ultra-fresh wine is remarkable for its mature overtones of yellow fruit and candied citrus peel and its notes of controlled oxidation. It brings out the herby aromas of the tea as well as the flavour of the caramel.

SERVES 8

Preparation time: 15 minutes
Cooking time: 30 minutes
Standing: 1 hour
Chilling: 1 hour

180ml (6½ floz) milk
2 teaspoons Assam tea
80g (3oz) granulated sugar
4 egg yolks
400ml (14fl oz) single cream
100g (3½oz) soft brown sugar

Preparing the crème brûlée

Bring the milk to the boil.

Remove from the heat, add the tea and cover.

Leave to infuse for 5 minutes, then strain through a fine sieve.

Add the granulated sugar, egg yolks, and single cream and mix together without whisking.

Pour this mixture into eight small dishes and cook in a bain-marie for about 30 minutes in a preheated oven – 110°C (225°F), Gas Mark ¼.

The creams are done if the centres are still quivering when they are taken out of the oven.

Leave to cool for 1 hour at room temperature, then chill for 1 hour in the refrigerator.

Finishing

When the crèmes brûlées are completely cool, sprinkle with brown sugar and place under a preheated grill until the sugar is caramelized.

Serve immediately.

Serving temperature

Condrieu Vendange Tardive Quintessence 1999, François Villard: 10°C (50°F).

Moscatel de Setubal Aged 20 Years, Jose Maria da Fonseca: 12°C (53°F).

Condrieu

The sensational Condrieu
appellation dates from 1940
and applies to six villages. The
100 hectares of vineyards, that
produce one of the finest white
wines in France, cling to the
steep hillsides, some forty-eight
kilometres (thirty miles) south
of Lyon. Viognier thrives in this
area: the acid soil is composed
largely of mica and granite
and the continental Rhodanian
climate gives hot summers.
As is the case with all hillside
vineyards, yields are fairly low.
The maximum permitted yield
is thirty-seven hectolitres per
hectare. In exceptional years,
this well-established appellation
has produced crisp, supple
wines ranging from *demi-sec*
to sweet: a feat that wine-
growers still attempt when
weather conditions permit.

CONDRIEU VENDANGE TARDIVE QUINTESSENCE 1999, FRANCOIS VILLARD

François Villard is one the
leading producers in the
Rhône valley. This meticulous
winemaker is passionate about
wine and keen to produce great
vins de terroir. Whether red
or white, his superb wines are
well-structured, concentrated
and delicate. His six hectares
are run with incredible attention
to detail. The Quintessence
vintage was made from
botrytized Viognier harvested
from the vineyard's various
Condrieu plots and produced
in new barrels. The wine
is rich and well-balanced with
a residual sugar content
of 105g per litre.

MOSCATEL DE SETUBAL AGED 20 YEARS, JOSE MARIA DA FONSECA

Moscatel de Setubal is an area
bounded, since 1907, by the
villages of Palmela, Freguesia, and
Sesimbra, in Portugal. Muscat of
Alexandria and Muscat Roxo
vines grow on the chalky slopes
of the Serra Arrabida
mountains. This wine is fortified
like French naturally sweet
wines. Moscatel Blanco and
Moscatel Roxo must have an
alcohol content between 16.5
degrees and twenty-two
degrees. Moscatel de Setubal
must be made from a minimum
of sixty-seven per cent Muscat
grapes and aged for at least
twenty-four months. When
labelled "Superior", the wine will
have been made from eighty-
five per cent Muscat grapes and
passed official tastings in its
second and fifth years.

Vanilla Cream Mille-feuille

(Mille-feuille à la crème vanillée)

This sweet, creamy dessert with its prominent vanilla flavours calls for wines with vanilla and woody notes. These wines can be very rich and concentrated, since their sweetness is absorbed by the flaky pastry. 1995 was a very good year for noble rot in Monbazillac. This Château Grand-Maison has a well-balanced palate that is perfect for the taste structure of the mille-feuille: an ageing period in new wood develops the aromas of vanilla and precious wood which underpin notes of apricot, peach and pineapple. This is a delightful combination. The Austrian TBA from Neusiedlersee is a rich wine with good acidity that has vanilla aromas and notes of yellow fruit. This superb wine works just as well with the vanilla mille-feuille.

SERVES 8

Preparation time: 30 minutes

Cooking time: 30 minutes

Chilling: 1 hour

Standing: 1 hour

FOR THE MILLE-FEUILLE

500g (1lb 2oz) Flaky Pastry
 (see page 52)

80g (3oz) icing sugar

FOR THE CONFECTIONERS'
CUSTARD

1 vanilla pod, split lengthways

500ml (18fl oz) milk

4 egg yolks

100g (3½oz) granulated sugar

30g (1oz) flour

30g (1oz) cornflour

TO SERVE

200ml (7fl oz) whipped cream

50g (1¾oz) icing sugar

Preparing the confectioners' custard

Add the split vanilla pod to the milk and bring to the boil. Cover and leave to infuse for 1 hour.

Beat the egg yolks vigorously with the sugar. Fold in the flour and cornflour and gradually add the vanilla-flavoured milk.

Pour the mixture into saucepan and bring to the boil, stirring well. Cook for a few minutes, stirring, until thickened.

Put to one side in a deep bowl, lay a sheet of clingfilm directly over the top of the cream and leave to cool.

Making the flaky pastry

Roll out the pastry into a rectangle about 30 x 40cm (12 x 16 inches) and 2mm (⅟₁₆ inch) thick.

Place on a baking sheet and cook for about 25 minutes in a preheated oven – 180°C (350°F), Gas Mark 4.

Sprinkle the flaky pastry with icing sugar and allow to caramelize for 5 minutes in the oven. Take out and leave to cool on a wire rack.

Finishing

Vigorously whip the confectioners' custard and add the whipped cream.

Cut the sheet of pastry lengthways into four strips. Cover three of the strips with vanilla cream.

Place one on top of the other and cover with the third strip.

Cut the mille-feuille into eight and serve, sprinkled with icing sugar.

Serving temperature

Monbazillac Château Grand-Maison, Cuvée du Château 1995, Thierry Després: 10°C (50°F).

Neusiedlersee TBA N°7 Nouvelle Vague 1998, Alois Kracher: 10°C (50°F).

Monbazillac

This appellation, which obtained its AOC in 1936, covers five villages in the Dordogne *département*. It applies only to sweet white wines or dessert wines made from Sémillon, Sauvignon Blanc, and Muscadelle with a minimum potential alcohol level of 14.5 degrees. The style of wine produced depends on the policy implemented by the wine-grower and its quality depends on the size of the yields and the meticulous selective harvesting processes used. Vintage is also a key factor in determining the wine's potential alcohol and sugar content because noble rot does not occur automatically every year. Raisining and overripening may be used to improve the level of concentration. The maximum yield of the Monbazillac appellation is also fairly high, which can compromise quality and concentration. Monbazillac has often been criticized for poor-quality wines and the image of its sweet wines has certainly suffered due to overzealous harvesting methods. Fortunately, a handful of producers are attempting to raise the profile of this appellation and enhance its image by adhering to low yields, top-quality selective harvesting methods, and rigorous winemaking processes. Wineries like Château Tirecul-La Gravière, Château Theulet, Château Grand-Maison, and Château La Borderie are now showing the way.

CHATEAU GRAND-MAISON, CUVEE DU CHATEAU 1995, THIERRY DESPRES

This Monbazillac vineyard has been completely biodynamic for several years. Thierry Després produced this Cuvée du Château at the Château Grand-Maison from the 1995 vintage. Made from an excellent harvest, picked in as many as five or seven successive passes through the vineyard, this wine is a beautiful light gold. The nose has prominent overtones of yellow fruit – apricot, mango, pineapple – underpinned by a delicate woody aroma. The wine is robust, sweet, and syrupy with good balance and the final acidity guarantees persistence. Produced using traditional winemaking processes, it was fermented and wood aged in barrels for twenty-one months.

Neusiedlersee

With 8,310 hectares of vines, this Austrian region is the foremost wine-producer in the Burgenland, stretching along the Hungarian border and the banks of Lake Neusiedl. The climate is conducive to the development of noble rot. The terrain is fairly flat and the soil is mainly loess, sand and silt. The most widely planted varieties of grape are Welschriesling, Muskateller, Pinot Blanc, Bouvier, and Furmint. Some excellent producers have made a name for themselves in the villages of Gols, Illmitz, and Apetlon. TBA is the highest category defined by Austrian wine laws and the minimum sugar content of these grapes must reach 156 Oechsle (22.1 degrees volume). These rich, syrupy wines age extraordinarily well.

NEUSIEDLERSEE TBA N° 7 NOUVELLE VAGUE 1998, ALOIS KRACHER

Probably the best wine producer in Austria, Alois Kracher makes sensational wines, including a number of TBA. He operates a ten-hectare vineyard in the village of Illmitz and favours Welschriesling, Traminer, Chardonnay, Muscat Ottonel and Scheurebe grape varieties. Alois Kracher uses two different winemaking processes. The first method is traditional and involves ageing in 300-litre acacia-wood barrels with residual sugar concentration ranging between 200 and 220g per litre. The second method produces the "Nouvelle Vague" (New Wave) family of wines, that are aged in French oak barrels and are much higher in alcohol – around thirteen per cent – with a high residual sugar content ranked on a scale between one and thirteen. Nouvelle Vague N°7 offers perfect balance between sugar alcohol acidity. This is an elegant wine with candied aromas of yellow fruit, mandarin, late-ripening peach, apricot, and candied citrus fruit. It has a subtle, well-integrated, vanilla-tinged woody palate and 195g per litre of residual sugar.

Banana Cakes with Sweet Spices

(Petits gâteaux de banane aux épices douces)

These moist little cakes are subtly flavoured with sweet spices like nutmeg and cinnamon. Married with the taste of the slightly caramelized cooked banana, these spices call for rich, generous wines that are starting to show development, preferably old vintages with woody, balsamic notes that can complement the flavour of the cinnamon. The South African Constantia 1987, made from raisined Muscat à Petits Grains, is this type of wine. Over fifteen years old, its array of aromatic notes include wood polish, old wood, and honey. Similarly, the white Banyuls is a crisp wine with prominent fruit overtones. It is also packed with spicy, banana, and white-fruit flavours and has the necessary progressive notes to balance this dessert perfectly.

MAKES 16 SMALL CAKES

Preparation time: 30 minutes

Cooking time: 20 minutes

Standing: 20 minutes

300g (10oz) flour

2 teaspoons baking powder

240g (8½oz) icing sugar

1 pinch table salt

150g (5¼oz) softened butter

2 eggs + 2 egg yolks

½ teaspoon freshly grated nutmeg

½ teaspoon ground cinnamon

400g (14oz) fresh bananas, peeled

juice of 1 lemon

40g (1½oz) finely diced dried apricots

Preparing the cake mixture

Sift the flour with the baking powder.

Mix the icing sugar and softened butter in a large bowl, add the salt then the whole eggs one at a time, followed by the yolks, whisking vigorously.

Mix in the flour and ground spices.

Blend the flesh of the peeled bananas with the lemon juice in a food processor.

Fold this purée into the cake mixture, add the dried apricots and mix with a wooden spoon.

Cooking the cake

Pour the mixture into sixteen individual greased tins and cook for about 20 minutes in a preheated oven – 170°C (325°F), Gas Mark 3.

Turn out the small cakes and stand them on a wire rack for 20 minutes to ensure they stay soft and moist.

Decorate with slices of fresh banana if desired.

Serving temperature

Banyuls Cuvée Rivage, Domaine Vial-Magnères 1999, Bernard Saperas: 10°C (50°F).

Klein Constantia 1987: 11°C (52°F).

Banyuls

The white version of Banyuls represents only three to four per cent of the appellation. Banyuls is made from white and rosé grape varieties authorized for the production of French *vins doux naturels*. These grapes are made into white wine using traditional methods, such as direct pressing, without any contact between juice and skins. The wine is fortified with neutral alcohol to stop alcoholic fermentation and the non-fermented (residual) sugar remains in the wine. However, white Banyuls is matured in a completely different way to red Banyuls: the wine is aged in wood or another oxidative environment for a limited period of time because it is important to preserve the fruit flavours, colour and crispness. Although well-balanced, white Banyuls is not as complex as *rancio*-style Banyuls or Banyuls *rimage*, since it lacks the characteristic tannic structure of red Banyuls: the tannin plays a key role in tempering the sweetness.

BANYULS CUVEE RIVAGE, DOMAINE VIAL-MAGNERES 1999, BERNARD SAPERAS
Monique and Bernard Saperas run this family vineyard with ten hectares of vines planted in small plots on the best land in the area. The vines are cultivated in terraces along the coast and harvesting is exclusively manual. The soil of these terraces is slate-based. This white Banyuls 1999 vintage is made from eighty per cent Grenache Blanc and twenty per cent Grenache Gris, pressed directly and fermented to an alcoholic strength of sixteen degrees at low temperatures. The wine is fortified, left on the lees for three months then aged for six months in new wood before bottling.

Constantia

The Constantia appellation, in South Africa's Cape region, was established in 1973. The vineyard of 750 hectares extends over the red granite slopes of Table Mountain. Constantia was one of the first wines to make a name for itself in the eighteenth century – Napoleon even had it shipped to Saint Helena to sweeten his exile. Part of the Coastal Region, this wine-producing zone enjoys a Mediterranean climate tempered by breezes from the Indian and Atlantic oceans. The vines have no need of irrigation as the area receives an average annual rainfall of 850 millimetres (thirty-three inches). This region is planted with classic grape varieties. The major sweet wines, both white and red, are made from Muscat à Petits Grains, Muscat of Alexandria, and dark red Pontac. The grapes are raisined, not infected by noble rot.

KLEIN CONSTANTIA 1987
This winery came into being when the former Groot Constantia estate was divided into two in the late eighteenth century. In 1987, the winery again began producing the famous "Vin de Constance", a wine made from Muscat à Petits Grains around 1870. This was the first vintage to be produced since this type of wine disappeared. The harvests were late, around the end of March and the grapes were raisined on the vine. The result is a wine of incomparable finesse. The nose is complex, the concentration superb, and the palate displays a fine balance of flavours.

Pineapple in a Spiced Caramel Sauce with Coconut Ice-cream

(Ananas au caramel épicé, glace coco)

Pineapple is naturally tart, even when candied, and this acidity should be brought out and complemented by the selected wines. The Jurançon Moelleux Clos Lapeyre 1999, produced from Petit Manseng grapes is perfect. When overripened, this classic grape variety from southwest France develops aromas of exotic fruit, particularly candied pineapple and mango. This is a semi-sweet wine with just the right balance between sugar and acidity. The raisined Muscat à Petits Grains from Austria has more prominent aromas of yellow fruit, apricot, and candied orange, but goes perfectly with this fruity pineapple dessert. In both cases, the tangy pineapple offsets the full-bodied sweetness of the wines whose candied, spicy notes complement the aromatic caramel sauce.

SERVES 10

Preparation time: 50 minutes

Cooking time: 30 minutes

Standing: 1 hour

Freezing: 1 hour

1 pineapple

FOR THE SAUCE

30g (1oz) butter

100ml (3½fl oz) water

200g (7oz) granulated sugar

100ml (3½fl oz) pineapple juice

2 star anise

4 cinnamon sticks

2 vanilla pods, diced

FOR THE COCONUT ICE-CREAM

250ml (9fl oz) milk

1 x 250g (9oz) tin of sweetened coconut cream

Preparing the caramel sauce

Heat the butter until it begins to melt.

Put the measured water and granulated sugar in a separate saucepan and heat for about 5 minutes to obtain a dark brown caramel.

Remove from the heat and gradually pour in the pineapple juice.

Add the melted butter, spices, and vanilla pods.

Remove from the heat, cover, and leave to infuse for 1 hour.

Cooking the pineapple

Peel and slice the pineapple.

Remove the core with a curved knife and arrange the slices in a dish.

Drench with the strained caramel sauce, cover and cook for 30 minutes in a preheated oven – 150°C (300°F), Gas Mark 2. Leave to cool.

Preparing the coconut ice-cream

Bring the milk to the boil then add the coconut cream.

Mix until the coconut fat has melted and leave to cool.

Pour into an ice-cream maker and churn for 20–25 minutes (or pour into a freezer-proof container and freeze until firm). Put in the freezer for 1 hour.

Place two slices of pineapple on each plate with some sauce, and serve with a scoop of coconut ice-cream.

Serving temperature

Jurançon Moelleux Clos Lapeyre 1999, Jean-Bernard Larrieu: 10°C (50°F).

Ruster Ausbruch Gelber Muskateller 1999, Robert Wenzel: 10°C (50°F).

Jurançon

The Jurançon AOC applies to twenty-five villages sandwiched between the Gave de Pau and the Gave d'Oloron rivers, in the Pyrénées-Atlantiques region. The vineyards form a patchwork of small plots. The average altitude is 300 metres (985 feet) and the soil is mainly clay and silica. This appellation produces dry white wines largely from Gros Manseng grapes with much smaller quantities of Courbu, Lauzet, and Camaralet. Jurançon Moelleux is dominated by the Petit Manseng grape. Unlike most sweet wines, its concentration is the result of raisining on the vine, as the grapes are harvested when overripe. The long, warm autumns are freshened by the *Foehn*, a warm, dry wind that blows in from Spain. The cumulative effect of the warm days and cool nights concentrates the grapes' sugars. The yield is limited to forty hectolitres per hectare. This wine may be labelled Vendange Tardive if made solely from Petit Manseng and Gros Manseng and not chaptalized for any reason. The natural sugar content should give at least sixteen degrees potential alcohol and the certificate of approval should have been awarded after a test sampling at least eighteen months after the harvest. The Jurançon is a harmonious blend with well-balanced sweetness and good acidity. Its complex aromas and flavours make it one of the finest dessert wines produced in France.

JURANCON MOELLEUX CLOS LAPEYRE 1999, JEAN-BERNARD LARRIEU

Jean-Bernard Larrieu produces wine at the village of La Chapelle-de-Rousse. His vines are planted in soil of great character at high altitudes and his wine bears the stamp of this location: Clos Lapeyre wines always display greater minerality and acidity than wines from the rest of the appellation area. Acidity is a key factor in the quality of these sweet wines, because it provides an underlying crispness. The Cuvée Sélection was made wholly from raisined Petit Manseng grapes, picked with nineteen degrees' potential alcohol in the second week of November. A third of the wine is fermented in new wood, the rest in older barrels. The residual sugar content is eight-five grams per litre. This wonderful well-balanced wine is delightfully sweet and displays great finesse for a year that was not one of the appellation's best.

RUSTER AUSBRUCH GELBER MUSKATELLER 1999, ROBERT WENZEL

According to Austrian wine laws, the Ausbruch category corresponds to a minimum ripeness of 138 Oechsle. The oechsle is a German system for calculating the sugar content of grape must by comparing the specific gravity of the must with the specific gravity of the water. If the water's specific gravity is 1,000, then grape must with a specific gravity of 1,100 will weigh 100 Oechsle. The Wenzel family has been growing vines since the seventeenth century on a seven-hectare estate in Rust, a village in Burgenland, near Lake Neusiedl. Robert Wenzel is probably the village's leading producer. His impressive wines are the product of top-quality selective harvesting methods. The Gelber Muskateller grape (similar to the Muscat Blanc à Petits Grains), which is used to make this wine, owes its name to its golden yellow skin. This variety accounts for only 0.2 per cent of the country's vine stock. The Ausbruch Gelber Muskateller vintage is remarkable for its balance: ten degrees alcohol with 12.5 per cent acidity and residual sugar of 300g per litre.

Chantilly Cream Puffs

(Choux à la crème Chantilly)

These light choux puffs filled with frothy Chantilly cream are complemented perfectly by effervescent wines. Your choice should be a slightly sparkling, delicate wine such as the Jacquesson Blanc de Blancs Champagne, which is an elegant match for the Chantilly cream. The texture of this minerally white Champagne works wonders with the delicate taste of the dessert, which is also complemented by its flavoursome mouth. The botrytized yet refined Moselle is also a good match, although more for its aromas than its texture. With its mineral tang, notes of green apple, and its lack of aromatic exuberance, it complements the Chantilly-filled choux buns perfectly. This is a great pairing for this type of dessert, as the sweetness of the wine is absorbed by the choux pastry.

SERVES 10

Preparation time: 30 minutes
Cooking time: 20 minutes

FOR THE CHOUX PASTRY
125g (4½oz) butter
80ml (2¾oz) water
125ml (4fl oz) milk
1 large pinch table salt
½ teaspoon granulated sugar
125g (4½oz) sifted flour
5 eggs

FOR THE CHANTILLY CREAM
500ml (18fl oz) well-chilled whipping cream
50g (1¾oz) icing sugar
1½ teaspoons vanilla sugar

TO SERVE
50g (1¾oz) icing sugar

Preparing the choux pastry

Melt the butter in a saucepan and add the measured water, milk, salt, and sugar.

Bring to the boil, remove from the heat and add the sifted flour.

Mix vigorously with a wooden spoon to thicken the paste.

Fold in four eggs one at a time, stirring to obtain a smooth, dense mixture.

Baking the choux puffs

Transfer to a piping bag with a plain 10-mm (½-inch) nozzle and pipe small balls of pastry the size of walnuts onto a baking sheet, spacing them at about 5-cm (2-inch) intervals.

Beat the remaining egg, strain through a sieve, then brush over the choux puffs.

Cook for 20 minutes in a preheated oven – 180°C (350°F), Gas Mark 4. When the choux puffs are well risen, golden and dry, take from the oven and leave to cool on the baking sheet.

Preparing the Chantilly cream

Pour the well-chilled cream into a large mixing bowl and whip energetically.

When the cream begins to form stiff peaks, add the icing sugar and vanilla sugar.

Mix carefully and pour into a piping bag with a wide fluted nozzle.

Finishing

Split the choux buns lengthways and pipe in some Chantilly cream.

Put them back together placing the top half over the cream.

Dust with icing sugar before serving.

Serving temperature

Blanc de Blancs Champagne Avize Grand Cru 1993, Jacquesson: 10°C (50°F).

Mosel-Saar-Ruwer Riesling BA Zeltingen Sonnenuhr 2000, Selbach-Oster: 10°C (50°F).

Blanc de Blancs Champagne

Champagne is frequently made from three grape varieties: Pinot Noir, Pinot Meunier, and Chardonnay. Champagne labelled "Blanc de Blancs" (white wine from white grapes) has been made entirely from Chardonnay, since this is the only variety of the three with white skin and white juice (Pinot Noir and Pinot Meunier are red-skinned grapes). Chardonnay vines are planted largely in the Côte des Blancs wine-growing area of the Champagne region. Other areas can make good Chardonnay wines, but the best in Champagne are produced in the Côte des Blancs; full of villages with *grand cru* ratings. Despite this, Chardonnay covers a smaller area than the other varieties and the production of Blanc de Blancs Champagne is limited, accounting for only seven per cent of the total volume of Champagne.

BLANC DE BLANCS CHAMPAGNE AVIZE GRAND CRU 1993, JACQUESSON

The Jacquesson company, in the village of Dizy, near Épernay and Ay, devotes a great deal of care and attention to making Champagne: the soil and yield are carefully monitored and the quality is remarkable. Brothers Jean-Hervé and Laurent Chicquet, who have taken the company from strength to strength, own twenty-eight hectares of vines, including eleven hectares in Avize. The Avize 1993 vintage is a *grand cru*, produced solely by the Champagne village of Avize, which has received a 100 per cent rating for quality. 1993 was a good year for Chardonnay grapes. Fifty-five per cent of the wine was wood fermented, in large barrels and half-hogshead casks. The Champagne was then aged for five years on the lees before being disgorged. The wine's purity and minerality was respected by a low dosage of 3.5g per litre. Jacquesson has acquired an excellent reputation as a Champagne producer.

Mosel-Saar-Ruwer

This is the fourth largest wine-growing region in Germany with 11,929 hectares under vine. It runs along the banks of the Saar and Mosel rivers and through the Ruwer valley in northern Germany. Its lush vineyards are planted on largely slate-based slopes. Divided into six areas, this region begins in the south with the Obermosel area, opposite the Luxembourg Mosel area, and stretches as far as Koblenz and the Rhineland vineyards in the north. The wines produced here are mainly Riesling-based. Small plots of Elbling are grown in the south and some Müller-Thurgau vines are found in the north. Wines from this region are renowned for their finesse, purity, and drinkability. The region has a moderate climate and July is the hottest month. The vines are susceptible to frost in the spring, while autumn and winter frosts do not automatically allow the annual production of Eiswein.

MOSEL-SAAR-RUWER RIESLING BA ZELTINGEN SONNENUHR 2000, SELBACH-OSTER

The Selbach-Oster winery is situated in the Bernkastel area, in the village of Zeltingen. The area is very steep and the soil is stony and slate-based. This wine is made from fifty- to eighty-year-old ungrafted vines. The 2000 harvest was very poor and only shrivelled or botrytized grapes were picked. Balance and finesse are the key notes of this wine which has only seven per cent alcohol, a residual sugar content of 154g per litre and an acidity of 7.9 per cent. It is ideal for cellaring.

Bavarian Rice Pudding

(Riz au lait bavaroise)

With a hint of vanilla, a dash of Grand Marnier, the zest of an orange, and some candied grapes, this aromatic rice pudding calls for a simple pairing: sweet wines with underlying acidity that complement and contrast with the dessert. The two wines selected, one from Alsace and the other from South Africa, are botrytized Rieslings. When this grape variety is infected by noble rot, its acidity allows it to balance the sugars and develop exquisitely sweet notes of lemon and candied orange. When drunk with the rice pudding, these wines bring out the flavour of the orange peel in the dessert, offering some sensational taste experiences and a good balance of flavours. The two Rieslings are very similar, although the wine from Stellenbosch, made in a warmer climate, is more highly developed than the Riesling from Alsace with its mineral tang and notes of old wood and furniture polish.

SERVES 8

Preparation time: 35 minutes
Cooking time: 30 minutes
Standing: 1 hour
Chilling: at least 1 hour

FOR THE RICE PUDDING

140g (5oz) pudding rice
500ml (18fl oz) milk,
vanilla pod, split lengthways
30g (1oz) raisins
grated zest of 1 orange

FOR THE BAVARIAN CREAM

150ml (¼ pint) milk
1 vanilla pod, split lengthways
2 egg yolks
100ml (3½fl oz) whipped cream
2 gelatine leaves
20g (¾oz) granulated sugar
1 dessertspoon Grand Marnier

FOR THE CARAMEL

100g (3½oz) granulated sugar
40ml (1½fl oz) water

Cooking the rice

Cover the rice with cold water and boil for 5 minutes. Rinse in cold water to cool.

Put the strained rice, milk, split vanilla pod, raisins, and orange zest in an oven-proof casserole dish. Cover with a lid and cook for 25 minutes in a preheated oven – 180°C (350°F), Gas Mark 4.

Take the dish from the oven and leave to cool before removing the lid.

Preparing the Bavarian cream

Bring the milk to the boil with the split vanilla pod, cover and leave to infuse for an hour. Strain and bring back to the boil.

Soak the gelatine leaves in cold water.

Beat the egg yolks with the sugar, pour the boiling milk over the mixture, stirring vigorously, and pour back into the saucepan. Stir continuously over a medium heat until the cream thickens. Remove from the heat and add the strained gelatine.

Mix to dissolves, then cool on a bed of ice.

Fold in the cooled rice and the Grand Marnier, followed by the whipped cream.

Finishing

Divide this mixture between eight small dishes and chill in the refrigerator.

Heat the sugar and the measured water over a medium heat to obtain a light-coloured caramel.

Leave to cool slightly before pouring over the rice.

Chill in the refrigerator for at least 1 hour before eating.

Serving temperature

Riesling Sélection de Grains Nobles, Cuvée Frédéric-Émile 1990, Trimbach: 10°C (50°F).

Stellenzicht Riesling Noble Late Harvest 1998: 10°C (50°F).

Riesling Sélection de Grains Nobles

The greatest white grape variety in the world, Riesling has many qualities: finesse, elegance, breeding, minerality, crispness, a unique regional taste, and a proven ability to preserve balance and drinkability at different stages of ripeness. Riesling has accounted for twenty-three per cent of the vine stock in Alsace since March 1, 1984. When overripened, it produces some wonderful dessert wines which are labelled Vendange Tardive. When infected by noble rot, these wines are labelled Sélection de Grains Nobles. However, this label is only given to Rieslings that are made from hand-harvested grapes, have a minimum natural sugar content of 276g per litre and must not have been chaptalized. In addition, a declaration of harvest must have been submitted in advance to the INAO (French National Institute for AOC and AOVDQS wines) and, last but not least, the wine must have passed an analytical examination at least twelve months after harvest.

RIESLING SELECTION DE GRAINS NOBLES, CUVEE FREDERIC-EMILE 1990, TRIMBACH

As well as being a vineyard-owner, the Trimbach winery also sells its own wine, although the company is so deeply committed to quality that there is little to choose between the two activities. Meticulous winemaking methods, rigorous selective harvesting techniques and extremely pure wines make this one of the best cellars in Alsace. Located in Ribeauville, Trimbach has 25.5 hectares of its own vineyards as well as contracts with neighbouring growers for a further fifty-seven hectares. Riesling accounts for forty-one per cent of production. Trimbach's prominent "Riesling culture" equates to a desire to produce great dry whites which favour balance, finesse, and crispness over lushness and excessive concentration. The two great Clos-Saint-Hune vintages –- *grand cru* Rosacker, produced at the village of Hunawihr, and Frédéric-Émile – are exemplary *vins de terroir*. However, the latter cannot be labelled *grand cru* because it is a blend of two *grand cru* vineyards (Geisberg and Osterberg), which is not permitted by the appellation. The sun-drenched 1990 vintage had a yield of eighteen hectolitres per hectare and was produced in stainless-steel vats. The alcohol content of the wine was eighteen degrees at harvest and the residual sugar content was sixty grams per litre.

Stellenbosch

The Stellenbosch region in South Africa produces a wide variety of wines. The quality of its sweet white wines and dessert wines is superb. The country has enormous potential for the production of overripened and nobly rotted wines. South African wines are classified by various labels indicating the natural sugar and alcohol content, the various stages of ripeness of the grapes when harvested and the minimum residual sugar level. White wine must have over twenty and less than thirty grams non-fermented sugar per litre to merit the "Late Harvest" label. The "Special Late Harvest" label denotes a maximum of fifty grams per litre; wines labelled "Noble Late Harvest" must exceed fifty grams per litre and the grapes used must be nobly rotten.

STELLENZICHT RIESLING NOBLE LATE HARVEST 1998

This vineyard in eastern Stellenbosch, east of Cape Town, has been owned for many years by the Cloeté family, the former owners of the Constantia winery. The vineyard on the slopes of Mount Helderberg extends over sixty hectares and produces white, red, and sweet wines. Some of its vines were recently replanted. Sea breezes from nearby False Bay play an important role in cooling and ventilating the rows of vines, which improves the health of the harvest by reducing the risk of bad rot.

Chocolate and Coffee

Chocolate Creams

(Moelleux au chocolat)

It is never easy to find the right wine to drink with chocolate. The best choice is a vintage with a chocolatey selection of aromas offering notes of praline and roasted coffee bean that will bring out the bitter taste of the dark chocolate. It should also be sweet enough to offset this bitterness, creating a balance of flavours that complement and contrast with the dessert. The best pairing for these chocolate creams is a liqueur or naturally sweet wine produced by extended wood ageing in casks or barrels. Various appellations of different origins will do an excellent job. Vintage or *rimage*-style wines, which have not been wood aged for long periods and have more prominent notes of red fruit, will also go perfectly with this dessert if it has a cherry or raspberry filling.

SERVES 8

Preparation time: 30 minutes

Cooking time: 10 minutes

FOR THE CHOCOLATE CREAMS

190g (6½oz) plain chocolate

190g (6½oz) butter, melted

3 large eggs + 4 egg yolks

120g (4¼oz) granulated sugar

80g (3oz) sifted flour

50g (1¾oz) crushed hazelnuts

FOR THE VANILLA SAUCE

250ml (9fl oz) milk

1 vanilla pod, split lengthways

50g (1¾oz) granulated sugar

2 egg yolks

TO SERVE

750ml (1¼ pints) vanilla ice-cream

Preparing the chocolate creams

Melt the plain chocolate in a bain-marie. When it has acquired smooth consistency, fold in 180g (6¼oz) of the melted butter.

Beat the eggs and sugar vigorously until smooth and frothy, add the flour, then beat to mix well. Fold in the chocolate and butter mixture.

Grease eight small soufflé dishes or manqué moulds with the remaining butter, then line with the crushed hazelnuts and pour in the chocolate cream mixture. Put to one side.

Preparing the vanilla sauce

Bring the milk to the boil and add the split vanilla pod. Cover and leave to infuse for several minutes.

Beat the granulated sugar and egg yolks, then gradually pour the boiling milk over this mixture, beating continually. Pour back into the saucepan and heat gently, stirring with a spatula until the cream thickens. Strain through a fine sieve and leave to cool on a bed of ice.

Chill in the refrigerator.

Cooking and finishing

Cook the creams for 8–10 minutes in a preheated oven – 170°C (325°F), Gas Mark 3: they are done when small cracks appear on the top.

Leave to stand for a couple of minutes before turning them out onto plates. Swirl a little vanilla sauce around them and put a scoop of vanilla ice-cream on each plate.

Serving temperature

Maury Cuvée Spéciale Dix Ans d'Age, Domaine du Mas-Amiel: 14–15°C (57–59°F).

Tawny Port 10 Year Old, Quinta do Infantado, João Lopes Roseira: 14–15°C (57–59°F).

Maury AOC

Maury is a naturally sweet wine that has been aged for at least two years. It is produced on black schist soil in an area comprising four villages in the north-west of the Pyrénées-Orientales *département*. The wine from this region has long been used to make aperitifs, including those produced by the Byrrh cellars. The Maury appellation applies to vintage and *rancio*-style wines – the highly distinctive aromas of the latter resulting from longer periods of wood ageing. The minimum sugar content when harvested is high at 252g per litre and the wine has an alcoholic strength of between fifteen and twenty per cent. There are five authorized grape varieties: Grenache (at least seventy-five per cent), Maccabeu (maximum ten per cent), as well as Carignan, Syrah, and Cinsault, which also must not exceed ten per cent.

MAURY CUVEE SPECIALE DIX ANS D'AGE, DOMAINE DU MAS-AMIEL

This Maury is made from 100 per cent hand-harvested Grenache, grown on well-exposed, slate-based soil. After extended maceration and a year outside in glass demi-johns called *touris*, which are exposed

to bad weather and changes in temperature, the wine is aged for a further nine years in oak casks. This mahogany-coloured wine with reddish-yellow highlights is brimming with warm notes of prune, cocoa, and caramel, supported by undertones of dried fruit and roasted nut. It has a strong, full-bodied mouth with a subtle sweetness and complex lingering aromas.

Port

It is impossible to do justice to this magnificent beverage and the 40,000 hectares of vineyards devoted to its production in just a few words. However, it is worth noting by way of an introduction that this was the first wine-growing sector in the world to become a demarcated region when Prime Minister José de Carvalho, Marquis of Pombal, implemented an appellation system in 1756. The region extends along the River Douro and takes in the districts of Villa Real, Bragança, Viseu, and Guarda. The slate and sandstone soil is fairly poor and the climate gives cold winters and blistering summers when temperatures can soar to 47°C (117°F). Port is fortified partway through fermentation by the addition of wine eau-de-vie with a maximum strength of seventy-seven per cent, giving a minimum alcohol content of 16.7 degrees. Although different ageing periods and production methods result in a variety of

port styles, there are two main groups: ports that are initially aged in wooden casks like all red ports, then bottle-aged (vintage, late-bottled vintage, vintage character, and ruby), and port that is exclusively aged in wood and subject to oxidation: *colheita* and regular or aged tawnies.

TAWNY PORT 10 YEAR OLD, QUINTA DO INFANTADO, JOAO LOPES ROSEIRA

Quinta do Infantado is a forty-five-hectare estate situated at an altitude of fifteen metres (forty-nine feet) on the north bank of the Douro, near Pinhão in the sub-district of Contelho. These vineyards are classified as A sites, which means they are ranked amongst Portugal's top vineyards. Before 1979, Quinta do Infantado used to sell its wine to Taylor's, but its port is now produced, blended, aged and bottled on the estate, then sold direct. The most widespread grape varieties are Touriga Nacional, Tinta Cão, Tinta Roriz, Touriga Francesa, and Tinta Barroca. These elegant ports are all produced from a blend of semi-dry wines. This ten-year-old tawny is made from old wood-aged wines blended with younger wines to give an average age of ten years. It is mahogany in colour with dark amber highlights and a reddish-yellow tinge. The nose has remarkable finesse and is overflowing with aromas of dried fruit, prune, coffee, and bitter cocoa. The mouth is full-bodied, oily, smooth, and perfectly balanced. It has good length, finishing on notes of chocolate and orange gâteau.

Coffee Religieuses

(Religieuses au café)

These classic cakes combine light choux pastry with a smooth, delicately flavoured cream filling. The strong coffee flavour calls for complex wines. An old *rancio*-style Rivesaltes Tuilé is ideal, particularly the 1985 vintage. Aged for an extended period in oak barrels and subjected to dramatic shifts in temperature between winter and summer – which speeds up the oxidation process – this wine gives off superb aromas of iced coffee, praline, and cocoa. Over time, it has acquired a controlled sweetness which makes it an ideal pairing for these choux buns. The same is true of the Cavendish 1979, a port-style dessert wine from South Africa, which also boasts an oxidative character. It immediately offers scorched, toasted aromas and boasts a superb sugar-alcohol balance.

SERVES 8

Preparation time: 40 minutes

Cooking time: 20 minutes

Chilling: 1 hour

FOR THE CHOUX BUNS

300g (10oz) Choux Pastry (see page 166)

1 egg yolk

FOR THE COFFEE CONFECTIONERS' CUSTARD

500ml (18fl oz) milk

1 vanilla pod, split lengthways

4 egg yolks

125g (4½oz) caster sugar

30g (1oz) cornflour

30g (1oz) flour

1 dessertspoon coffee essence

FOR THE COFFEE FONDANT

75g (2½oz) caster sugar

50ml (2fl oz) water

150g (5¼oz) white fondant

2 dessertspoons coffee essence

FOR THE BUTTER CREAM

180g (6¼oz) butter

90g (3¼oz) praline

270g (9½oz) Confectioners' Custard (see above)

Making the choux buns

Transfer the choux pastry to a piping bag with a plain nozzle and pipe out eight balls the size of small eggs and eight balls the size of small walnuts on a baking sheet.

Brush with beaten egg yolk and cook for 20 minutes in a preheated oven – 180°C (350°F), Gas Mark 4. Leave to cool on a wire rack. Make a split in the side of each.

Preparing the coffee confectioners' custard

Bring the milk to the boil with the split vanilla pod. Cover and leave to infuse. Beat the egg yolks and sugar until the mixture whitens, then fold in the cornflour and flour.

Add a little hot milk, stir and pour into the saucepan with the rest of the milk. Bring to the boil over a low heat until the custard thickens.

Add the coffee essence, take out the pieces of vanilla, and leave to cool. Eliminate any lumps, separate out 270g for the butter cream. Cover with clingfilm and chill in the refrigerator.

Filling and finishing

Pour the remainder of the coffee confectioners' custard into a piping bag and fill the choux buns. For the fondants, add the sugar to the measured water and bring to the boil, cover, and leave to cool.

Heat the white fondant, coffee essence and 20–30ml of cooled syrup to 40°C (104°F) in a bain-marie.

Coat the upper part of each choux bun with fondant icing and place the smaller buns on top of the larger ones.

Prepare the butter cream. Mix the butter and praline to obtain a cream. Add the well-whisked confectioners' custard and stir vigorously.

Transfer this mixture to a piping bag with a fluted nozzle and decorate the cakes. Chill for 1 hour in the refrigerator.

Serving temperature

Rivesaltes Tuilé 1985, Domaine Cazes: 14°C (57°F).

Port Style Wine KWV, Cavendish 1979: 14°C (57°F).

Rivesaltes Tuilé

The Rivesaltes appellation comprises several families that correspond to colour type (red, white), grape variety, and wood-ageing period (Ambrés, Tuilés, Vintage). Rivesaltes Tuilés, which are usually made from the red Grenache grape, are wood aged for extended periods. The porous wood encourages an exchange of air and the development of controlled oxidation, conferring distinctive coffee, and praline flavours with notes of cocoa and aromatic wood. According to French wine laws, Rivesaltes Tuilés must be made from a minimum of fifty per cent Grenache if they are to be matured in an oxidative environment. The wine must also be aged for at least two years before sale.

RIVESALTES TUILE 1985, DOMAINE CAZES

This well-structured wine is not too sweet and has a beautiful mahogany colour with coppery highlights and a complex aromatic palette. Subtle notes of praline and coffee are mingled with aromas of dried fruit: date and fig with undertones of Havana cigar and tobacco. The mouth is full-bodied and robust, with a slightly bitter tang. There are also rich notes of *rancio*, cocoa, and balsamic essence.

Port Style Wine

South Africa produces a fairly large quantity of excellent fortified wines, usually made from Portuguese grape varieties. Certain regions with very hot or exposed climates like South Africa produce wines that are too alcoholic and lacking in finesse, so fortification and the production of dessert wines can actually provide a useful solution to this problem. This type of wine is harvested in the Wine of Origin (WO) region of Klein Karoo, throughout the Breede River Valley and the Boberg Region, and is strictly regulated. The range includes all the various port families: pale, golden, brown, amber, tawny, ruby, each having its own style, colour, strength, taste, qualities, and level of sweetness. Residual sugar content per litre must be between 75g and 160g. This particular wine comes from the Boberg Region: the appellation only applies to fortified wines from the Paarl and Tulbagh districts. The 1979 Cavendish was made from a blend of Portuguese grape varieties. It was fortified, then wood aged for over fifteen years, which accounts for its rich aromatic character bursting with notes of coffee, praline, and cocoa.

PORT STYLE WINE, KWV CAVENDISH 1979

The KWV (*Kooperatieve Wijnbouwers Vereniging van Zuid-Afrika Beperkt*), founded in 1918, is both a commercial wine-growing company and a state-subsidized cooperative for monitoring and regulating wine laws. It is also responsible for locating fresh market openings by designing new products and boosting international demand for wine. This association, originally a national body, has safeguarded the country's wine-growing industry over the years, playing a key role during periods of economic isolation. Its role has now changed and, although the company is still the controlling body of the South African wine sector, it is no longer answerable to the government.

Mocha Gâteau

(Gâteau moka)

Well-aged, mellow wines are the perfect accompaniment for this mocha dessert – combining a creamy filling, moist sponge, and strong coffee flavour – because their sweetness and strength offsets the complex mix of tastes. The Rivesaltes Rancio Hors d'Age 1976 has developed notes of controlled oxidation after an extended period of wood ageing without losing any of its finesse and crispness. Notes of praline, cocoa, hazelnut and coffee combine with its woody character to produce a superb aromatic palate that is not too sweet. The excellent Primitivo di Manduria is a naturally sweet, rich, generous dessert wine with aromas of roasted coffee bean. This 1959 vintage is just as luscious as the Rivesaltes and offers well-balanced sweetness. It is a smooth wine with a strong oxidative edge that adds texture and undertones of prune, coffee, roasted fig, and iced mocha.

SERVES 8

Preparation time: 40 minutes
Cooking time: 25 minutes
Chilling: 1 hour

FOR THE GENOESE SPONGE

100g (3¾oz) granulated sugar
3 eggs
100g (3¾oz) sifted flour
 + 20g (¾oz) for the cake tin
20g (¾oz) butter, melted

FOR THE COFFEE SYRUP

100ml (3½fl oz) water
100g (3¾oz) granulated sugar
1 tablespoon instant coffee

FOR THE COFFEE BUTTER
CREAM

200g (7oz) Butter Cream
 (see page 177)
1½ tablespoons coffee essence

FOR THE TOASTED ALMONDS

200g (7oz) chopped almonds

Making the sponge

Mix the sugar and eggs in a bowl and stand in a bain-marie. Heat this mixture to 45°C (113°F), whisking until completely cool. Fold in the sifted flour and melted butter.

Pour this mixture into a greased and floured cake tin and cook for about 25 minutes in a preheated oven – 170°C (325°F), Gas Mark 3.

Turn out and leave to cool on a rack.

Preparing the syrup and the coffee butter cream

For the syrup, bring the measured water and sugar to the boil. Add the coffee and leave to cool. For the cream, mix this coffee essence with the butter cream.

Assembling and finishing

Cut the sponge cake into four even horizontal slices with a serrated knife or palette knife. Drizzle each layer except the top with syrup and cover with coffee butter cream, then reassemble the cake.

Coat the top and sides of the sponge cake with butter cream. Chill in the refrigerator.

Lightly toast the almonds in a preheated oven – 160°C (320°F), Gas Mark 2–3. Leave to cool slightly then use to decorate the sides and top of the mocha cake. Chill in the refrigerator for at least an hour.

Serving temperature

Rivesaltes Cuvée Aimé Cazes 1976: 14°C (57°F).

Primitivo di Manduria Solaria Jonica, Cantine Ferrari 1959: 14°C (57°F).

Rivesaltes AOC

The Rivesaltes appellation produces a wide range of wine styles (red or white, Ambré, Tuilé, Hors d'Age), from Grenache or Muscat grapes, with varying aromas and tastes. Although Rivesaltes make excellent dessert wines, whatever the category, and are the perfect pairing for virtually any sweet, cake or pastry, they are unfortunately often overlooked, particularly as a dessert accompaniment.

RIVESALTES CUVEE AIME CAZES 1976

The 1976 vintage is a Rivesaltes Hors d'Age, aged in oak barrels for twenty-two years. The "Hors d'Age" label refers to Rivesaltes Tuilés or Ambrés that have been aged for a minimum of five years. The "Rancio" label is given to wines that have acquired a *rancio* flavour during the extended ageing periods required by local winemaking methods. However, this 1976 Rivesaltes Ambré (made from 100 per cent white Grenache vines between forty and forty-five years old and grown on clay and chalk soil) is completely different from a *rancio*. Picked when perfectly ripe, the grape clusters are not de-stalked and are pressed directly, then fermented for four days. The wine is then fortified and aged in barrels for twenty-two years. Bottled in 1998, this sensational Rivesaltes is dark topaz in colour and has complex aromas of coffee, dried fruit, and praline. Its complexity revolves around hints of sweet spices, bitter orange, and cinchona. The palate is racy and powerful. The overall effect is well-balanced and sophisticated.

Primitivo di Manduria

Puglia, a vast region of hills and plains stretching for 400 kilometres (249 miles) at the southernmost tip of the peninsula (forming the heel of the boot), is the second largest wine region in Italy. The Phoenicians were making wine in this area, lapped by both the Adriatic and Ionian seas, as early as 2000BC. Puglia produces a wide variety of DOC appellations and types of wine. The dessert wines are particularly worthy of interest because many native grape varieties, both white and red, grow in this area. The Primitivo grape is one such variety. Long associated with Zinfandel and thought to be a relative of the Croatian Plavac Mali, it produces dense, florid wines with a rich, generous structure that are high in alcohol. Wine producers use it to make an unfortified Primitivo Dolce Naturale, which is ideal with desserts.

PRIMITIVO DI MANDURIA SOLARIA JONICA, CANTINE FERRARI 1959

This 1959 vintage comes from the Salice Salentino region, which is currently classified as a DOC. Although this naturally sweet Primitivo was made in the region, it was aged in the Ferrari cellars, in Piedmont. It has been aged for ten years in oak barrels then in cement vats. It has a well-developed garnet colour with orangey highlights. The complex nose is overflowing with notes of coffee, cocoa, wine, and spices. The palate is wonderfully balanced, its sweetness offset by a good tannic structure, and it has a generous, full-flavoured finish with notes of iced coffee and Havana cigar.

Bitter Chocolate Flan

(Tarte au chocolat amer)

As is the case with any chocolate dessert, the selected wine should have a strong, well-developed character to counterbalance the bitterness and enough sweetness to temper it. The sweet *rancio*-style wine from Louis Puig Santenach is a non-fortified, naturally fermented wine made predominantly from Grenache grapes. Aged for extended periods in barrels, using a *solera* system dating from 1880, it has very little residual sugar – just enough sweetness for this dessert – and its oxidative qualities combine with the bitterness and complexity of the cocoa aromas to accentuate their persistence. The 1937 Colheita Port boasts a wonderfully complex array of tastes. Nothing comes close to its length and richness. It has balsamic accents with ultra-rich flavours of praline, cocoa, and coffee. This well-balanced blend finishes well, marrying sweetness with notes of oxidation.

SERVES 8

Preparation time: 45 minutes

Cooking time: 25 minutes

Chilling: 1 hour

FOR THE SABLE BASES

120g (4¼oz) butter

75g (2¾oz) icing sugar

30g (1oz) ground almonds

1 egg

½ teaspoon table salt

200g (7oz) flour

FOR THE CHOCOLATE CREAM

200g (7oz) plain chocolate
  (min 60% cocoa)

80ml (2¾fl oz) milk

1 egg

200ml (7fl oz) single cream

TO SERVE

20g (¾oz) cocoa powder

Preparing the sablé bases

Mix the butter and icing sugar together. Add the ground almonds, egg, and salt and mix with a wooden spoon. Add the flour, knead rapidly, and chill the pastry dough for 1 hour in the refrigerator, wrapped in clingfilm.

Roll out the pastry to a thickness of 3mm (⅛ inch) and cut into rounds 7.5cm (3 inches) in diameter. Put into individual flan tins, prick the pastry bases all over with a fork, and bake blind in a preheated oven – 200°C (400°F), Gas Mark 6 – for 10 minutes. Leave to cool.

Lower the oven temperature to 160°C (320°F), Gas Mark 2-3.

Preparing the chocolate cream

Break the plain chocolate into small pieces. Beat the milk and egg together.

Bring the single cream to the boil and pour over the plain chocolate.

Mix carefully to melt the chocolate. Leave to cool slightly then add the milk and egg mixture.

Strain this mixture through a sieve and pour into the cooked flan bases.

Finishing

Bake the flans in the oven for about 15 minutes. Leave to cool before turning them out.

Serve dusted with cocoa powder.

Serving temperature

Rancio Doux Solera 1880, Louis Puig Santenach: 15°C (59°F).

Colheita Port 1937, Burmester: 15–16°C (59–61°F).

RANCIO DOUX SOLERA 1880, LOUIS PUIG SANTENACH

This *rancio* wine from the Pyrénées-Orientales *département* is not a Rivesaltes because it was not fortified with wine alcohol. Nothing was done to this natural, unfiltered wine after barrelling. It was made from ninety-five per cent white Grenache and five per cent Maccabeu. The bunches of grapes were picked when overripe and the same methods used as for a classic white wine. The potential alcohol level was high. After vinification, the wine was matured in chestnut barrels over 100 years old and topped up every four to five years in order to prevent the wine level from dropping in the barrel due to evaporation through the wood. The wine was stored in a cellar subject to considerable temperature changes between summer and winter which created a wonderful complexity with subtle undertones of prune, dried fruit, cocoa, and praline. This *solera* system, which dates from 1880, produces a maximum of fifty bottles per year.

Port

The Demarcated Douro region covers some 250,000 hectares, including about 40,000 under vine. These fine vineyards extend from Barqueiros, sixty-five kilometres (forty miles) upstream from Oporto, to Barca d'Alva, some 220 kilometres (137 miles) further away, on the Spanish border. The region is divided into three sub-regions: Baixo-Corgo, located downstream of the River Corgo, which tends to produce red Douro wines because the climate is cooled by Atlantic breezes; Cima-Corgo, located further upstream of the same river, which produces the great ports, made from vineyards planted in steeply sloping mountainside terraces with slate-based soil; and Douro-Superior, which covers the vineyards in the Upper Douro near the Spanish border and enjoys a hotter climate, while the terrain is not so steep. The Douro has more than ninety grape varieties, both red and white, but the five most popular are Touriga Nacional, Tinta Roriz, Tinta Barroca, Touriga Francesa, and Tinta Cão. Port is a dessert wine fortified with neutral alcohol, which has an alcohol content of between nineteen and twenty-two degrees. It belongs to one of two main families: late-bottled vintage ports (LBVs) and vintage-style ports, that are aged in a reducing environment (bottles) and are ruby-red, even deep-purple in colour; or ports whose character is determined by barrel oxidation and whose colours are lighter and more faded. These latter ports offer aromas of coffee, chocolate, caramel, and praline and include tawnies, aged tawnies, and *colheitas* – vintage ports made from single-vintage grapes. They are wood aged from the moment they are made until they are bottled, seven years later. The label should show vintage, date of bottling, and should specify "wood aged".

COLHEITA PORT 1937, BURMESTER

This company, founded in the eighteenth century by a German family, enjoys a sterling reputation for tawny and *colheita* ports. It is now owned by the Amorim group, which manufactures cork stoppers. It has ninety-three hectares of vines and owns a single *quinta* (a vineyard that only blends grapes from a single estate), Quinta do Nova. Dark topaz in colour, this 1937 Colheita is a wine of great finesse. The superb nose is complex, with subtle tones of cocoa, praline, nougatine, and fine notes of controlled oxidation. The mouth is full-bodied and robust. This is a well-balanced, smooth port with perfectly balanced sweetness and a great deal of class. The lingering finish offers accents of caramel, tobacco, and smoke.

Creamy Chocolate Mille-feuille

(Mille-feuille au chocolat crémeux)

This light dessert combining chocolate cream with layers of flaky pastry calls for delicate wines which are not too heavy or rich and which should bring out the texture and taste of this chocolatey dessert. The *rancio*-style Grand Roussillon, wood aged for extended periods, is similar to the closely related Rivesaltes, with its accents of praline, cocoa, coffee, wood, tobacco, and Havana cigar. Its notes of controlled oxidation complement the cocoa, whose bitterness is also offset by the wine's sweetness. The Catalan Priorat, made from similar grape varieties, offers the same blend of flavours. This highly concentrated, *rancio*-style fortified wine also boasts notes of coffee, praline, and chocolate with controlled sweetness, the usual qualities found in very old wines whose taste owes more to oxidation than to the fruit.

SERVES 8

Preparation time: about 45 minutes

Cooking time: 25 minutes

Chilling: 8 hours

FOR THE COCOA PASTRY

150g (5¼oz) flour

100g (3¾oz) softened butter

20g (¾oz) cocoa powder

FOR THE PLAIN PASTRY

2 teaspoons salt

150ml (¼pint) water

350g (10½oz) flour

400g (14oz) butter, melted

FOR THE CHOCOLATE CREAM

125ml (4fl oz) single cream

125g (4½oz) plain chocolate (60% cocoa), broken into small pieces

250g (9oz) Confectioners' Custard (see page 157)

TO FINISH

icing sugar

Preparing the two types of pastry

Cocoa pastry: mix all the ingredients together and knead the mixture vigorously. Shape the pastry into a ball and chill in the refrigerator for 1 hour.

Plain pastry: dilute the salt in the measured water and add the flour and butter. Shape into a ball and chill in the refrigerator for 2 hours.

Making the flaky pastry sheets

Roll out both balls of pastry into two rectangles, 15 × 30cm (6 × 12 inches). Lay the cocoa pastry on top of the plain pastry, fold the bottom third of the rectangle up towards the centre, then fold the top third down to make a square: this will give you 6 layers.

Give the pastry a quarter turn and roll out into a long rectangle, 15 × 30cm (6 × 12 inches). Fold into thirds as before and chill for 2 hours in the refrigerator. Fold and chill twice more.

Roll the pastry into a sheet 30 × 40cm (12 × 16 inches) and 3mm (⅛ inch) thick. Place on a baking sheet and cook for about 20 minutes in a preheated oven – 170°C (325°F), Gas Mark 3.

Sprinkle with icing sugar and cook for a further 5 minutes. Leave to cool.

Preparing the cream

Bring the single cream to the boil and pour over the chocolate. Cool to 30°C (86°F). Whisk the confectioners' custard gently to eliminate any lumps and fold in the chocolate cream.

Assembling the mille-feuille

Cut the layered pastry into three strips, 13 × 30cm (5 × 12 inches). Cover two with cream and place one on top of the other. Top with the third strip of flaky pastry. Cut into eight pieces. Arrange the mille-feuilles in a dish and sprinkle with icing sugar.

Serving temperature

Grand Roussillon VDN, Cuvée Georges Puig 1977, Domaine Puig-Parahy: 15°C (59°F).

Arrels del Priorat Rancio, 60 Year Old: 14°C (57°F).

Grand Roussillon

The popularity of this time-honoured appellation has waned. It applies to naturally sweet wines produced in the regions of Pyrénées-Orientales and Aude. Grand Roussillon is made from classic authorized grape varieties: Muscat à Petits Grains, Tourbat, Grenache, and Maccabeu, with a maximum of ten per cent Carignan, Aramon, Cinsault, Syrah, or Listan. The minimum ageing period is two years from September 1 of the harvest year.

GRAND ROUSSILLON VDN CUVEE GEORGES PUIG 1977, DOMAINE PUIG-PARAHY, GEORGES PUIG

The Puig-Parahy winery stretches over 110 hectares planted with Grenache, Carignan, Mourvèdre, Syrah, and Muscat vines in the commune of Sainte-Colombe. The soil consists of roundstones, morainic debris, quartz, gneiss, granite, and slate in a sandy clay loam. This estate, now owned and run by the sole heir,

Georges Puig, continues the great tradition of *rancio* wines. The winery won its first medal with its 1896 vintage. The 1977 Georges Puig was made from red Grenache and small quantities of Carignan. The wine was fortified and macerated in wooden barrels or vats. The old oak or chestnut barrels used were *demi-muid* with a capacity of 600 litres (132 gallons).

Priorat DOC

This Spanish appellation has just attained top ranking with a DOC, well-deserved both for the quality of its soil and for the high number of first-class wine-growers producing sensational wines in the region. The Priorato is located to the west of Tarragona, in southern Catalonia. The vineyards are spectacular: vines are planted in sheer terraces, sometimes at altitudes of 800 metres. This region has a distinctive soil called llicorella, a mixture of sandstone, mica, quartz, and slate. The area has a well-established tradition of *generoso*-style wines (between fourteen and eighteen degrees) and *vino rancio* (between fourteen and twenty degrees), aged for at least four years.

ARRELS DEL PRIORAT RANCIO, 60 YEAR OLD

This *rancio* wine is made from Garnacha Tinta, Peluda, and Carignano. The grapes are picked in October and November and pressed during November. This venerable wine is made from overripened fruit, the product of meticulous artisanal wine-growing techniques. The wine is fermented in 500-litre barrels for twelve to eighteen months and has an initial alcohol content of between sixteen and eighteen degrees. It is then aged in old barrels which are stored in lofts open to the weather as natural changes in temperature are vital for the production of great rancios. A *solera*-style system (called "la mare" in the Priorato) is then used to age the wine. The wine is placed in 300-litre barrels which are partially decanted into each other from year to year. A maximum of thirty per cent per year is drawn off from the sixth barrel onwards in the case of *rancios* intended for sale. The wine improves over time and the barrels become more valuable. The last barrel, known as the *carretell*, is small, containing between 100 and 150 litres. This concentrate, which forms the heart of the wine, often has an average age of between sixty and 100 years old.

Dark Chocolate Orange Cake

(Gâteau au chocolat noir parfumé à l'orange)

This moist chocolatey cake calls for complex wines. The aromatic palette of an aged tawny port, with its typical notes of cocoa and coffee, dried fruit, cocoa powder, mocha, and praline, is a great pairing for this dessert, which is not too sweet. The port has a lingering fresh fruit taste that goes well with the orange syrup and zest used to flavour this cake. The Jerez Pedro-Ximénez is a very sweet, smooth wine that creates a similar blend of flavours. It also has aromas of cocoa and roasted coffee bean as well as notes of dried fruit – dried fig, candied grape – that bring out the tang of the orange peel. This is a perfect match, since the bitter cocoa and orange zest counterbalance the rich sweetness of the wine.

SERVES 8

Preparation time: 15 minutes
Cooking time: 35 minutes
Standing: 12 hours

FOR THE CHOCOLATE CAKE
220g (8oz) flour
2 teaspoons baking powder
40g (1½oz) cocoa powder
50g (1¾oz) plain chocolate
200g (7oz) softened butter
180g (6¼oz) icing sugar
3 eggs
30g (1oz) honey, melted
grated zest of 1 orange

FOR THE ORANGE SYRUP
100ml (3½fl oz) orange juice
grated zest of 2 oranges
20g (¾oz) granulated sugar

Preparing the chocolate cake

Sift the flour, baking powder and cocoa powder. Break the plain chocolate into very small pieces. Grease an 18-cm (7-inch) cake tin and line with greaseproof paper.

Put the butter and icing sugar in a large mixing bowl. Fold in the eggs one at a time, followed by the cocoa flour and melted honey. Then add the grated orange zest and the plain chocolate.

Pour this mixture into the cake tin and cook for about 35 minutes in a preheated oven – 160°C (320°F), Gas Mark 2–3. A knife inserted into the centre of the cake will come out clean when it is fully cooked. Turn out the cake and put it on a plate.

Preparing the syrup

Meanwhile, put the orange juice, orange zest and granulated sugar in a saucepan. Bring to the boil and leave to infuse for a few minutes.

Put this syrup through a fine sieve and leave to one side until the cake is ready.

Finishing

Drizzle the orange syrup over the still hot cake, wait for it to soak in for a few seconds, then cool the cake on a wire rack.

Wrap in clingfilm and keep on the bottom shelf of your refrigerator or in a cool place for at least 2 hours.

Serving temperature

Tawny Port 20 Year Old, Ferreira: 15°C (59°F).

Jerez Pedro-Ximénez, El Candado Valdespino: 15°C (59°F).

Aged Tawny Port

Aged tawny ports are labelled with an age of ten, twenty, thirty or forty years. This category covers wines that have been produced by blending old tawny ports with younger ports, although not necessarily in identical proportions. The age labels refer to characteristics associated with the wine's average age, rather than its exact age: the wines' colour, bouquet, and taste should reflect the qualities expected of an aged port. The port-makers' skill involves creating an aromatic palate and style of taste that satisfy these criteria. The key qualities of a twenty-year-old port are balance and a subtle aromatic character. It will have complex notes of controlled oxidation, while retaining a crisp fruitiness.

TAWNY PORT 20 YEAR OLD, FERREIRA

This renowned Portuguese family business was founded in 1715. It owes its reputation to Doña Antonia Adelaide Ferreira, a Portuguese noblewoman who took the company from strength to strength. The vast winery was bought in 1989 by the Symington's group (already an umbrella company composed of Sogrape, Forrester, and Offley). The group now owns many single quintas: Quinta do Seixo, Quinta do Port, Quinta Caedo – near Pinhao – and Quinta da Leda in the Alto Douro region. This winery has a sterling reputation for its tawny ports, particularly this twenty-year-old Duque da Bragança.

Jerez Pedro-Ximénez

These attractive sweet wines are very rich in sugar and are made from Pedro-Ximénez grapes. When picked, the grapes are sun dried, as in Malaga: as the grapes shrivel, they concentrate the sugars. The wines are fortified to an alcoholic strength of eighteen degrees and often aged using a *solera*-system comprised of a number of tiers of stacked barrels called *criaderas* (that allow wines of different ages to be blended). A long period of ageing is usually needed for Pedro-Ximénez to achieve a good balance. Extended ageing tempers the wine's sweetness, conferring structure and complexity.

JEREZ PEDRO-XIMENEZ, EL CANDADO VALDESPINO

This small family business was founded in Jerez in 1864. Run by Don Miguel for many years, it was bought in 1999 by Herederos del Marqués del Real Tesoro. Connoisseurs rank their range of wines amongst the best of the appellation. The small wine cellars in Valdespino are now grouped together in a vast wine storehouse that controls the temperature, humidity and atmosphere and stands opposite the famous Jerez Macharnudo, Anina, Balbaina and Carrascal vineyards. This El Candado vintage was made from Pedro-Ximénez grapes. Sun-dried for two weeks, fortified to an alcoholic strength of eighteen degrees and aged for twelve years using a *solera* and *criadera* system, this wine has 450g per litre of residual sugar. Deep brown in colour, its nose presents aromas of dried fig, coffee, and chocolate and it has a rich, dense palate. It has a high sugar content but the overall effect is well-balanced.

Dark Chocolate Mousse

(Mousse au chocolat noir grand cru Cuba)

As this mousse is made with dark, strong chocolate, it needs full-flavoured wines that are sweet enough to offset the bitterness of the cocoa and offer prominent notes of controlled oxidation. The sweetness and oxidative character of both the Fondillon from Alicante and the Sicilian Marsala work wonders with chocolate, praline, and coffee flavours. The Marsala Vecchio is a fortified wine that has been aged for an extended period: its well-developed, pale red hue is caused by ageing for around twenty years in oxidative conditions. The wine gives off incredible aromas of wood and smoke, with notes of cocoa and praline. Both this *rancio*-style wine and the Fondillon make a superb accompaniment for this type of dessert. The notes of controlled oxidation come into their own when paired with bitter cocoa. Both wines complement and contrast with this dark chocolate mousse.

SERVES 6

Preparation time: 30 minutes

Chilling: 3 hours

5 eggs

75g (2½oz) butter, melted

370g (13oz) plain chocolate
  (minimum 70% cocoa)

75g (2½oz) caster sugar

375g (13oz) whipped cream

Preparing the mousse

Break the eggs and separate the whites from the egg yolks. Break the chocolate into small pieces and melt in a bain-marie, stirring carefully with a spatula to eliminate lumps. Fold in the melted butter, followed by the egg yolks one at a time.

Beat the egg whites stiffly and add the caster sugar as soon as they begin to form stiff peaks. Using a flexible spatula, gently fold this into the chocolate mixture, carefully stirring in a circular motion.

Finally, fold in the whipped cream and pour into individual small bowls. Leave for at least 3 hours in the refrigerator and serve well chilled.

Serving temperature

Marsala Vecchio Samperi Riserva 20 Anni, Marco de Bartoli: 15°C (59°F).

Fondillon Gran Reserva 1964, Bodegas Brotons: 15°C (59°F).

Marsala

The oldest document featuring Marsala dates from 1773, when a ship left the Sicilian port of Trapani for England with a cargo of barrels filled with a wine that had already been fortified with alcohol to brace it for the voyage. The area of production takes in the province of Trapani, excluding the villages of Pantelleria, Favignana, and Alcamo. The climate is hot and dry and the arid soil is known locally as *sciare*. Marsala can be dry, semi-sweet or sweet, and the different styles are produced from wines made from native grape varieties: Marsala Oro (gold) and Marsala Ambra (amber) are made from Grillo, Catarrato, and Inzolia grapes and Rubino (ruby) wines are made from Calabrese, Perricone, and Nerello Mascalese, which are all red grape varieties. The dry base wine is sometimes supplemented with a concentrated must, called *musto cotto*, which has been cooked and reduced and/or *sifone*, a mixture of grape alcohol and sweet must, sometimes called *mistella* (similar to the French *mistelle*). Marsalas are classified depending on the length of the ageing period and there are several varieties.

Marsalas labelled "fine" must be at least one year old; the term "*Superiore*" refers to Marsalas that have been aged for at least two years; "*superiore riserva*" wines have been aged for a minimum of four years; "*vergine*" must have been aged for five years and "*vergine stravecchio*" for a minimum of ten years. The minimum alcohol content varies between seventeen and eighteen degrees.

MARSALA VECCHIO SAMPERI RISERVA 20 ANNI, MARCO DE BARTOLI

This Riserva 20 Anni from Marco de Bartoli, an excellent Marsala producer, is made using a *solera* system. It is aged in 350-litre barrels from which only ten per cent is drawn off each year. Made from white Grillo or Inzolia grapes, this vintage has all the complexity of an aged Marsala: aromas of coffee, dried fruit, cinnamon, and a hint of cocoa. The palate is full-flavoured and the controlled oxidation, which is a product of the *solera* system, gives a long aromatic finish.

Alicante DO

The Spanish region of Valencia takes in the appellations of Valencia and Utiel-Requena. This region is hot and dry, despite the cooling Mediterranean winds. The Alicante appellation is divided into two regions: La Marina and

Alicante. The vineyards in the latter are planted in predominantly clay and chalk soil and can reach altitudes of between 300 and 400 metres (984 and 1312 feet). This area supplies a wide variety of white and red wines, as well as many dessert wines. The production of dessert wines is a time-honoured tradition in Alicante, thought to date back to the fifteenth century. Called Fondillon, this dessert wine is made predominantly from Monastrell, identical to the French grape Mourvèdre, which is also known as Mataro in Spain. There are two styles of wine in the Fondillon category. According to Spanish wine laws, the appellation applies to wines aged for at least eight years using a *solera* system. However there are also *rancio*-style wines, still made predominantly from Monastrell, that have been lightly fortified (to at least sixteen degrees) and aged in a *solera* system for longer periods.

FONDILLON GRAN RESERVA 1964, BODEGAS BROTONS

The 1964 Fondillon is the beautiful deep amber brown of a Jerez oloroso. The nose is characterized by a fine aromatic nose with overtones of dried fig, cocoa, praline, and iced coffee. The palate has prominent notes of mocha. This is a powerful wine, with great balance and a well-structured sweetness. The flavours linger in the mouth for an incredibly long time.

Colombian Coffee Crème Brûlée

(Crème brûlée au grain de café de Colombie)

The ideal pairing for this coffee dessert is a fortified wine with an oxidative character which has acquired depth, complexity, and length through extended ageing, a process which has also tempered its sweetness. The Banyuls Grand Cru, which has been wood aged for thirty months, is a beautiful mahogany colour. Its notes of iced coffee, Arabica, tobacco, cappuccino, and mocha make it the perfect accompaniment for the custard cream base, particularly as it is not too sweet. The same is true of the Moscatel de Malaga, whose dark colour with greenish-brown highlights is reminiscent of coffee grounds. Although its aromas are situated midway between praline, cream caramel, cocoa, and notes of dried fig, it has dominant coffee overtones and thus offers a perfect blend of flavours combining sweetness, notes of oxidation, and aromatic persistence.

SERVES 8

Preparation time: 30 minutes

Cooking time: 30 minutes

Chilling: 1 hour

CREME BRULEES

125ml (4½fl oz) milk

15g (½oz) freshly ground Colombian coffee beans

150g (5¼oz) caster sugar

5 egg yolks

380ml (13oz) single cream

FOR THE TOPPING

80g (3oz) light brown sugar

1 teaspoon instant coffee

Preparing the crème brûlées

Bring the milk to the boil then add the ground coffee beans. Remove from the heat, cover, and leave to infuse until completely cool. Add the caster sugar and egg yolks and whisk well. Pour in the single cream, stir, and put through a fine sieve.

Pour this mixture into eight individual ramekins or heatproof bowls, and cook for 30 minutes in a preheated oven – 110°C (225°F), Gas Mark ¼.

Remove the crèmes brûlées from the oven and leave to cool before chilling for at least 1 hour in the refrigerator.

Finishing

Dust the crème brûlées with a mixture of brown sugar and instant coffee and place under the grill for a few moments until this topping has caramelized. Serve immediately.

Serving temperature

Banyuls Grand Cru, Cuvée Président Henry Vidal 1985, Cellier des Templiers: 14°C (57°F).

Moscatel de Malaga Don Salvador, Lopez Hermanos: 14°C (57°F).

Banyuls Grand Cru

This appellation, obtained in 1936, produces sensational, naturally sweet wines. The Banyuls vineyards are planted in hillside terraces along the Mediterranean coast in the communes of Port-Vendres, Banyuls-sur-Mer, Cerbère and Collioure. The Banyuls Grand Cru designation was added in 1962 and is the appellation's top category. It must be made from a minimum of seventy-five per cent Grenache and additional grape varieties must not exceed ten per cent. The yield is still set at thirty hectolitres per hectare, but the wine must be wood aged for at least thirty months. The Banyuls may be labelled "sec" (dry) if the residual sugar content is no higher than fifty-four grams per litre. Banyuls Grand Cru is a *rancio*-style wine: extended wood ageing has caused the colour to fade and has resulted in greater complexity and a wider range of flavours.

BANYULS GRAND CRU, CUVEE PRESIDENT HENRY VIDAL 1985, CELLIER DES TEMPLIERS
The Cellier des Templiers, founded in 1950 and located in Banyuls-sur-Mer, is a group of 750 wine-growers operating 1,202 hectares, including 869 planted with Banyuls vineyards. This Cuvée Président Henry Vidal 1985 was sourced from all the communes in the appellation and produced from 100 per cent Grenache vines grown on slate-based soil. The picked grapes were destalked, fortified on the lees with neutral alcohol, then macerated for twenty days. The wine was wood aged, then bottle aged in an underground cellar for three to four years. This vintage was made exclusively from top-quality harvests. The residual sugar content for 1985 was 112g per litre.

Malaga DO

Both Malaga's vineyards, south of Andalusia, and its wine-growing tradition date back to 600BC. In the seventeenth and eighteenth centuries, Malaga's wine was exported throughout the world and the vineyards extended across almost 100,000 hectares. There are now only 11,500 hectares of vines. Not only was this region the first to be devastated by phylloxera, but other factors, including high production costs, workforce shortages, competition with other vineyards, and the Spanish civil war, contributed to the slump in the wine sector. The region is divided into sub-zones. The largest, on the Antequera plateau, fifty kilometres (thirty-one miles) from Malaga, produces a wine that is made predominantly from the Pedro-Ximénez grape, while Moscatel is the most widespread grape variety grown in the coastal zone of La Axarquia and in the cooler mountain zone, north of Malaga. Traditionally, Malaga wine is fortified with wine eau-de-vie after fermentation. It owes its complex character and sweetness to the addition of sweet wine, syrup, and concentrated must. Malaga is made from grapes dried in the sun for between seven and twenty days on trays made of woven grass and the wine is aged using a *solera* system. This traditional method of blending Jerez and Malaga wines consists in periodically drawing off a quantity of wine from the oldest barrels (known as *soleras*), which is then replaced by wine from the previous year, and so on. This ageing system is very expensive and labour intensive since it usually requires about 100 barrels.

MOSCATEL DE MALAGA DON SALVADOR, LOPEZ HERMANOS
This winery, founded in 1885 by Salvador Lopez, now has 250 hectares of vines in Fuentepiedra, where the main grape varieties are Pedro-Ximénez and Muscat of Alexandria. It possesses an immense wine storehouse, comprising 6,000 American oak barrels. The Don Salvador vintage came from Sector 32 of the cellar. The wine is the product of a *solera* system; it is deep mahogany in colour with olive brown highlights. The aromatic nose has notes of coffee, praline, and dried fruit, with a hint of chocolate. The palate is syrupy, full-bodied, smooth, and complex.

Chocolate and Coffee Mascarpone Cream

(Fraîcheur de mascarpone chocolat-café)

This mascarpone cream is a delicate blend of chocolate and coffee, offering a mix of textures, both crunchy and smooth. Its complex array of lingering, roasted flavours with a slightly bitter edge goes marvellously with wines that have been wood aged for extended periods. The prominent notes of praline, cocoa, and hazelnut acquired through ageing, along with their gentle sweetness, make the selected wines the best pairing for this fresh, simple dessert. Too often passed over for Rivesaltes, the Rasteau Ambré makes a wonderfully subtle accompaniment, complementing the chocolate and coffee aromas. The Australian port-style wine is also ideal. Despite its characteristic richness and strength, it does not drown the chocolate and coffee flavours of the mascarpone cream.

SERVES 8

Preparation time: 30 minutes

Cooking time: 10 minutes

Chilling: at least 1 hour

FOR THE CHOCOLATE CREAM

100ml (3½fl oz) single cream

200ml (7fl oz) plain chocolate

200g (7oz) whipped cream

FOR THE LIGHT MASCARPONE CREAM

1 gelatine leaf

3 egg yolks

35g (1¼oz) granulated sugar

125ml (4½fl oz) whipped cream

125g (4½oz) mascarpone cheese

FOR THE COCOA AND COFFEE PETIT FOURS

2 tablespoons single cream

50g (1¾oz) sugar crystals

1 teaspoon cocoa powder

30g (1oz) butter

50g (1¾oz) crushed hazelnuts

½ teaspoon instant coffee

Preparing the chocolate cream

Bring the single cream to the boil and pour over the plain chocolate which has been broken into small pieces. Mix, leave to cool to 30°C (86°F) then fold in the whipped cream. Mix gently to obtain a smooth mousse and eliminate any lumps.

Half fill eight small glass containers and chill in the refrigerator.

Preparing the light mascarpone cream

Melt the gelatine leaf in cold water. Beat the egg yolks and sugar in a large mixing bowl until the mixture is very white. Drain the gelatine and melt in a bain-marie. Add it to the egg yolk mixture, stir, and fold in the whipped cream and the mascarpone cheese.

Fill the glass containers with this cream to 5mm (¼ inch) below the lip. Chill in the refrigerator.

Making the cocoa and coffee petit fours

Put the single cream, sugar crystals, butter, cocoa powder, hazelnuts, and instant coffee in a saucepan. Bring to the boil then spread this mixture onto a sheet of greaseproof paper and cook for 10 minutes in a preheated oven – 170°C (325°F), Gas Mark 3.

Finishing

Immediately cut this crunchy topping into circles using a small pastry-cutter with the same diameter as the serving glasses.

Leave to cool and top each mascarpone cream with a petit four.

Serving temperature

Rasteau Ambré, Domaine de la Soumade, André Roméro: 14°C (57°F).

D'Arenberg Nostalgia, Tawny Port, McLaren Vale: 14°C (57°F).

Rasteau AOC

The Rasteau *vin doux naturel* appellation covers an area comprising Rasteau, Sablet, and Cairanne, three villages in the Vaucluse with an established reputation for top-quality Côtes-du-Rhônes. Unfortunately, the number of excellent naturally sweet wines produced in this appellation area is on the decline, as wine-growers prefer to concentrate on the production of red Côtes-du-Rhône-Villages. Wine legislation states that Rasteau must be made from ninety per cent Grenache Noir, Gris, or Blanc. The yield must not exceed thirty hectolitres per hectare and the mandatory ageing period is one year. This naturally sweet wine begins with a fruity, intense mouth, then offers a more oxidized taste caused by extensive wood ageing. Its amber and dark topaz colour and its developing aromas of coffee, cocoa, praline, and dried fruit are also products of this prolonged ageing.

RASTEAU AMBRE, DOMAINE DE LA SOUMADE, ANDRE ROMERO

This golden Rasteau, made from 100 per cent Grenache Noir, is pressed directly without maceration. The grapes are so ripe that, despite using this method, a certain amount of colour is released, giving this wine a slightly amber hue. The wine is fortified partway through fermentation. During the year-long ageing period in oak casks, caramel is added to the wine to enhance its colour. The residual sugar content varies between eighty-five and 100g per litre. The alcoholic content (15.5 degrees) is fairly high without being overpowering. This wine offers aromas of pine nut, walnut, dried fruit, and a hint of cream caramel, with notes of cocoa and praline. The mouth is full-bodied, generous and the alcoholic strength is well-balanced by gentle sweetness.

South Australia

South Australia is the second largest wine-producing region on the continent. As in other Australian states, the first vines date back to the nineteenth century: they were planted in 1836 around Adelaide, in Magill. Adelaide's progressive urbanization has spared only a few hectares of the historic Penfolds vineyards, which are now surrounded in the city's outskirts. The vineyards were planted in the north, in the Barossa Valley, by German immigrants and initially spread into the Southern Vales and McLaren Vale. This hot, dry region is cooled in the early eveningby ocean breezes. It specializes traditionally in the production of sweet port-style wines, dessert wines, and well-structured reds.

D'ARENBERG NOSTALGIA, TAWNY PORT, MCLAREN VALE

The D'Arenberg winery is located on the hillside, four kilometres (2.5 miles) from the town of McLaren, on the Fleurieu peninsula. The climate is arid and Mediterranean, with mild winters and hot, dry summers, but the estate has an exceptional microclimate, gently cooled by the proximity of the Gulf of Saint-Vincent, as well as by an annual rainfall of between 600 and 700 millimetres. For sixty years, the Osborn family merely tended the vineyards – they did not begin to make and sell wine from their grapes until 1928. The first bottles bearing the now famous red stripe appeared on the market in 1967. The estate now grows all the popular grape varieties in Australia – those from the Rhône valley are particularly well-represented. D'Arenberg Nostalgia is made from fifty-year-old Grenache vines and Syrah. The wine is made in the same way as port, being fortified and aged in wood for long periods. Delicate notes of coffee and tobacco box with superb woody accents are a clear indication that this wine has a *rancio* quality: its chocolate-coffee character is unmistakable.

List of Contents

Useful Addresses

Alicante Vino Dulce de Moscatel Casta Diva,
Guttierez de la Vega 2001
68, rue du Colonel-Fabien, 51530 Dizy
Tel.: 00 33 (0)3 26 55 68 11/Fax: 00 33 (0)3 26 51 06 25
Jacquesson

Amigne Grains Nobles 1999, Fabienne Cottagnoud
Rue de Maligny 28, CH-1196 Gland
Tel.: 00 41 22 354 20 20/Fax: 00 41 22 354 20 24
www.cavesa.ch
Cavesa

Anton Bredell Port Wine, Bredell Wine Estate 1998,
Stellenbosch
La Vigna, bd de la Madeleine, 75008 Paris
Tel.: 00 33 (0)1 42 97 20 20

Arbois Vin de Paille 1995
Caveau de Dégustation du Domaine (Tasting Cellar),
Rue de l'Hôtel-de-Ville, 39600 Arbois
Tel.: 00 33 (0)3 84 66 00 05/Fax: 00 33 (0)3 84 37 47 41
Domaine Rolet

Arrels del Priorat Rancio 60 Year Old,
214, avenue du Président-Wilson,
93210 Saint-Denis-La Plaine
Tel.: 00 33 (0)1 49 17 57 29/Fax: 00 33 (0)1 49 17 57 17
Vinespa

Banyuls Cuvée Rivage, Domaine Vial-Magnères 1999
14, rue Herriot, 66650 Banyuls-sur-Mer
Tel.: 00 33 (0)4 68 88 31 04/Fax: 00 33 (0)4 68 88 02 43
Bernard Saperas

Banyuls Grand Cru, Cuvée Président Henry Vidal 1985,
Cellier des Templiers
GICB, Route du Balcon de Madeloc,
66650 Banyuls-sur-Mer
Tel.: 00 33 (0)4 68 98 36 70/Fax: 00 33 (0)4 68 88 00 84

Banyuls L'Oublée, Domaine de la Rectorie, Marc and
Thierry Parcé
54, avenue du Puig-Delmas,
66650 Banyuls-sur-Mer
Tel.: 00 33 (0)4 68 88 13 45/Fax: 00 33 (0)4 68 88 18 55

Banyuls Vintage 2000, Cuvée Léon Parcé, Domaine de
la Rectorie, Marc and Thierry Parcé
54, avenue du Puig-Delmas,
66650 Banyuls-sur-Mer
Tel.: 00 33 (0)4 68 88 13 45/Fax: 00 33 (0)4 68 88 18 55

Barsac Château Doisy-Védrines 1989, Casteja
1, rue Védrines, 33720 Barsac
Tel.: 00 33 (0)5 56 27 15 13/Fax: 00 33 (0)5 56 27 26 76

Bodegas Insulares de Tenerife,
Vina Norte Tinto 1999, Dulce Humbolt
68, rue du Colonel-Fabien, 51530 Dizy
Tel.: 00 33 (0)3 26 55 68 11/Fax: 00 33 (0)3 26 51 06 25
Jacquesson

Bonnezaux Château de Fesles 1997, Bernard Germain
49380 Thouarcé
Tel.: 00 33 (0)2 41 68 94 00/Fax: 00 33 (0)2 41 68 94 01
www.vgas.com

Breganze Torcolato 1998, Fausto Maculan
44260 La Chapelle-Launay
Tel.: 00 33 (0)2 40 56 75 75/Fax: 00 33 (0)2 40 56 75 76
vinsdumonde@wanadoo.fr
Vins du Monde

Bugey-cerdon Rosé Pétillant,
SARL Alain Renardat-Fache, 01450 Mérignat
Tel.: 04 74 39 97 19/Fax: 04 74 39 93 39
cerdon.renardat-fache@wanadoo.fr
Alain Renardat-Fache

Cabernet-d'Anjou 2001
Tel.: 00 33 (0)2 41 78 30 53/Fax: 00 33 (0)2 41 78 43 55
44, rue Belle-Angevine,
49750 Saint-Lambert-du-Lattay
Vincent Ogereau

Cabernet-de-Saumur, Domaine de la Tour-Grise 2000
1, rue des Ducs-d'Aquitaine,
49260 Le Puy-Notre-Dame
Tel.: 00 33 (0)2 41 38 82 42/Fax: 00 33 (0)2 41 52 39 96
Philippe Gourdon

Cadillac Château Reynon 1998
Château Reynon, 33410 Béguey
Tel.: 00 33 (0)5 56 62 96 51/Fax: 00 33 (0)5 56 62 14 89
denisdubourdieu.com
Denis and Florence Dubourdieu

Champagne Blanc de Blancs Avize Grand Cru 1993
68, rue du Colonel-Fabien, 51530 Dizy
Tel.: 00 33 (0)3 26 55 68 11/Fax: 00 33 (0)3 26 51 06 25
Jacquesson

Champagne Rosé de Saignée Dry Duval-Leroy
69, avenue Bammental, 51130 Vertus
Tel.: 00 33 (0)3 26 52 10 75/Fax: 00 33 (0)3 26 52 12 93
www.duval-leroy.com

Cidre Doux Château de Hauteville
Château de Hauteville, 53250 Charchigné
Tel.: 00 33 (0)2 43 03 95 72/Fax: 00 33 (0)2 43 08 18 21
Éric Bordelet

Commandaria Saint John, Keo
Maison Laplace, 94190 Villeneuve Saint-Georges
Tel.: 00 33 (0)1 43 82 11 20/Fax: 00 33 (0)1 43 82 05 11

Condrieu VT Quintessence 1999
42410 Saint-Michel-sur-Rhône
Tel.: 00 33 (0)4 74 56 83 60/Fax: 00 33 (0)4 74 56 87 78
vinsvillard@aol.com
François Villard

Coteaux-de-l'Aubance Les Fontenelles,
Domaine de Haute-Perche
9, chemin de la Godelière,
49610 Saint-Melaine-sur-Aubance
Tel.: 00 33 (0)2 41 57 75 65/Fax: 00 33 (0)2 41 57 75 42
Christian Papin

Coteaux du Layon Beaulieu-Les Rouannières 1997
Château Pierre-Bise, 49750 Beaulieu-sur-Layon
Tel.: 00 33 (0)2 41 78 31 44/Fax: 00 33 (0)2 41 78 41 24
Claude Papin

Coteaux du Layon-Villages, Clos des
Bonnes-Blanches 1997
44, rue Belle-Angevine,
49750 Saint-Lambert-du-Lattay
Tel.: 00 33 (0)2 41 78 30 53/Fax: 00 33 (0)2 41 78 43 55
Vincent Ogereau

Cotnari Château Cotnari Grasa VSOC CIB 1993
Le Bourg, 69530 Orliénas
Tel.: 00 33 (0)4 72 31 02 06/Fax: 00 33 (0)4 72 31 01 84
dionis@wanadoo.fr
Sté Dionis

D'Arenberg Nostalgia, Tawny Port, McLaren Vale
44260 La Chapelle-Launay
Tel.: 00 33 (0)2 40 56 75 75/Fax: 00 33 (0)2 40 56 75 76
vinsdumonde@wanadoo.fr
Vins du Monde

Ermitage Flétri 2000, Nicolas Zufferey
68, rue du Colonel-Fabien, 51530 Dizy
Tel.: 00 33 (0)3 26 55 68 11/Fax: 00 33 (0)3 26 51 06 25
Jacquesson

Floc de Gascogne Blanc Château de Tariquet
Château de Tariquet, Saint-Amand, 32800 Eauze
Tel.: 00 33 (0)5 62 09 87 82/Fax: 00 33 (0)5 62 09 89 49
www.tariquet.com

Floc de Gascogne Rosé Château de Tariquet
Château de Tariquet, Saint-Amand, 32800 Eauze
Tel.: 00 33 (0)5 62 09 87 82/Fax: 00 33 (0)5 62 09 89 49
www.tariquet.com

Fondillon Gran Reserva 1964, Bodegas Brotons
Partida Culebron 59 e 3658 Culebron, Pineso Alicante
Tel.: 00 34 965 477 267/Fax: 00 34 965 477 267
Bodegas Brotons

Gaillac Doux Cuvée Renaissance 1999
Petit Narèye, 81600 Cadalen
Tel.: 00 33 (0)5 63 41 75 14/Fax: 00 33 (0)5 63 41 54 56
EARL Rotier Marre

Gewurztraminer Burg VT 1997, Marcel Deiss
15, route du vin, 68750 Bergheim
Tel.: 00 33 (0)3 89 73 63 37/Fax: 00 33 (0)3 89 73 32 67
marceldeiss@marceldeiss.com
Jean-Michel Deiss

Gewurztraminer SGN 1994
15, route de Bergheim, 68150 Ribeauvillé
Tel.: 00 33 (0)3 89 73 60 30/Fax: 00 33 (0)3 89 73 89 04
Trimbach

Grand-Roussillon VDN, Cuvée Georges Puig 1977,
Domaine Puig-Parahy
2, chemin de l'Étang, 66510 Saint-Hippolyte
Tel.: 00 33 (0)4 68 28 16 62
gaikjeremie@aol.com
Jérémie Gaik

Gonzalez Byass, Elegante Cream Sherry, Jerez
Manuel Maria Gonzales, 12
11403 Jerez de la Frontera (Spain)
Tel.: 00 34 956 357 000/Fax: 00 34 956 357 045

**Jumilla Olivares Dulce Monastrell 1998,
Bodegas Olivares**
44260 La Chapelle-Launay
Tel.: 00 33 (0)2 40 56 75 75/Fax: 00 33 (0)2 40 56 75 76
vinsdumonde@wanadoo.fr
Vins du Monde

Jurançon Moelleux Clos Lapeyre 1999
Chemin du Couday, 64110 Jurançon
Tel.: 00 33 (0)5 59 21 50 80/Fax: 00 33 (0)5 59 21 51 83
Jean-Bernard Larrieu

Klein Constantia 1987
Le Bourg, 69530 Orliénas
Tel.: 00 33 (0)4 72 31 02 06/Fax: 00 33 (0)4 72 31 01 84
dionis@wanadoo.fr
Sté Dionis

La Palma Malvasia Dulce 1999,
Bodegas Teneguia
68, rue du Colonel-Fabien 51530, Dizy
Tel.: 00 33 (0)3 26 55 68 11/Fax: 00 33 (0)3 26 51 06 25
Jacquesson

Liqueur Cédratine Mattei
Mattei Cap Corse, Lieu-dit Rasignani, 20290 Borgo
Tel.: 00 33 (0)4 95 59 17 17/Fax: 00 33 (0)4 95 38 34 18

Liqueur Suprême de Noix
9, boulevard du Maréchal-Lyautey
19100 Brive-la-Gaillarde
Tel.: 00 33 (0)5 55 74 34 27/Fax: 00 33 (0)5 55 84 81 69
www.denoix.com
Denoix

Loupiac Château du Cros, M. Boyer
94, route de Saint-Maraire, 33410 Loupiac
Tel.: 00 33 (0)5 56 62 99 31/Fax: 00 33 (0)5 56 62 12 59

Madeira Verdelho 1933, Barbeto
Épicerie de Longueil, 78600 Maison Laffitte
Tel.: 00 33 (0)1 39 62 00 50

Moscatel de Malaga Don Salvador, Lopez Hermanos
44260 La Chapelle-Launay
Tel.: 00 33 (0)2 40 56 75 75/Fax: 00 33 (0)2 40 56 75 76
vinsdumonde@wanadoo.fr
Vins du Monde

Malvasia Passito di Lipari 1999, Pietro Colosi
68, rue du Colonel-Fabien, 51530 Dizy
Tel.: 00 33 (0)3 26 55 68 11/Fax: 00 33 (0)3 26 51 06 25
Jacquesson

Marsala Vecchio Samperi Riserva 20 Anni, Marco de Bartoli
Contrada Fornara Samperi 292,
91025 Marsala (TP)
Tel.: 00 39 923 962 093
www.marcodebartoli.com

Maury 2000, Domaine Pouderoux
2, chemin de l'Étang, 66510 Saint-Hippolyte
Tel.: 00 33 (0)4 68 28 16 62
gaikjéremie@aol.com
Jérémie Gaik

Maury Cuvée Spéciale Dix Ans d'ge,
Domaine du Mas-Amiel
66460 Maury
Tel.: 00 33 (0)4 68 29 01 02/Fax: 00 33 (0)4 68 29 17 82

Maydie or Tan'nage Château d'Aydie 2000
Laplace les Vignobles, 64330 Aydie
Tel.: 00 33 (0)5 59 04 08 00/Fax: 00 33 (0)5 59 04 08 08
www.pierre-laplace.com
M. Laplace

MEL 2000, Antonio Gaggiano
68, rue du Colonel-Fabien, 51530 Dizy
Tel.: 00 33 (0)3 26 55 68 11/Fax: 00 33 (0)3 26 51 06 25
Jacquesson

Monbazillac Château Grand-Maison,
Cuvée du Château 1995
La Grande Maison 24240 Monbazillac
Tel.: 00 33 (0)5 53 58 26 17/Fax: 00 33 (0)5 53 24 97 36
grandemaison@aquinet.tm.fr
Thierry Desprès

Montilla-Moriles Don Pedro 1972, Toro Albala
44260 La Chapelle-Launay
Tel.: 00 33 (0)2 40 56 75 75/Fax: 00 33 (0)2 40 56 75 76
vinsdumonde@wanadoo.fr
Vins du Monde

Montlouis Moelleux Cuvée Romulus 1997
Domaine de la Taille aux Loups,
8, rue des Aitres, 37270 Montlouis-sur-Loire
Tel.: 00 33 (0)2 47 45 11 11/Fax: 00 33 (0)2 47 45 11 14
Jacky Blot

Moscatel de Lanzarote 1972, Solera Mozzagua
Rue de Malagny 28, CH-1196 Gland
Tel.: 0041 22 354 20 20/Fax: 0041 22 354 20 24
www.cavesa.ch
Cavesa

Moscatel de Setubal Aged 20 Years,
Jose Maria da Fonseca
Rua Jose Augusto Coelho, 11/13
P-2925 Azitao
Tel.: 00351 212 197 500/Fax: 00351 212 197 501

Moscato d'Asti Bricco Quaglia 2001,
Giorgio Rivetti
68, rue du Colonel-Fabien, 51530 Dizy
Tel.: 00 33 (0)3 26 55 68 11/Fax: 00 33 (0)3 26 51 06 25
Jacquesson

Moscato Passito 1999 La Spinetta, Giorgio Rivetti
68, rue du Colonel-Fabien, 51530 Dizy
Tel.: 00 33 (0)3 26 55 68 11/Fax: 00 33 (0)3 26 51 06 25
Jacquesson

Moscato Passito di Pantelleria, Pietro Colosi
68, rue du Colonel-Fabien, 51530 Dizy
Tel.: 00 33 (0)3 26 55 68 11/Fax: 00 33 (0)3 26 51 06 25
Jacquesson

Mosel-Saar-Ruwer Riesling BA Zeltingen Sonnenuhr 2000, Selbach-Oster
68, rue du Colonel-Fabien, 51530 Dizy
Tel.: 00 33 (0)3 26 55 68 11/Fax: 00 33 (0)3 26 51 06 25
Jacquesson

Murfatlar, Muscat Ottonel VSOC, CIB 1984
Le Bourg, 69530 Orliénas
Tel.: 00 33 (0)4 72 31 02 06/Fax: 00 33 (0)4 72 31 01 84
dionis@wanadoo.fr
Sté Dionis

Muscat de Beaumes-de-Venise Clos des Bernadins 2000
Cave Castaud, Domaine Bernardins,
Avenue Léon-Gambetta, 84190 Beaumes-de-Venise
Tel.: 00 33 (0)4 90 62 94 13/Fax: 00 33 (0)4 90 65 01 42

Muscat de Rivesaltes 1999
4, rue Francisco-Ferrer, 66600 Rivesaltes
Tel.: 00 33 (0)4 68 64 08 26/Fax: 00 33 (0)4 68 64 69 79
Jean-Michel Cazes

Muscat de Saint-Jean-de-Minervois, Domaine de Barroubio
34360 Saint-Jean-de-Minervois
Tel.: 00 33 (0)4 67 38 14 06/Fax: 00 33 (0)4 67 38 14 06
baroubio@club-internet.fr
Raymond Miquel

Muscat du Cap Corse 2000, Domaine Antoine Arena
Lieu-dit Morta Majo, 20253 Patrimonio
Tel.: 00 33 (0)4 95 37 08 27/Fax: 00 33 (0)4 95 37 01 14

Samos Nectar
Le Bourg, 69530 Orliénas
Tel.: 00 33 (0)4 72 31 02 06/Fax: 00 33 (0)4 72 31 01 84
dionis@wanadoo.fr
Sté Dionis

Neusiedlersee Scheurebe Auslese 1998, Alois Kracher
44260 La Chapelle-Launay
Tel.: 00 33 (0)2 40 56 75 75/Fax: 00 33 (0)2 40 56 75 76
vinsdumonde@wanadoo.fr
Vins du Monde

Neusiedlersee Schilfwein The Red One 1999, Weingut Gerhard Nekowitsch
44260 La Chapelle-Launay
Tel.: 00 33 (0)2 40 56 75 75/Fax: 00 33 (0)2 40 56 75 76
vinsdumonde@wanadoo.fr
Vins du Monde

Neusiedlersee TBA N° 7 Nouvelle Vague 1998, Alois Kracher
44260 La Chapelle-Launay
Tel.: 00 33 (0)2 40 56 75 75/Fax: 00 33 (0)2 40 56 75 76
vinsdumonde@wanadoo.fr
Vins du Monde

Noble One Botrytis Sémillon 1996, De Bortoli 1996
44260 La Chapelle-Launay
Tel.: 00 33 (0)2 40 56 75 75/Fax: 00 33 (0)2 40 56 75 76
vinsdumonde@wanadoo.fr
Vins du Monde

Pacherenc-du-Vic-Bilh Passion de Frimaire 1995
Château Bouscassé, 32400 Maumusson-Laguian
Tel.: 00 33 (0)5 62 69 74 67/Fax: 00 33 (0)5 62 69 70 46
Alain Brumont

Pineau des Charentes Rosé
Le Château, 16300 Ambleville
Tel.: 00 33 (0)5 45 80 54 57/Fax: 00 33 (0)5 45 80 56 46
raymond.ragnaud@freesbee.fr
Raymond Raynaud

Colheita Port 1933, Burmester
La Vigna, bd de la Madeleine, 75008 Paris
Tel.: 00 33 (0)1 42 97 20 20

Tawny Port 20 Year Old, Ferreira
Épicerie de Longueil, 78600 Maison Laffitte
Tel.: 00 33 (0)1 39 62 00 50

Tawny Port 10 Year Old, Quinta do Infantado, João Lopes Roseira
Lieu-dit Crière, 69380 Charnay
Tel.: 00 33 (0)4 78 47 93 45/Fax: 04 78 47 93 38
Jean-Paul Brun

Primitivo di Manduria Dolce Il Madrigale 1997
19 via Fabio Massimo, 74024 Manduria
Tel.: 00 39 99 973 5332
Consorzio Produttori Vini

Primitivo di Manduria Solaria Jonica,
Cantine Ferrari 1959
Via Santo Stasi 1, 74024 Manduria
Tel.: 00 39 99 973 8929
Pervini

Quarts-de-chaume Château de Bellerive 1989
49190 Rochefort-sur-Loire
Tel.: 00 33 (0)2 41 78 33 66/Fax: 00 33 (0)2 41 78 68 47

Rancio Doux Solera 1880, Louis Puig Santenach
44, avenue de la Méditerranée, 66670 Bages

Rappu, Domaine Gentile
Lieu-dit Olzo, 20217 Saint-Florent
Tel.: 00 33 (0)4 95 37 01 54/Fax: 00 33 (0)4 95 37 16 69

Rasteau Ambré, Domaine de la Soumade, André
Roméro
Quartier Saint-Martin, 84110 Rasteau
Tel.: 00 33 (0)4 90 46 11 26/Fax: 00 33 (0)4 90 46 11 69

Rasteau Vintage 1999, Domaine de la Soumade,
André Roméro
Quartier Saint-Martin, 84110 Rasteau
Tel.: 00 33 (0)4 90 46 11 26/Fax: 00 33 (0)4 90 46 11 69

Recioto Della Valpolicella 1995,
Romano Dal Forno
68, rue du Colonel-Fabien, 51530 Dizy
Tel.: 00 33 (0)3 26 55 68 11/Fax: 00 33 (0)3 26 51 06 25
Jacquesson

Recioto di Soave Col Foscarin 1997,
Claudio e Sandro Gini
68, rue du Colonel-Fabien, 51530 Dizy
Tel.: 00 33 (0)3 26 55 68 11/Fax: 00 33 (0)3 26 51 06 25
Jacquesson

Riesling Eiswein Zeltingen Himmelreich 1998, Selbach-
Oster
68, rue du Colonel-Fabien, 51530 Dizy
Tel.: 00 33 (0)3 26 55 68 11/Fax: 00 33 (0)3 26 51 06 25
Jacquesson

Riesling Grand Cru Altenberg de Bergheim 1998 VT
Marcel Deiss
15, route du vin, 68750 Bergheim
Tel.: 00 33 (0)3 89 73 63 37/Fax: 00 33 (0)3 89 73 32 67
marceldeiss@marceldeiss.com
Jean-Michel Deiss

Riesling Ice Wine Inniskillin Silver,
Niagara Peninsula 1989
44260 La Chapelle-Launay
Tel.: 00 33 (0)2 40 56 75 75/Fax: 00 33 (0)2 40 56 75 76
vinsdumonde@wanadoo.fr
Vins du Monde

Riesling SGN, Cuvée Frédéric-Émile 1990
15, route de Bergheim, 68150 Ribeauvillé
Tel.: 00 33 (0)3 89 73 60 30/Fax: 00 33 (0)3 89 73 89 04
Trimbach

Rivesaltes Ambré 1991
4, rue Francisco-Ferrer, 66600 Rivesaltes
Tel.: 00 33 (0)4 68 64 08 26/Fax: 00 33 (0)4 68 64 69 79
Jean-Michel Cazes

Rivesaltes Cuvée Aimé Cazes 1976
4, rue Francisco-Ferrer, 66600 Rivesaltes
Tel.: 00 33 (0)4 68 64 08 26/Fax: 00 33 (0)4 68 64 69 79
Jean-Michel Cazes

Rivesaltes Tuilé 1985
4, rue Francisco-Ferrer, 66600 Rivesaltes
Tel.: 00 33 (0)4 68 64 08 26/Fax: 00 33 (0)4 68 64 69 79
Jean-Michel Cazes

Rubis Demi-Sec Bouvet-Ladubay
11, rue Jean-Ackerman,
49400 Saint-Hilaire Saint-Florent
Tel.: 00 33 (0)2 41 83 83 83/Fax: 00 33 (0)2 41 50 24 32

Ruster Ausbruch Gelber Muskateller 1999,
Robert Wenzel
44260 La Chapelle-Launay
Tel.: 00 33 (0)2 40 56 75 75/Fax: 00 33 (0)2 40 56 75 76
vinsdumonde@wanadoo.fr
Vins du Monde

Ruster Ausbruch Pinot Noir 1999, Feiler-Artinger
44260 La Chapelle-Launay
Tel.: 00 33 (0)2 40 56 75 75/Fax: 00 33 (0)2 40 56 75 76
vinsdumonde@wanadoo.fr
Vins du Monde

Sainte-Croix-du-Mont Château Loubens 1985
Arnaud de Sèze,
3, Loubens, 33410 Sainte-Croix-du-Mont
Tel.: 00 33 (0)5 56 62 01 25/Fax: 00 33 (0)5 56 62 01 28

Saussignac Château des Eyssards, Cuvée Flavie 1997
Pascal and Gérard Cuisset
24240 Monestier
Tel.: 00 33 (0)5 53 24 36 36

Sauternes Château d'Yquem 1990, Lur-Saluces
Château d'Yquem, 33210 Sauternes
Tel.: 00 33 (0)5 57 98 07 07/Fax: 00 33 (0)5 57 98 07 08

Savennières Clos du Papillon 1997, Cuvée d'Avant,
Pierre Soulez
Château Chambourreau, 49170 Savennières
Tel.: 00 33 (0)2 41 77 20 04/Fax: 00 33 (0)2 41 77 27 78

Sélection de Grains Nobles 1999, Dominique
Rouvinez
68, rue du Colonel-Fabien, 51530 Dizy
Tel.: 00 33 (0)3 26 55 68 11/Fax: 00 33 (0)3 26 51 06 25
Jacquesson

Sherry Oloroso
Europvin,
65, cours Saint-Louis, 33300 Bordeaux
Tel.: 00 33 (0)5 57 87 43 21/Fax: 00 33 (0)5 57 87 43 22
www.europvin.com
Europvin

Sherry Pedro-Ximenez, El Candado Valdespino
Rue de Maligny 28, CH-1196 Gland
Tel.: 00 41 22 354 20 20/Fax: 00 41 22 354 20 24
www.cavesa.ch
Cavesa

Stellenzicht Riesling Noble Late Harvest 1998
44260 La Chapelle-Launay
Tel.: 00 33 (0)2 40 56 75 75/Fax: 00 33 (0)2 40 56 75 76
vinsdumonde@wanadoo.fr
Vins du Monde

Terra Alta Tinto Dulce Con Criança, Millennium 2000
Tel.: 0034 968 186 072/Fax: 0034 968 179 153
topwine@expandexport.com
Expand Export

Tokaji Aszú 5 puttonyos 1993, Domaine Disnókó
PF 10 H 3910 Tokaj Hungria
Tel.: 00 36 47 361 371/Fax: 00 36 47 369 138

Tokaji Aszú 6 puttonyos 1972, Oremus
44260 La Chapelle-Launay
Tel.: 00 33 (0)2 40 56 75 75/Fax: 00 33 (0)2 40 56 75 76
vinsdumonde@wanadoo.fr
Vins du Monde

Tokaji Aszú Eszencia 1983, Oremus
44260 La Chapelle-Launay
Tel.: 00 33 (0)2 40 56 75 75/Fax: 00 33 (0)2 40 56 75 76
vinsdumonde@wanadoo.fr
Vins du Monde

Vin de Glacière Muscat Canelli Bonny Doon 1999,
Randall Graham
44260 La Chapelle-Launay
Tel.: 00 33 (0)2 40 56 75 75/Fax: 00 33 (0)2 40 56 75 76
vinsdumonde@wanadoo.fr
Vins du Monde

Port Style Wine, Cavendish 1979
44260 La Chapelle-Launay
Tel.: 00 33 (0)2 40 56 75 75/Fax: 00 33 (0)2 40 56 75 76
vinsdumonde@wanadoo.fr
Vins du Monde

Slovenia San Leonardo 1999,
Edvin Smimcic
Tel.: 00 38 641 363 193/Fax: 00 38 653 959 211
slowfFoodGo@guest.neticom.si
Vinos Noble Eslovénia

Vin Noble du Minervois Cuvée 1998, Domaine Tour-
Boisée, Jean-Louis Poudou
11800 Laure-Minervois
Tel.: 00 33 (0)4 68 78 10 04/Fax: 00 33 (0)4 68 78 10 98
info@domainelatourboisee.com

Vino Santo Chianti Classico Fattoria di Felsina 1996
44260 La Chapelle-Launay
Tel.: 00 33 (0)2 40 56 75 75/Fax: 00 33 (0)2 40 56 75 76
vinsdumonde@wanadoo.fr
Vins du Monde

Vino Santo Nobile di Montepulciano 1990, Avignonesi
44260 La Chapelle-Launay
Tel.: 00 33 (0)2 40 56 75 75/Fax: 00 33 (0)2 40 56 75 76
vinsdumonde@wanadoo.fr
Vins du Monde

Vouvray Premier Tri Haut-Lieu 1989, Domaine Huet
11-13, rue de la Croix-Buisée, 37210 Vouvray
Tel.: 00 33 (0)2 47 52 78 87/Fax: 00 33 (0)2 47 52 66 51

Wachau BA 2000, Freie Weingartner
68, rue du Colonel-Fabien, 51530 Dizy
Tel.: 00 33 (0)3 26 55 68 11/Fax: 00 33 (0)3 26 51 06 25
Jacquesson

Wachau TBA 2000, Freie Weingartner
68, rue du Colonel-Fabien, 51530 Dizy
Tel.: 00 33 (0)3 26 55 68 11/Fax: 00 33 (0)3 26 51 06 25
Jacquesson

Weingut Franz Kunstler Hochheimer Kirchenstück
Eiswein 2001
Freiherr-vom-stein-ring, 3
D-65239 Hochheim
Tel.: 0049 61 46 82 57/Fax: 0049 61 46 57 67

Welschriesling TBA 1998 Neusiedlersee-Hügelland,
Gunther Schönberger
68, rue du Colonel-Fabien, 51530 Dizy
Tel.: 00 33 (0)3 26 55 68 11/Fax: 00 33 (0)3 26 51 06 25
Jacquesson

Wine Index

Glossary

AOC: the top category in the French system for ensuring quality wines. Appellation d'Origine Contrôlée is sometimes shortened to *Appellation Contrôlée* and abbreviated as either AOC or AC.

AOVDQS: *Appellation d'Origine Vin Délimité de Qualité Supérieure*, a designation replacing the VDQS label. These wines come in a very close second to AOC wines in quality but are still precisely controlled.

AUMONIERE: from the French for "purse". This is a parcel made of shortcrust pastry or pancake dough with a sweet or savoury filling.

BABA: a cake made from leavened dough, steeped in rum or Kirsch syrup.

BAIN-MARIE: (Mary's bath) this utensil is used for melting ingredients without burning them, or for keeping mixtures warm for later use. The basic method involves placing a pan of food in another pan containing hot water to stabilize the heat reaching the food.

BAKING BLIND: a term used to describe pastry cooked on its own in the oven before the filling is added. Air trapped under the base, which sometimes causes the pastry to "balloon" during cooking, can be released by pricking the base all over with a fork before putting it in the oven. Lining papers and/or baking beans are also used to weigh the pastry down.

BEERENAUSLESE (BA): the German term for "selected single berries", used to refer to very sweet QmP wines made from overripe, botrytized grapes, individually picked.

BIODYNAMICS: a regulated system of farming that obeys certain principles (close observation of weather conditions, the timing of activities to coincide with the phases of the moon, the use of natural soil improvers and the refusal to use chemical fertilizers or pesticides). Biodynamic farming is not synonymous with organic farming although the two approaches share many similarities.

BOTRYTIZATION: condition of grapes infected by noble rot (*Botrytis cinerea*).

BOURBON VANILLA: vanilla from the Indian Ocean.

BRIOCHE: a soft loaf, cake or bun made from a yeast dough enriched with butter and eggs.

BRIX SYSTEM: *see* Oechsle.

CHAPTALIZATION: the legal addition of sugar during fermentation to increase the alcohol content of a wine. It is more prevalent in cool climates where the grapes have a lower natural sugar content.

CHIBOUST CREAM: a type of confectioners' custard (pastry cream), usually flavoured with vanilla and blended when warm with stiffly beaten egg whites.

CLAFOUTIS: a traditional dessert from the Limousin region of France. It is made by pouring pancake batter over fruit in a dish and baking in the oven.

COLLIOURE: a red wine from the Roussillon, made mainly from the Grenache Noir grape. It is aged in wooden barrels and cannot be bottled and sold until the July following the year of harvest. It is a dry, robust, and full-bodied wine, about 12–15 degrees of alcohol.

CRYOEXTRACTION: French term for the practice of subjecting grapes to very low temperatures (around –7°C or 19°F) so that only the most concentrated grape juice will be extracted during pressing.

CUVEE: a term used to refer to the contents of a (vat) or a blended wine.

DACQUOISE: traditional gâteau from southwestern France. It consists of two or three layers of light, crisp meringue flavoured with hazelnuts and almonds, sandwiched together with a cream (fresh whipped cream or French butter cream) and fruit filling.

DEGORGEMENT (DISGORGING): a stage in the Champagne method, following remuage. The cork is removed and the bottle simultaneously flipped upright to remove the plug of yeast sludge.

DO (SPAIN): *Denominación de Origen*. The Spanish equivalent of French AOC wines. There are now over forty DO wines, including wines from the best-known regions.

DOC (SPAIN): *Denominación de Origen Calificada*. New top category for Spanish wines.

DOC (ITALY): *Denominazione di Origine Controllata*. The Italian equivalent of French AOC wines.

DOCG (ITALY): *Denominazione di Origine Controllata e Garantita*. Top category of Italian wines, examined, and tasted by government testers.

DOSAGE: a sugar-and-wine mixture added to sparkling wines after *dégorgement*. The amount of sugar varies depending on how sweet or dry the wine is required to be.

EAU-DE-VIE: literally means "water of life". This term describes any colourless, potent brandy, or other spirit distilled from fermented fruit juice. Among the grape-based eaux-de-vie are: *eau-de-vie de marc* (from *marc*), *eau-de-vie de lie* (from lees), and *eau-de-vie de vin* (from wine). Probably the two most popular eaux-de-vie in the world are Kirsch (from cherries) and Framboise (from raspberries).

FLETRI: term used to denote a wine made from shrivelled, botrytized grapes.

INAO *Institut Nationale des Appellations d'Origine*. French organization that establishes the broad guidelines for AOC and AOVDQS wines.

ITALIAN MERINGUE: a type of meringue made by slowly beating hot sugar syrup into stiffly beaten egg whites. The resulting meringue is very dense, shiny and smooth. Italian meringue is used as cake frosting.

KLOSTERNEUBURGER MOSTWAAGE (KMW): the Austrian method of measuring the natural sugar content of the must in weight percentage. 1 degree KMW is approximately 5 degree oechsle.

KOOPERATIEVE WIJNBOUWERS VERENIGING VAN ZUID-AFRIKA BEPERKT (KWV): (Cooperative Wine Growers' Association, South Africa).

LIQUEUR D'EXPEDITION: a sugar-based preparation added for the commercialisation of quality sparkling wines.

LIQUEUR DE TIRAGE: a blend of sugar and yeasts, used in the Champagne method to start bottle fermentation.

MANQUE MOULD: *moule à manqué* – the classic French cake tin – 18–23cm (7–9 inches) in diameter – made from aluminium or tinned steel. The slightly sloping sides – about 5cm (2 inches) deep – give the finished cake an attractive shape.

MILLE-FEUILLE: thin layers of flaky (puff) pastry filled with pastry cream, jam or some other filling and topped with icing sugar, fondant icing or royal icing. Mille-feuilles are usually small rectangular pastries but can also be made as larger gâteaux.

MISTELLE AND MISTELLA: grape juice to which spirits have been added to prevent fermentation, so that the natural sweetness of the fruit is retained. This fortified grape juice is used in the making of various aperitifs and vermouths

MUTAGE: the process of stopping fermentation either by using sulphur dioxide and sterile filtering or by adding grape alcohol or brandy; in other words, fortification.

MUTAGE SUR GRAINS: the wine is fortified (see *mutage*) by pouring alcohol onto the grapes before pressing. The grapes are then macerated for at least 20 days.

NOBLE ROT: *Botrytis cinerea*, a fungus that attacks white grapes in warm, humid autumn weather. It shrivels the grapes and concentrates the natural sugars – see botrytization.

OECHSLE: a German method of measuring the specific gravity (therefore, the sugar content) of must or grape juice prior to fermentation. Developed in the ninteenth century by Germany's Christian Ferdinand Oechsle, this method is similar to the Brix system used in the United States and the Baumé scale used in France.

PASSITO: an Italian term indicating that a wine has been made from grapes dried by raisining. The French equivalent is *passerillé*.

QUALITATATSWEIN MIT PRADIKAT (QMP): Top German quality designation for wines made in specific areas and from grapes that do not require additional sugar to achieve the correct alcohol level. It has five categories, from the light Kabinett to the intensely rich Trockenbeerenauslese.

RAISINING: partial drying of the grapes, either naturally (on the vine) or artificially (on racks, straw, stone or the ground, by means of warm air, etc), so that the sugar content of the juice and the flavour are increased by concentration.

RANCIO: a VDN that owes its smoothness and distinctive flavour to the oxidative conditions under which it is aged – in wooden barrels and technically in the sun – for several years. In France, it describes wines such as Banyuls or Muscat, in Spain, the nutty flavour of sherry and Málaga wines, in Portugal, the distinctive taste of some ports and Madeiras and, in Italy, Marsala and other fortified wines.

RELIGIEUSE: a cake consisting of a large choux (cream puff pastry), filled with confectioners' custard or Chiboust cream, topped with a smaller choux, similarly filled, then iced with fondant icing and decorated with cream.

REMUAGE: a stage in the Champagne method, during which the bottles are gradually tipped from horizontal to upside down by being given a slight turn and a knock every day for a number of weeks. The process encourages the sediment to collect in the neck of the bottle so that it can be removed during *dégorgement*.

RIMAGE: a regional term for a vintage Banyuls. *Rimage* is used to denote an early bottled style that places the emphasis on the fruit.

SAVARIN MOULD: ring-shaped mould with a hole in the centre.

SABLE: a sweetened shortcrust (or shortbread) pastry.

SELECTION DE GRAINS NOBLES (SGN): very sweet and concentrated wines made with late-harvest grapes infected by noble rot.

SOLERA AND CRIADERA: a traditional system of blending and ageing wines, particularly popular in the regions of Jerez and Malaga (but not restricted to Spain). A quantity of wine is periodically drawn off from the oldest tier of barrels (the *solera*) and replaced with wine from the next oldest tier or criadera of barrels and so on, finishing with the criadera containing the youngest wine.

TARTLET TIN: tinned steel fluted individual tins, variously shaped, for petits fours and pastries.

TERROIR: a French term that refers to a wine-growing area or the type of soil in a particular area. It is also used to refer to the natural and cultural specificity of the area in which the wine is produced.

TROCKENBEERENAUSLESE (TBA): the German term for "dry berries select picking" and the sweetest category of German QmP wines. Made from late-harvested, individually selected berries which are allowed to overripen and shrivel on the vine almost to raisins. These are rich, sweet, luscious, honey-like wines.

ULLAGE: the empty space that forms in barrels, bottles or casks as a result of evaporation or the wine used to top up the levels.

VARIETAL: wine made from, and named after, a single grape variety.

VIN DE LIQUEUR (VDL): dessert wine.

VIN DOUX NATUREL (VDN): naturally sweet wine. These wines are fortified with strong grape spirit, added during fermentation when around half the natural sweetness has been converted to alcohol. White VDNs are made from Muscat, the reds are made from Grenache.

VDQS: *Vins Délimités de Qualité Supérieur* is a label that designates excellent regional wines. This designation has now been replaced by the AOVDQS label.

VIN DE PAILLE: a sweet, golden-coloured wine from the Jura wine area. The grapes are traditionally dried on layers of straw (*paille*) to concentrate their sugars before fermentation.

VINS DE PAYS: these French "country wines" are of a less stringent quality than AOC wines.

VINS DE TERROIR: (wines of the soil). Wines from vineyards over twenty years old grown in named vineyards (*lieux-dits*).

VINIFICATION: the various processes carried out in order to make wine from grape must.

VSOC: Romania's highest quality wine classification.

VENDAGES TARDIVES (VT): (Late Harvest).

WINES OF ORIGIN (WO): Wine certification laws in South Africa. When the term "Wine of Origin" or the abbreviation 'W.O.' together with the name of a production area, such as Stellenbosch, Durbanville or Robertson appears on a label, it confirms that 100% of the grapes from which the wine was made come from that specific area.

Acknowledgments

Valérie Lhomme would like to express warm thanks to Riedel Crystal, the Cristallerie de Sèvres, l'Atelier du Vin, l'Esprit du Vin, and Leonardo for their kind help and support.

Deep appreciation also goes to: ceramicist Christiane Perrochon; Quartz stores, La Forge Subtile, the CFOC, Christofle and Lubi; and Kyoko Yamada for Living Talk.

Last but not least, a big thank you to Philippe Gobet for his immense kindness and his mouth-watering desserts, and to Olivier Poussier for his superb wines.

Olivier Poussier would like to express his gratitude to Vialis Création for the highly original design of their Laguiole Sommelier knife.